The Origins of
Our Founding Principles

The Origins of Our

FOUNDING PRINCIPLES

THE MORRIS FAMILY CENTER FOR LAW & LIBERTY
at Houston Baptist University

Published by Periclitus Press.

Authors may be contacted through
Houston Baptist University
7502 Fondren Road, Houston, Texas 77074
www.hbu.edu

Book and cover design by Marisa Jackson
Front cover image: Independence Hall in Philadelphia

ISBN: 978-1-7341282-0-8
Manufactured in the United States of America
First Paperback Edition

FOR ALL THOSE WHO
SUPPORT OUR MISSION—
WITH GRATITUDE FOR YOUR KINDNESS,
PATRIOTISM, AND LOVE OF HISTORY.

OUR MISSION

The Morris Family Center for Law & Liberty is dedicated to the promotion of American founding principles, the rule of law, the preservation of liberty, and free enterprise. Our mission is 1) to educate our fellow Texans about the principles that make America an exceptional nation; 2) to train and equip teachers, lawyers, and the business community to articulate and defend these principles; and 3) to facilitate civil discourse among diverse groups about the political, social, and economic implications of a nation truly committed to liberty and justice for all.

It has been frequently remarked
that it seems to have been reserved
to the people of this country,
by their conduct and example,
to decide the important question,
whether societies of men are really capable or not
of establishing good government
from reflection and choice,
or whether they are forever destined
to depend for their political constitutions
on accident and force.

ALEXANDER HAMILTON, FEDERALIST PAPER #1

TABLE OF
CONTENTS

INTRODUCTION

The fact that you are reading this book indicates three things. First, you have a desire to learn more about the Constitution. You probably already know much of our nation's constitutional story and many of the key events of the American Founding. Now you'd like to understand our constitutional government on a deeper level. While the Constitution itself is a relatively small document, with just seven Articles and 27 Amendments, the history and philosophy behind the document can be overwhelming. It's difficult to find a good starting place to learn more.

Second, you are concerned about some of the things you hear in the news, social media, and on many college campuses today. Maybe you are at a college that tends to concentrate on "sociological history." You'll focus on what it was like for certain groups of people who lived during the American Founding—women, slaves, indigenous peoples—while focus on Constitutional history gets overlooked. Or maybe you've heard on social media that the United States was a country founded on greed and exploitation. Or that we've become a super power only because of military and economic imperialism. Or maybe you've heard pundits in the news or on talk radio claim that America has lost its way and will fall like the Roman Republic of old. If you are feeling unsure about what to believe, you've made a good decision to start reading and learning on your own.

Third, you are concerned about the future of our country. We live in an age when an increasing number of citizens no longer have faith in the political institutions that govern our nation. Many have begun to doubt the principles on which our nation is based and discuss them with indifference or outright rejection. You believe that this country is worth fighting for and that there are political principles and institutions worth preserving. You're just not sure how to articulate it. If ever there was a time to take a deeper look at the origins, principles, and importance of our constitutional government, now is the time.

You are doing the right thing by educating yourself about our Constitution. By taking responsibility, you've made an important first step toward understanding what our constitutional system is all about and how unique it is in the annals of human history. What you'll discover in the story to come is that America *is* an exceptional country, regardless of what you might see in social media, read in the news, or hear on a college campus. That exceptionalism is institutionalized in our constitutional government, and that Constitution is based on important principles drawn from history, philosophy, religion, and law. The story of American constitutionalism is unique in the history of mankind … and it's a story worth telling.

Reflection and Choice

Not everyone enjoys studying history, philosophy, religion, or law. For some people, these areas of study seem irrelevant and useless. The people who wrote our Constitution knew otherwise. Our Founding Fathers loved to study these topics because they understood that important lessons could be learned from the past. Remember, the Founders were trying to set up a constitutional government that they hoped would last for generations. This had never been attempted before, and there weren't any contemporary case studies or historical examples of working constitutional republics they could simply adopt. Most of history was marked by the rise and fall of monarchies due to war or power struggles.

Two exceptions from the ancient world were the Athenian democracy and the Roman Republic. These systems were a favorite topic for our Founders. Ancient Greece and Rome were not, however, without their flaws. Eventually both imploded, ending in failed government and civil war. To this end, the examples of Greece and Rome provided important lessons on government both as to what worked and what didn't work.

The Founders were equally fascinated with English history. This was not only because they had strong cultural and historic ties to England, but also because they had considered themselves as Englishmen up until the Revolution. Most importantly, English history provided a relatively recent example of what happens when rights and liberties are violated by a tyrannical government. The English Civil Wars (really a series of wars between 1642 and 1651) pitted parliament against king in a battle for supremacy. The subsequent Glorious Revolution of 1688 resulted in a Parliamentary victory over the monarchy and the adoption of an English Bill of Rights that effectively codified limitations on the government.

The Founding Fathers studied ancient and modern history—from Ancient Greece to 17th-century England—to learn as much about bad government as good government, and took these lessons to heart when designing our Constitution. And it's this *designing* part that is so critical to understanding how we got our Constitution.

Our country is unique in the annals of history because we designed our own government. What makes America unique is that we established a nation based on principles of our own choosing and instituted a government of our own creation. Alexander Hamilton, who would later act as a strong advocate for the adoption of the Constitution, wrote in the *Federalist Papers (#1)* that the founding of the American nation was basically an experiment to see whether human beings could rule themselves in a government of their own making:

> It has been frequently remarked that it seems to have been reserved to the people of this country, by their conduct and example, to decide the important question, whether societies of men are really capable or not of establishing good government from reflection and choice, or whether they are forever destined to depend for their political constitutions on accident and force.

Think about this. For almost all of human history, mankind had been accustomed to government that was established in one of two ways. The first would be by force, when one group of people overpowers another, who then agree out of fear to submit themselves to the rule of their conqueror. This was the pattern for much of human history, as great rulers like Darius, Alexander, and Julius Caesar swept the ancient world by force. In most of these cases, the conquered were offered the choice to submit or die. Government was largely a product of the sword. In our own world, there are still many places that are essentially controlled by dictators or powerful ruling factions who use fear and violence to maintain power.

The second way governments could come about, wrote Hamilton, was by accident. Hamilton meant that all the weird twists and turns of history, fate, economics, politics, and so forth would elevate one person or group to the top of the heap. These people would become the ruling class or power in society. If not by war, then kings and nobles came to power via birthright, wealth, marriage, or some other political machination. Leadership and political power in ancient Greek and Roman societies, for instance, were based heavily on class structure, social mores, ancient traditions, and a heavy dose of intrigue. The "accidents" Hamilton refers to were these long, convoluted ways of man by which rulers came to power.

The origins of our country, however, are different. Hamilton and the other American Founders rejected the premise that governments must be products of accident or force. To the contrary, our Founders *designed* a government that would be *freely* adopted by the people it would serve. They wanted to see if government could be a product of carefully laid out principles and plans and freely implemented with the consent of the people to be governed. In Hamilton's words, the Founders wanted to establish a government based on *reflection* and *choice*.

It was a novel idea, and one that wasn't necessarily guaranteed to work. The entire idea of "self-government" is based on a risky proposition. Ask yourself this basic question: "Why do people need government?" Your response is probably something along the lines that people need government because human nature is such that we are unable to live peacefully without it. In stronger words, you might argue that men are incapable of living without government because we are basically self-interested, selfish, or evil. James Madison, writing in the *Federalist Papers (#51)* expressed the same sentiment when he wrote, "It may be a reflection on human nature … But what is government itself, but the greatest of all reflections on human nature?"

This skepticism about human nature was widespread among the Founding Fathers. They were profoundly influenced by Christian theology regarding the fallen nature of man, historical lessons from the ancient world, and political philosophy. The Founders understood that the desire for glory, wealth, and power are potent forces in human affairs. The Bible; the histories of Herodotus, Thucydides, Tacitus, and Polybius; and the political writings of thinkers such as Thomas Hobbes and John Locke confirmed this. When Madison writes that "government is basically a reflection of our nature," he really means that government is tragic evidence of our fallen nature, and necessary to compensate for that condition.

Madison also writes, "If men were angels no government would be necessary." But men aren't angels, so this is where it gets tricky. The fallen nature of man creates real problems regarding the operation of government. The dilemma with government, Madison argues, is that it's comprised of the same fallen, fallible, passionate human beings who can't survive without it in the first place. Madison's concern, shared by all the Founders, was that since governments are run by men, these men will struggle with the same passions that make government necessary in the first place. Only now these same men have real power—the power of the government—to use as they will!

The result is that government has the very real potential to become abusive because men might use the powers of government to get stuff (money, power, property, and so forth) for themselves. If rulers come to power via intrigue, war, or happenstance, then we're just stuck with whatever bad government we have the misfortune to live under. About all we can do is hope for a better ruler next time. The only alternative is to fight back, and of course this is dangerous and risks chaos, violence, and death. It's not a pleasant choice to make.

But perhaps there is another option. If we can create a government from "reflection and choice," then perhaps we can *design* a system of government to compensate for human weakness. After all, no sane person would want to design a government to live under that resulted in their own abuse or oppression. That would defeat the very purpose of designing our own government. The government must have limits. Madison makes this clear in one of his most famous passages from *Federalist #51*: "In framing a government which is to be administered by men over men, the great difficulty lies in this: you must first enable the government to control the governed; and in the next place oblige it to control itself."

What would such a government look like? **The Constitution that our Founders created, from conception to ratification, was based on thought-**

ful and carefully asserted principles. This book is the story of those principles, where they came from, and how they influenced the design of our Constitution. Understanding the key principles that inform our Constitution is necessary for understanding what makes this country unique.

Foundational Principles

Our Constitution is framed around six foundational principles. You'll learn more about them in the chapters that follow, but here they are in brief:

1. **Natural Law.** This is the fundamental principle of American constitutionalism. Natural law teaches that our rights exist prior to the establishment of government, that these rights are God given, and that they are part of our nature. Natural law theory lays the groundwork for the idea that the government has limits. There are certain things that even the government should not be able to do.

2. **Liberty.** This principle provides the *purpose* of government, which is to protect our natural rights while promoting order and stability. The protection of our liberty is the ultimate goal of government. Liberty is related to freedom, but they are not the same thing, and the Founders rarely used the latter term except in a cautionary sense. You'll learn that in American constitutionalism, liberty and natural law are inherently related.

3. **Limited Government.** This is the principle that our government is one of limited rather than absolute powers. There are certain things the government is allowed to do, and certain things it is prohibited from doing. Arguments over the scope of governmental power were central to debates over ratification of the Constitution. This remains an important principle of American constitutionalism yet one that is constantly tested.

4. **Popular Sovereignty.** This is the idea that legitimate government only exists with the consent of the people. You might think of it as democracy, though that's not necessarily the best definition of the principle. We'll explore the differences between a democracy and a republic, and the Founders' concerns about the former and preference for the latter.

5. **The Rule of Law.** One of the cornerstones of our political system is our belief in the rule of law. This is the idea that the law must be properly made, applied equally to all persons, and properly enforced. A political system based on the rule of law is essential to preventing the abuse of political power. If you believe in liberty, the rule of law is essential.

6. **Equality.** Equality before the law is a key element of American exceptionalism. It stems from the Founders' belief that "all men are created equal" and should be treated the same in the "eyes of the law." While government must maintain one set of laws for all citizens, the Founders' belief in political equality must not be construed as a desire for "equality of outcomes." You'll understand why soon.

By the end of the book, you'll have a much better understanding of these six principles and why they are important to our Constitution. Our professors at Houston Baptist University, who write and teach in the fields of history, religion, law, and philosophy, will be your guides. They'll help you understand where these six principles came from and how they influenced the construction of our Constitution. By the end of the book, you'll know much more about our Constitution than most people, you'll understand why it's structured the way it is, and how that structure reflects important principles.

The book has four sections, demonstrating the diverse influences that informed our Founding Fathers' views on constitutional government. The first section covers the influences of history on our Founders. You'll explore the lessons of Greek democracy, the fall of the Roman Republic, and the rise of the Roman Empire. You also look at the influence of another empire—England—from the Middle Ages through the English Civil Wars and Glorious Revolution. Then you'll trace the evolution of many of our constitutional principles through the American Revolution, learning that the fight for American independence was really a fight for a return to constitutional government rather than the creation of something new.

The second part of the book explores the numerous philosophical influences on the Founders. Many of that generation were classically educated and studied Herodotus, Thucydides, Plato, Aristotle, Cicero, and Polybius. But even those who lacked a classical education would have been familiar with the ideas espoused by more contemporary thinkers like Locke, Montesquieu, and Blackstone. Jefferson took many of these ideas and synthesized them in a single document called the Declaration of Independence, which provides the philosophical mission statement for our country.

The third section of the book references the many religious ideals that informed our Founding Fathers' views on government. Concepts like natural law, liberty, and equality have strong theological connections that early Americans found familiar and appealing. It is not our intent to revisit the perennial question as to whether America is or is not a "Christian nation." Rather, we emphatically make the case that Christianity was an important influence on the American Founders that cannot be ignored.

The final section of the book traces the legal influences on the U.S. Constitution. Our Founders didn't create the Constitution merely from philosophical ideas or historical anecdotes. To the contrary, our Founders had a long tradition of constitutional law that informed their plans. In this section you'll learn about the Magna Carta, the English Bill of Rights, the Mayflower Compact, early colonial charters and state constitutions, and the

Articles of Confederation. Our Founders had a good idea as to what a new national constitution might look like because there were many existing templates from which to choose.

In sum, we write this book because we want you to understand where the principles in our Constitution come from and why they are important. Our Founders had no shortage of material to draw from, but also no idea as to whether the document they produced would actually work. Our Constitution is more than just words on paper. **Our Constitution is a document based on important principles—principles that must be preserved and passed from generation to generation in order for constitutional government to succeed. American constitutionalism is a culture that will not survive on its own, and is increasingly in danger of being forgotten.**

Alexander Hamilton was right about us—*this is an experiment*. How long our "experiment" in self-government lasts is really up to us to decide. The great powers of the ancient world—Persia, Greece, Rome—eventually faded away. The fate of the United States has yet to be determined. The experiment goes on … for as long as we care to make it last.

Chris Hammons, PhD
Director, Morris Family Center for Law & Liberty
Professor of Political Science
Houston Baptist University

HISTORICAL
INFLUENCES

ATHENIAN DEMOCRACY

By Collin Garbarino, PhD

PROFESSOR OF ANCIENT HISTORY

The purpose of this chapter is two-fold—to give a brief history of the origins of democracy and to think about whether or not it's a good form of government. Regarding that second point, our contemporary society assures us, "Of course it's a good form of government!" Many argue that it's the only good form of government. People have begun to think of democracy, whatever they have in mind by using that word, as the evolutionary conclusion of human political interactions. For the last 60 years or so, we've watched the steady increase in the number of liberal democracies around the globe, but is every government that someone labels as a "democracy" really a democracy?

The word "democracy" has come to mean little more than "I approve of this form of government." In the 21st-century, everyone in the West is in favor of democracy, and everyone knows it must be a good thing. Everyone knows that it has something to do with voting. Everyone knows we need more of it. If only more people would vote! Then we'd have more democracy, and the world would be a better place. Unfortunately, most of these ideas are vague and are not based on much of a historical understanding of what democracy is and where it comes from. So let's start with our first point and look at the origins of democracy.

The Seeds of Democracy

Athens wasn't born a democracy. Human ideas have to start somewhere. In Athens, the seeds of democracy can be found in the archonship of Solon in 594 B.C.

At the beginning of the 6th century B.C., the city of Athens was experiencing social and political turmoil. Many Athenians had fallen into crushing debt, and the aristocracy had lost the ability or the willingness to deal with the problem. Athens had become a city on the verge of political collapse. In order to avoid catastrophe, the city took the extraordinary step of choosing a single man to lead the state. At this point in their history, the Athenians usually chose three archons, or magistrates, to oversee the laws of the city, but in 594 they chose only one: Solon.

Solon had a reputation for great wisdom. In fact, the Greeks would later refer to him as one of the seven sages. During his year in office, he applied that wisdom to creating a constitutional framework to protect the citizens of Athens.

The sources aren't clear as to what exact reforms he made or how he made them. Some aspects of the story haven't survived in the historic record, and the sources occasionally contradict each other. Perhaps some political developments in Athens took place later but then were attributed to Solon. Even so, we have a general idea about some of his most important reforms.

Part of the crisis had to do with the high levels of debt owed by some Athenians who owned small farms. Solon initiated some form of relief for these farmers, though it's unclear to what extent this relief was given. An important aspect of this relief is that Solon outlawed debt slavery, which would have a lasting impact on the way Athenians thought about the intersection of politics and economics. The state's job was to protect its citizens.

Solon also seems to have divided the citizens into political divisions based on wealth. These divisions coincided with the military needs of the city. The richest Athenians were in the top bracket. After them, came Athenians who were wealthy enough to bring a horse to the battlefield. The third group might be analogous to what we'd today call the middle class. These Athenians had small farms and were wealthy enough to equip themselves for battle: able to afford the armor and weapons necessary to defend the city. The last group were day labors without significant wealth who couldn't afford to fight in the city's wars.

Those in the top bracket were eligible to stand for the topmost offices in Athens, while other political service was open to those in the next two brackets. Those at the bottom had little opportunity to influence the direction of the state.

This might not sound like a radical reorganization of political power to modern ears, but Solon's reforms shook up the political landscape of Athens. For the first time, access to political power was tied to economic power rather than birth. No one can change their birth, but people can create wealth. Upward mobility became possible in Athens. In later years, the Athenians extended this principle beyond Solon's intent by opening offices to all citizens no matter how much wealth they had. Solon gave Athenians their first steps toward equality.

After his year as archon expired, Solon left Athens. The city was supposed to live by the laws that he had given them for at least 10 years, and he wanted to avoid the temptation to tinker with them. Solon gave the

Athenians a chance to prove that they could govern themselves without heavy-handed leadership.

The Soil of Tyranny

Solon's reforms settled the civic strife in Athens for about a generation. By 560 B.C., factionalism had reemerged, and the old aristocracies attempted to exploit these rifts for political gain. Megacles led the Athenians of the coast, Lycurgus lead those of the plains, and a young Aristocrat named Pisistratus became the champion of the hillmen. Some historians have speculated that these three factions might represent economic or political distinctions, but probably they merely represent regional loyalties to powerful dynastic families.

The struggle must have led to occasional violence, which gave the opportunistic Pisistratus an idea. The historian Herodotus tells us that Pisistratus wounded himself and told the Athenians that he had been attacked. He managed to convince the city of Athens to give him a bodyguard to protect him from further assaults. With the aid of this bodyguard, Pisistratus proceeded to seize the Acropolis in Athens and install himself as tyrant of the city. Solon, an old man by this time, tried to convince the Athenians to resist Pisistratus's tyranny. When no one listened, he retired from public life.

When modern-day people talk about tyranny it has a wholly negative connotation, but this wasn't the case in ancient Greece. Tyrants could be good or bad, loved or hated by their people. Tyranny merely meant that one man ruled the city without constitutional mandate. Tyrants were often quite popular in Greek cities.

Pisistratus's first tyranny was short-lived. He continued to clash with the other aristocratic families, and it took him two more attempts before his rule over Athens took root. His final tyranny lasted about 20 years, and he ruled as tyrant until his death in 527 B.C., much loved by the common people of Athens.

Since he had trouble with other aristocratic families, Pisistratus spent his last tyranny trying to undermine their authority. He attempted to replace the people's loyalty to various aristocratic dynasties with loyalty to Athens itself. Pisistratus instituted many reforms to promote this end. He constructed great buildings in the name of Athens. He offered low-interest loans to farmers from the state's coffers. He sent out traveling judges who dispensed justice to the countryside in the name of Athens. He began Athens's most important festivals, which helped develop the people's national identity.

Athenians began to rely on Athens itself rather than the goodwill of their local aristocrat. Pisistratus changed the way Athenians thought about what it meant to be citizens of Athens, and for the most part no one noticed much had changed.

The city was contented enough with Pisistratus, but his sons eventually wore out their welcome when they instituted their own tyranny after Pisistratus's death. With the help of the Spartans, the Athenians threw out their tyrants, and the old aristocratic families went back to fighting for influence over the state.

But this time it was different. Pisistratus's tyranny changed how people saw Athens. His habit of ruling in the name of the city rather than his own name created an atmosphere in which the concept of "Athens" began to take up more space in the imaginations of the common people, who the Greeks called the *demos*. Ironically, this left less room for the rule of aristocrats like the sons of Pisistratus and their rivals.

One of the aristocrats, Cleisthenes, understood this shift in the people's thinking, and in 508 B.C. he took a bold step. In order to enact his political policies, Cleisthenes "took the people, the *demos*, into his party." The people no longer needed the aristocrat. The aristocrat needed the people. This move was the birth of the Athenian democracy—rule by the people.

The Blooming of Democracy

What does rule by the people look like? In America we tend to think that rule by the people means that the people elect officials to form a government. The Athenians rejected this premise. Elections don't indicate that the people rule. They merely mean that the people have some say over who rules over them. For an Athenian, democracy meant that every Athenian citizen had equal political opportunity.

Ruling the city fundamentally lay with the Assembly, which comprised all the citizens of Athens. The citizens would meet on a hill in the city and debate policy and vote on laws. No law was too big or too small for the Assembly to debate and consider. At any given meeting they might declare war, evaluate the performance of magistrates, or designate moneys for public works. They might bestow the gift of citizenship on someone who previously didn't qualify. They might even change their mind and vote to repeal the law they had passed the previous day. No Athenian governmental institution could check the Assembly's power. Only speeches filled with persuasive words could sway the citizens of Athens.

How could all those citizens effectively debate policy and vote? Athens was a big city by ancient standards, and at its height it probably had about 350,000 people living in its boundaries. Could 350,000 people function in one legislative body? They didn't have to because not all residents of Athens were citizens.

At the most, Athens probably had 50,000 men who enjoyed the rights of citizenship. Only free, native, adult men counted. As the city grew, the

Athenians took steps to limit citizenship even further by requiring that both of a man's parents had to be from Athenian families. Disenfranchising those who had foreign-born mothers might seem to us an oppressive and anti-democratic policy, but the opposite is actually the case. This law championed the interests of the *demos*, the common people. The only Athenians with non-Athenian wives were the richer, aristocratic Athenians. As the democracy developed, the *demos* looked for more ways to limit the power of the upper classes.

Even with a citizenship of only 50,000, conducting business in the Assembly would have been unwieldly. Debate was somewhat more manageable because the full number of citizens never showed up. Most men had their own business to attend to, and many lived too far away for an easy commute to the Assembly's hill. In some years the Assembly might meet 50 times, and individual citizens would make as many meetings as was practical. When was the last time all 535 members of the United States Congress managed to show up for a vote? The Athenians knew that not everyone would be able to attend, but they decided that at least 6,000 citizens were needed for a quorum.

In order to facilitate the work of the Assembly, Athens had a Council of 500. Solon had created a Council of 400 during his reforms whose membership was limited to the top three economic brackets. Solon's council served as a sort of high court in Athens, but Cleisthenes expanded the council to 500 citizens who would take on some administrative duties in addition to their judicial role. As the democracy developed, all four economic classes began to participate.

The Council of 500 created loose agendas for the Assembly and oversaw some of the day-to-day operations of the city. Not all 500 members worked all the time. They were divided into 10 groups of 50, and each group was responsible for coordinating civic functions for a month. During the month, the 50 active members would rotate the chairmanship.

The Council of 500 played an important role in making sure Athens ran smoothly. You might think that elections would have been competitive for this position, but the Athenians didn't hold elections. Every year, they held a lottery for the 500 seats on this council. Councilmen served one-year terms, and their names would not go into the lottery the next year. An Athenian citizen could only serve twice in his lifetime. After serving twice he would never participate in the lottery again.

The Athenians believed this lottery system to be a cornerstone of democracy. Democracy demands broad participation by the people. By having a lottery and by limiting someone's eligibility to two years, the Assembly ensured that many of the 50,000 citizens would one day serve on this council. In addition to everyone having an equal chance to serve, the large number of men with its rotating leadership meant that no one could gain outsized influence over the government.

During Solon's day, the chief magistrates of Athens were the archons, three aristocrats responsible for the operations of the state. As the common man's role increased, the archons' role changed to accommodate the new political system. Their number was increased to nine, which further shows the Athenian ideal that more leaders means more accountability. The city diminished the archons' powers, taking away responsibilities for war and policy. Rather than creating policy, they executed laws under the oversight of the Council of 500 and the Assembly. At first the Assembly elected the archons, but in the 5th century B.C., lottery replaced elections here too.

In Athens, elections came to be seen as a tool of oligarchy. Who wins elections? Popular men—who too often happen to be the richest men from the "best" families. However, the Assembly knew that a lottery wasn't the best way to select someone for every office. The defense of the city couldn't be left to chance, so the Assembly voted for the members of the Board of Ten Generals. These ten men planned Athenian strategy in times of war and helped shape the city's foreign policy. They served at the pleasure of the Assembly for as long as the Assembly desired. Certain men, like Pericles, served in this capacity year after year, providing the only consistent element in Athens's free-flowing government. Even so, the board functioned like other institutions, with a daily rotation of the chairmanship. Athens trusted the wisdom of the people, but they didn't trust any single person.

These are the institutions of democracy that ushered in Athens's golden age. During the 5th century B.C., Athens built the Parthenon, built an empire, and built the foundation for Western civilization's political theory. **The Athenian democracy left a legacy that people can be loyal to the state rather than certain individuals and that the common people can direct the political institutions.** All citizens participate, so all citizens share in the glory of the city rather than seeing a king claim the glory for himself. But this reality can be a double-edged sword. When the state gets the glory, individuals can appropriate victories for themselves, victories to which they might have contributed very little.

People today often talk about Athens's democracy as the pinnacle of political achievement in the ancient world. This reputation has much to do with the fact that the Athenians devoted many hours to developing the art of rhetoric. After all, how does one sway the Assembly? With fine words. Athenians rewarded the ability to give good speeches, and many of the wealthy spent their money on the best tutors who would teach them how to talk.

The man most responsible for democracy's good name is Pericles, a wealthy aristocrat who devoted his life to making Athens's democracy more democratic. The Assembly loved Pericles, and he served as one of the 10 generals almost continuously for 30 years in the mid-fifth century. During these years, often called the Age of Pericles, he promoted policies that further increased the democratic nature of Athenian politics and gave even more power to the common man.

Pericles was a patriotic Athenian who wanted the rest of the world to see Athens as the preeminent Greek city-state. To this end, he promoted many public works, and he provoked war with Athens's rival Sparta. Beating Sparta in a war would show that democracy was superior to oligarchy (the Spartan form of government).

In 429 B.C., after the first year of the war with Sparta, Pericles gave a speech at a funeral for those who died in battle. In it he encourages his fellow Athenians to continue to fight and to believe in the superiority of their way of life. The historian Thucydides recorded this speech, which we call "the Funeral Oration," and many have looked to it as a summary of the virtues of democracy. After some introductory remarks, Pericles says:

> Our system of government does not copy the institutions of our neighbors. It is more the case of our being a model to others, than of our imitating anyone else. Our constitution is called a democracy because power is in the hands not of a minority but of the whole people. When it is a question of settling private disputes, everyone is equal before the law; when it is a question of putting one person before another in positions of public responsibility, what counts is not membership of a particular class, but the actual ability which the man possesses. No one, so long as he has it in him to be of service to the state, is kept in political obscurity because of poverty. And, just as our political life is free and open, so is our day-to-day life in our relations with each other. We do not get into a state with our next-door neighbor if he enjoys himself in his own way, nor do we give him the kind

of black looks which, though they do no real harm, still do hurt people's feelings. We are free and tolerant in our private lives; but in public affairs we keep to the law. This is because it commands our deep respect.

Pericles goes on to say that all the blessings of Athens stem from its democracy. Athenians are wealthy people and successful in business because of democracy. Athens's military can go toe to toe with the Spartans even though the Spartans bring allied cities with them and the Athenians fight alone. The blessings of democracy make Athens a beautiful place characterized by arts and culture. Pericles believes that no other city in Greece can compare to Athens, and his fine words sway us into believing that he must be right.

The Fading of Democracy

Often, when we read this paean to democracy, we forget about its context in Thucydides's history of the war with Sparta. Thucydides recorded Pericles's speech, but he doesn't want us to forget that Athens's war with Sparta is one that it will not win. Placing this speech on the lips of Pericles becomes a piece of literary irony. Athens, and Pericles with it, becomes the hero of a Greek tragedy. **In Greek tragedies, heroes fall because of their pride. In this case, Athens's pride in its democracy becomes its undoing.**

Just a few pages after Thucydides records Pericles's inspiring speech, he tells us the rest of the story. A plague hit Athens shortly after this, and instead of acting with the virtue that Pericles credits them, the city descended into "lawless extravagance." Everyone lived like there was no tomorrow, and Thucydides says, "Fear of gods or law of man there was none to restrain them."

The plague devastated the city, but worst of all, it killed Pericles, robbing the city of its greatest leader. Politics began to spin out of control, and Spartans eventually handed the Athenians a military humiliation. Some might say that when Pericles died, the Athenian democracy died with him. But actually, our eye witness, Thucydides, believed otherwise.

Thucydides suggested that the democracy under Pericles was a democracy in name only. The city was actually ruled by Pericles as a monarch under the guise of democratic principles. We might think of this as a criticism, but Thucydides meant it as a compliment. After Pericles was gone, the democracy was free of restraints. Demagogues rose up to fill the power vacuum, telling the people what they wanted to hear rather than what they needed to hear. The Assembly acted recklessly and often unjustly. Most disturbingly, anyone who questioned the wisdom of the mob suffered its wrath.

In 416 B.C., Athens had a temporary truce with Sparta and looked for more allies in case of renewed hostilities. The Assembly sent the army and navy to the small island city of Melos to encourage its inhabitants to join Athens's league. Athens expected the Melians to pay money to them every year as members of the league. The Melians declined to join Athens, pointing out that they'd prefer to remain neutral in the conflict between the two larger states. The Athenians would have none of it. They told the Melians that an alliance would be mutually beneficial. It would benefit Athens because they would profit from the money paid by Melos. It would benefit the Melians because otherwise Athens would destroy them. The Melians tell the Athenians that this extortion violates the principles of justice. The Athenians tell the Melians that the strong get to determine what is just. When the Melians resist, the Athenians attack the island, killing all the men and selling all the women and children into slavery. According to the Assembly, freedom is only for Athenians.

Athens continued to act without wisdom or justice in its war with Sparta, and eventually Sparta succeeded in gaining victory in 404 B.C. After the Athenians surrendered, Sparta's allies begged her to kill all the Athenian men and sell the women and children into slavery. The other cities of Greece blamed Athens for the suffering that this 30-year war had caused. Sparta demurred. The Spartans believed that Athens itself wasn't the problem. The problem was that the Athenians had a bad form of government, democracy. The Spartans installed an oligarchy in Athens and withdrew to their own territory.

A short time later, Athens overthrew this oligarchy and reinstituted democracy. Far from learning from mistakes, the Assembly began to act recklessly without justice. In 399 B.C., they executed the philosopher Socrates because his continued questions about justice and ethics didn't sit well with the populace. In 351, the Assembly ignored Demosthenes's warnings about the growing threat of Macedonia. They continued to vote more money for the theater subsidies rather than prepare for their defense. By 338 B.C., it was too late. Philip of Macedonia defeated the Athenians in battle, absorbing them into the empire that would be made famous by his son Alexander the Great.

The Limits of Democracy

Some people blame the demagogues for Athens decline, saying unprincipled men led the Athenians astray. However, Athens had prudent men with sense at every stage who warned them of their peril. Nicias warned them of the peril of provoking the Spartans and not being satisfied with what they had. Socrates warned them of the danger of acting without justice. Demosthenes warned them against their foolish disregard of future dangers. The Assembly decided to listen to rascals and fools instead. Might it be because they themselves were nothing but rascals and fools? A city consumed with greed and pride?

Too often in today's political discussions, the answer to every problem is more democracy. At the risk of sounding heretical, what if we need the opposite? Could it be that we are living in an age with too much democracy? We talk about democracy as if it's an inherent good, so if it's good, more of it must be better. We should probably imagine democracy as a method by which we can bring about good, rather than a good in and of itself.

When we think of the four cardinal virtues—prudence, justice, temperance, and courage—and the three theological virtues—faith, hope, and love—we notice that democracy doesn't make the list. Democracy could be a means of manifesting those virtues, but it can only manifest those virtues if the people voting possess those virtues. **Democracy contains nothing but what we bring to it.** The champions of unfettered democracy often miss this point. Many people have the belief that human beings are basically good and that if we ask enough people's opinion we'll arrive at a good answer.

The goodness of humanity has been a point of contention for much of the history of the West. The Athenians seemed to have a great deal of confidence in the moral judgement of the common man. The Romans, on the other hand, seemed to think that every generation of Romans was morally worse than the one before it. The Church taught that all human beings are tainted with original sin and that government must act as a viceroy for God to restrain it. The Enlightenment claimed that the human race was infinitely perfectible. During the Industrial Revolution we felt as if we had become the masters of the universe, but two world wars taught us that human beings are more vicious than any of nature's beasts.

If our government lacks virtue, it's because we ourselves, like the Athenians before us, have failed to be virtuous. If our elected officials lack virtue, whose fault is it but our own? When we look at our toxic political context, we're actually staring at our own society through the mirror of the democratic process.

Is Democracy a good form of government? Well, it certainly doesn't make people good. We've seen that in the history of Athens. The best anyone can say for democracy is that it gives a people the government that they deserve.

Better than Democracy

America's Founders sought to give us a government better than we deserve—a government that includes the checks and restraints that democracy lacked. Many of our Constitution's framers had a rather dim view of Athens and its democracy. In *Federalist #6*, Hamilton blames Athens's destruction on Pericles and the democracy. In *Federalist #10*, Madison explains the necessity of checks on the people: "To secure the public good and private rights against the danger of [majority rule], and at the same time to preserve the spirit and the form of popular government, is then the great object to which our inquiries are directed." The Founders believed that the purpose of the Constitution—the purpose of the rule of law—is to prevent the majority from doing what it pleases!

Democracies are unstable, and the authors of our Constitution wanted to create a form of government that would last. Madison writes, "Hence it is that such democracies have ever been spectacles of turbulence and contention; have ever been found incompatible with personal security or the rights of property; and have in general been as short in their lives as they have been violent in their deaths." According to our Founding Fathers, the world doesn't need more democracy. *Federalist #63* says, "What bitter anguish would not the people of Athens have often escaped if their government had contained so provident a safeguard against the tyranny of their own passions?" People don't need more voice. They need more restraint.

The Constitution provided Americans with the checks and restraints they needed to ensure good government. Branches of government could restrain each other for the good of the young nation. The people could hold their officials accountable through voting, but the indirect voting of the Constitution was meant to be a safeguard against demagogues telling the people what they wanted to hear.

Athenian-style freedom embodied in its democracy has proven to be a seductive ideal. For almost 200 years, American society has been slowly succumbing to the fine words of Pericles. Our Founding Fathers disliked Athenian democracy, but its reputation has experienced an almost complete rehabilitation. We tend to listen to the high-minded idealism of the Athenians, but we forget to look at the suffering and destruction that that idealism wrought. We must establish our government upon sound principles because we cannot find sound men to establish it upon. Humans have proven time and time again to be unreliable.

We've lost part of what was distinctive about our Constitution. *Federalist #63* said that the distinctiveness of American government "lies IN THE TOTAL EXCLUSION OF THE PEOPLE, IN THEIR COLLECTIVE CAPACITY, from any share in the government." These words, written by our Founders, sound strikingly un-American to 21st-century ears. They were so concerned about the abuses of freedom that they conceived of the Senate as being wholly removed from the people's control. But the Founders believed that government composed of the people's representatives had a better chance at promoting human flourishing than did a true democracy. The Constitution sought to restrain the relativistic idea that every man's opinion is as good as another's.

The Athenians only understood liberty, and their Spartan rivals only understood law. However, the Founders believed in both law and liberty. American constitutionalism rejects this false dichotomy that the Greeks present to us. In looking for models for America's Constitution, the Founders had to look beyond Greece. They found the inspiration in the histories of Rome and Britain—systems with a more balanced view of law and liberty. This balance of law and liberty in our Constitution is a delicate thing, and emphasizing one over the other could destroy both.

RECOMMENDED READING

Aristotle, *The Athenian Constitution*

Herodotus, *The Histories*

Thucydides, *The History of the Peloponnesian War*

THE
FALL OF ROME

By Steve Jones, PhD
PROFESSOR OF CLASSICS

The fall of Rome was a focal point for our Founding Fathers, but not in the way we often think. The Founders attempted to emulate the Roman Republic, not the later Empire, so they thought long and hard about how to avoid the Republic's fate. They aimed at the preservation of liberty, not the consolidation of power. This chapter will consider the ways in which our Founders sought to imitate and improve upon the Roman Republic. They wanted to create a new republic that imitated the strengths of Republican Rome but mitigated its weaknesses so as to hopefully avoid its fall.

Rome's Genius: The Mixed Constitution

The Roman Republic was itself an innovation. The Roman historian Polybius distinguished between three basic types of government: monarchy, rule by one person; aristocracy, rule by an elite group of people; and democracy, rule by the people themselves. He also acknowledged men could distort each type of government. In its ideal state, monarchy is the benevolent rule of an individual eager to create government that benefits all members of society. But monarchy can become tyranny when a single person preys upon the people for his own benefit. In its ideal form, aristocracy is the guiding of a government by a small group of talented individuals. When distorted, aristocracy degenerates into oligarchy, where only a closed group of a privileged few have access to the mechanisms of government. Democracy, where the government is managed by the people, when distorted, descends into ochlocracy, a Greek word meaning "mob rule."

In determining which form of government was best, people sometimes argued that in a perfect world full of good people and just leaders, monarchy was the ideal form of government. But in an imperfect world, monarchy is the most prone to abuses. Democracy was seen as the weakest form of government, but it had the most checks on the abuses of powerful men. Polybius suggested that political history oscillates between the various forms of governments. As one form descended into corruption, another form would rise to replace it. When that one became distorted, it too would be replaced.

The genius of the Roman Republic was that it replaced a broken and corrupt monarchy that had descended into tyranny with a mixed constitution, blending all three forms of government, in the hopes that the strengths of each would be a check on the weaknesses of the others. The power of monarchy was represented by the consuls of Rome. The Roman Senate represented Aristocracy. The Council of the Plebs represented democracy.

The idea of a mixed constitution, however, was not the original idea of a single individual or group created in the course of an afternoon. It grew and developed over generations, but the final product of Rome's Republic inspired America's Founders to create their own mixed constitution in their own lifetimes.

The Origin and Development of the Republic

According to tradition, Rome was founded in 753 B.C. by Romulus. Its initial system of government was monarchy, and for almost 250 years, kings ruled Rome. In 509 B.C., the Roman aristocracy rose up in revolt. Led by a man named Brutus, they deposed the kings of Rome and founded the Republic.

The world "republic" comes from the Latin phrase "res publica," which means "the public thing." Romans did not want the power of government to be the private concern of a single person or family. They transferred power from the king to the Senate, a group of powerful and wealthy aristocrats. The name "Senate" comes from a Latin word meaning "Old Guys." Founded during the time of the kings, the Roman Senate was not an elected body but a board of advisors representing the major aristocratic clans of Rome. The Senate divided the power of the single king between two consuls, who were elected yearly by popular vote and who served as an executive body and the generals of Rome's citizen army.

The birth of the Republic began as a conflict between a king and the nobility, but this conflict became the catalyst for larger cultural developments. This struggle between the kings and the patricians, the term the Romans used to refer to their aristocracy, grew into a new crisis, called by historians "the Conflict of the Orders." This conflict led to the further expansion and development of the Republic.

Roman society comprised two orders or classes of people: patricians—the aristocrats—and plebeians—the common people. From 494 to 287 B.C., the plebeians struggled, protested, demanded, and negotiated to gain equal protection from government, fair treatment by government, and greater participation in government.

One early victory for the plebeians was the publication of the so-called "Twelve Tables." Around 450 B.C., plebeians began to demand equal treatment under the law. To placate the plebeians, the magistrates wrote down the laws on 12 bronze tablets and posted them in a public space so that all Romans could read the laws for themselves. The Twelve Tables are an important milestone in the development of the Republic because the law was no longer in the custody of a few elite magistrates, but was publically codified for all citizens. Though unfair application of the law no doubt continued to exist, the content and nature of the law was publicly known.

Over the next few hundred years, plebeians gained the right to run for political offices once open only to patricians. Along with the right to hold political office came entrance to the Senate. During the Republic the Senate gradually gained more influence than it had under the kings, but it was still basically an advisory council. Its decrees advised and directed the actions of the magistrates. The magistrates originally came from patrician families, and the Senate served as a pool from which future magistrates were drawn. After their year of political service ended, magistrates returned to the Senate as perpetual members. It became customary that once a person had held certain high-level political offices (consul, praetor, quaestor, aedile), he was guaranteed admission to the Senate. By earning the opportunity to run for these offices, the Plebeians also gained access to participation in the Senate.

In addition to gaining access to offices and institutions previously reserved for patricians, the plebeians also gained recognition for their own institution, the Council of the Plebs, and the creation of their own representatives, the tribunes of the plebs.

The Council of the Plebs began as an informal plebeian gathering during the early days of the Conflict of the Orders, and it petitioned the patricians for redress of certain grievances. The plebeians gained political concessions from the patricians by withdrawing from civic life and work for periods of time. These periodic withdrawals, called Secessions of the Plebs, demonstrated the importance of the plebeians in all aspects of the Roman economy. They also underscored that the plebeians were numerically superior. A secession of the plebs was a powerful demonstration, and it always led to the Patricians giving in. However, the plebs knew that secessions were serious and extreme, so they were careful and strategic in using them. From 494 to 287 B.C., only five successions of the plebs occurred.

The First Secession of the Plebs in 494 B.C. led to the creation of a political representative for the plebeian class: the tribune of the plebs. Tribunes gained several important powers that made them integral to the working of the state. First, they were sacrosanct, which meant that it was against the law to physically intimidate or assault them. They could convene the Senate, propose legislation, and, perhaps most importantly, veto the acts of the consuls or other magistrates. These extensive powers ensured that the plebeians always had a voice in the Republic. The Senate didn't know that the creation of this office and its powers planted the seeds that would lead to the downfall of the Republic. But more about that later.

The Last Secession of the Plebs in 287 B.C. led to the Senate acknowledging that the decrees of the Council of the Plebs carried the full force of law and were binding on all Romans. We call these laws plebiscites. By granting this power to the Council of the Plebs, the Senate legitimized the Council of the Plebs and made it a formal part of the Roman government. What had started as an informal meeting to address the problems of the Plebs, in barely 200 years, had become the primary legislative body in Rome.

With the recognition and incorporation of the Plebeian Council into the formal structure of the government, the Roman Republic reached its full form. Over the next few hundred years, Rome gained strength and extended its influence through the Mediterranean world. Eventually, though, the scope of Rome's territory strained these political systems that were designed to govern a single city. Understanding why the Roman Republic collapsed was just as important to the Founders as the reasons for its rise.

Crisis of the Late Republic

Rome's Republic can be divided into three main sections: Early Republic (509–390 B.C.), Middle Republic (390–146 B.C.), and Late Republic (146–27 B.C.). The Early Republic encapsulates the rise of the Republic. Most of the institutions and offices of the Republic emerged and developed during this time, and Rome is one city among several in central Italy beginning to vie for prominence.

The Sack of Rome by the Gauls in 390 B.C. marks the transition from the Early to the Middle Republic. Traumatized by the destruction, the Romans determined never to let Rome be sacked again. The Middle Republic is the story of how Rome began to make defensive alliances with neighboring towns and gradually grew from a crossroads river town perched atop seven hills into a city-state ruling the Mediterranean and eventually much of Europe. During this period Rome fought three wars against Carthage, a powerful rival on the northern coast of Africa. With Carthage gone, there were few rivals left to challenge the power of Rome across the Mediterranean basin, but as Rome's power expanded, the larger territory stressed its political systems.

The last stage of the Republic, called the Late Republic, is the period that sees the Republic collapse. Because of Rome's military successes, certain leaders gained immense power and wealth. Strongmen discovered cracks in the Republic and began to exploit them to their own advantage.

The first of the great men to take the stage in the Late Republic were Tiberius Gracchus and his brother Gaius. As tribunes of the plebs, Tiberius in 133 B.C. and his brother following in 123 B.C., they attempted to enact laws to distribute to the common people land, grain, and money that the government had acquired in its expansion. The Senate violently opposed the Gracchi and their reforms. Both brothers died at the hands of angry mobs organized by the patricians.

It might be tempting to reduce the senatorial response to the Gracchi to greed, jealously, and power mongering. But in truth, the Gracchi's actions panicked the Roman Republic because the brothers had created a cult of personality by proposing measures popular with the people. The Patricians weren't necessarily against land distribution. They were angered because the Gracchi attempted to have themselves appointed as the head of the land redistribution commission. Such actions raised the suspicion of the senators that the Gracchi sought to make themselves kings. Ever since the expulsion of the kings in 509 B.C., the primary political fear in Rome was that some individual would attract to himself too much personal political power from the people. Such men, dubbed "populares," were seen as dangerous and were looked on with suspicion.

The next blow to the Roman Republic came from Gaius Marius, a Roman soldier who professionalized the Roman Army and upended traditional limits on serving as consul. His actions unleashed almost a century of civil war in Rome. Up until the time of Marius, citizen soldiers made up the Roman Army. Each citizen's tax bracket determined his role in the army, and those without property could not serve. Most soldiers were farmers. They planted their crops in the spring, went off to war for the summer, and returned to their fields in time for harvest. This regular pattern occurred each year since the time of the kings. As the Roman sphere of influence grew, the distance Roman armies had to travel increased. It became harder and harder for armies to end their campaigns in time to return home before harvest. Many farms failed and fell into foreclosure, and many soldiers' families fell into poverty while they were gone. A change was needed, but no one knew what other options would be possible.

The opportunity for reform came to Marius in 107 B.C. Ever since Rome's sack in 390 B.C., the idea of Gauls struck terror in the hearts of Romans. When a band of Gauls appeared on Rome's northern frontier, the Senate sent both consuls and their legions to face this threat. Marius knew that the more serious threat to Rome lay in the North African province of Numidia. He had no more troops to send, but he persuaded the Senate to allow him to recruit an army from the property-less citizens and equip them at the expense of the state.

Marius's reforms transformed the army from a citizen to a professional army with several consequences that changed Rome forever. First, it created a class of career soldiers who were able to serve for long periods of time away from Rome. These soldiers, after their years of service ended, could retire to outlying regions to Romanize uncivilized territory and to provide reserve troops in time of need. The reforms also standardized the equipment of the Roman Army. What had been a hodgepodge of whatever military equipment each person was able to provide became a Roman equivalent of "Government Issue." The American military has "G.I. Joe." The Roman Army had "Marius's Mules," nicknamed for the large amount of standardized government gear that these soldiers were expected to carry.

These innovations increased the number of legions that could be in the field and increased the time and distance they could remain on campaign. But this new army also came at a cost, literally. Previously, the army was limited to citizens with property, and the planting season constrained how long they could be gone. Now the only limiting factor was the amount of money needed to outfit such an army. The money to pay these soldiers didn't come from the coffers of the state but from the conquest of the generals. Initially this change relieved the penny-pinching Roman Senate, but this method for paying soldiers ended up being the primary catalysts in the downfall of the Republic. In order for soldiers to get paid, they needed to win. The more they won, the more loyalty they felt, not to Rome, but to their own generals. Suddenly strongmen interested in seizing control of the government had veteran soldiers loyal to them and willing to go wherever the general led.

Marius also undermined the Republic by running for multiple consulships in a row. He was elected consul in 107 B.C. He then held the consulship for a series of years in succession from 104 to 100 B.C. This might not seem like a big deal, but one of the purposes of the Republic was to ensure that one person didn't acquire too much power. The consuls already had the power of a king. What checked their kingly potential was that they were elected annually and only served for a year. How would a consul be different from a king if he was elected every year? Earlier in the Republic, a gentleman's agreement existed among the senators requiring a 10-year gap between consulships, and eventually they gave up second consulships altogether. Marius argued the necessity of holding multiple consulships in succession based on external threats. Rome needed a proven, successful leader to guide the city in troubled times.

After Marius, various strongmen rose through the ranks of the army, gained commands for themselves, and took control of the state by force. Marius's reform of the army led to almost a century of civil war and culminated in the rise and fall of Julius Caesar.

Julius Caesar was from an ancient and prestigious Roman family that had fallen into obscurity. His family's return to prominence started when Gaius

Marius married Julius Caesar's aunt. The Julius family claimed descent from one of Rome's founders, Iulus, the son of Aeneas, and through him from the God Venus herself. Marius was successful and wealthy, but he lacked a prestigious family. Marius hoped that by marrying into the Julius family he could gain at least the attention, and hopefully the approval of, the senatorial aristocrats. It worked.

Caesar watched the career of his uncle and set out to accomplish something similar. He knew that in Rome political power came through wealth and military experience, neither of which he had much of. To remedy this, he made a deal with the people who did have them. He made a secret agreement with Pompey and Crassus to manipulate the Roman government. They formed an alliance known to history as the First Triumvirate. Pompey was Rome's most powerful general and Crassus was one of Rome's wealthiest citizens. Caesar asked these two powerful men to help him get elected to the consulship. In exchange, Caesar promised to spend his year in office promoting the agendas of his two benefactors. Caesar asked to be governor of Gaul when his year in office was over. By Caesar's day, it had become custom for consuls to spend their year of office in the city, then in the following year be sent out to govern a province.

Caesar chose Gaul strategically. Roman politicians needed military victories, and the best military victories were over the hated Gauls who had sacked Rome centuries before. Caesar spent 10 years "pacifying" Gaul after his term as consul. His fortune grew, and his army became seasoned soldiers. His reputation among the people grew as well thanks to the *Gallic Wars*, a book that he wrote describing his campaigns.

The Senate grew fearful of Caesar's popularity and looked for a reason to remove him from power. In 49 B.C., as Caesar's time in the province was ending, he asked the Senate for the right to run for consul again, this time *in absentia*. The Senate refused, telling him that if he wanted to run for office, he would need to return to Rome. They did this hoping to separate him from his army. Roman generals didn't have the authority to command their armies outside of the province where they were assigned. Caesar, fearing a trap, made the fateful decision to take his armies with him when he returned to Rome. In January of 49 B.C., he took his army over the shallow stream that marked the boundary between Gaul and Italy, and in doing so immortalized it as a metaphor for the point of no return. Caesar crossed the Rubicon.

This act sparked another round of civil wars. When Caesar returned victorious to Rome, he granted clemency to all who had opposed him. He hoped to put civil war behind him, but the Senators he spared were still suspicious of his growing power. They formed a conspiracy to assassinate Caesar. If any single event led to Caesar's assassination, it was his obtaining the office "Dictator for Life." The Roman government had the power to create an office called "dictator." It was the Roman equivalent of declaring martial law. It happened in times of emergency and gave the person total control of all aspects of Rome's military and political life. The primary check on the power of the dictator was the term of office: 18 months. In many people's eyes, the only difference between a king and a dictator was the time frame. If Caesar was dictator for life that meant he was a king.

In Caesar's defense, he most likely sought the office to insulate himself from senatorial prosecutions. He saw the problems facing the Roman state and believed it needed a single hand to guide it, but in doing what he did, he alienated enough people that on March 15, 44 B.C., the so-called "Ides of March," a group of senators surrounded Caesar as he entered the Senate and stabbed him to death. One of the chief assassins was a man named Marcus Junius Brutus whom the conspirators had recruited to demonstrate their just intentions. An earlier Brutus had saved Rome from the corrupt kings: this Brutus would deliver Rome from the man who would be king.

Unfortunately for the conspirators, most of the Roman people were sad to hear of Caesar's death. Some feared his armies. Some loved him as a benefactor. Some were exhausted by generations of civil war and were willing to endure autocracy. They were right to fear more bloodshed. Mark Antony and Lepidus, two of Caesar's lieutenants, teamed up with Octavian, the heir to Caesar's estate, to form what history knows as the Second Triumvirate. These three men chased Caesar's murderers out of Rome and defeated them, before eventually turning on each other. The last battle of this century of Roman civil war was fought off the northwest coast of Greece at a place called Actium. In 31 B.C., Octavian defeated Anthony and his new wife, the Egyptian queen Cleopatra, in a decisive sea battle. Octavian was the last strongman standing. He had tremendous wealth, sole control of Rome's military power, and, as a product of the other two, total political control of the state.

When Octavian returned to Rome, everyone expected him to solidify perpetual control, but he did something no one expected. In 27 B.C., he entered the Senate House and said, "I restore the Republic." Over the next 40 years through a series of compromises and settlements, Octavian ruled Rome as a sole ruler but without angering the senatorial elite like Caesar had. How did he survive, where Caesar was killed? He claimed to restore the Roman Republic. He wanted people to see him as the strong man able to keep other people from sabotaging the state. He was elected consul several times, but he eventually gave up all official positions of power. He was a patrician, and not eligible to become a tribune of the plebs, but the common people loved him so much that they voted to give him the power of the tribunes. Even without official position, he had the authority to convene the Senate, to propose legislation, and to veto the acts of magistrates. Octavian had the power he needed to rule Rome without angering Romans. The city bestowed on him the honorary name that history knows him by: "Augustus."

Augustus was the first Roman emperor. He transitioned the Republic to one-man rule, but he did it so quietly that most Romans did not know the Republic was dead. The Roman elites believed everything had returned to the way it was supposed to be. Senators gave speeches. The city elected consuls. Tribunes proposed legislation. But one man off to the side made sure that the state ran smoothly and that no other strongmen could disrupt it again. The Republic was dead, but it took almost a hundred years before the Romans realized it.

Imitating and Improving Upon Rome

The fall of the Republic escaped the notice of most people at the time, but later history saw the change clearly. The American Founders understood the roles that the Gracchi, Marius, and Caesar played. **In founding the American Republic, our Founding Fathers determined to replicate many of Rome's institutions while at the same time improving them in order to avoid or at least delay its downfall.**

Hopefully, as you read the narrative above on the founding and fall of the Republic, you noticed points where American institutions mimic Roman ones, as well as perhaps some innovations or modifications. This imitation was done consciously to replicate the blended government that the Roman Republic developed into.

To replace the deposed kings, the Roman Republic created two executives called consuls and elected them annually. The American Founders imitated this office, giving the American Republic two executives. Two consuls prevented one person from consolidating too much power, but this division created its own problems. On occasion, the two consuls fought over who had preeminence. To counter this new problem, American Founders came up with a slight innovation and subordinated one executive to the other when they created the offices of president and vice-president. Originally, the office of vice-president was conceived to be not the president's running mate but his chief rival, the person who received the second-most votes.

The Founders also mirrored the Roman Republic's multiple legislative bodies. The American Senate replicated the functions of its Roman equivalent. The House of Representative reproduced the democratic functions of the Council of the Plebs.

One weakness that the Founders saw in the Roman Republic was that it lacked a written constitution. Much of the Roman government was unwritten, relying upon the *Mos Maiorum* which means "the custom or tradition of our ancestors." When men arose who had no respect for these customs, nothing prevented people from disregarding the traditional forms of government. The Founders sought to remedy this problem by writing down the Constitution and formalizing the mechanisms of government and the basis for legislation.

A third major innovation was the subordination of the military to the civil authority. The Declaration of Independence lists as one of its complaints that the British Crown had rendered "the Military independent of and superior to the Civil Power." They also saw this as a central flaw in the Roman system. The military reforms of Gaius Marius had the consequence of making the military difficult for the state to control. America attempted to solve the problem by making the president the commander-in-chief of the military and requiring him to be a civilian. It's important that the president wears a suit, not a military uniform. Even when the president is a former military general, he must lay aside the uniform in order to be president.

America & Rome

One wonders if America will fall prey to similar problems that befell the Roman Republic. The current size and population of America puts stress on the political systems of the American Republic. Time will tell what the effects of such stress will be. Will strongmen exploit these stresses to take control of the state? Will we experience the unsuspecting loss of liberty? Will America be reorganized into a form different but hard to distinguish from itself? Would we notice it happening? Will America fall like Rome did?

Today, some claim that Rome is an unworthy model. The history of Rome, they argue, is a story of slavery, oppression, and conquest, and therefore is not worthy of imitation. Those who copy Rome's successes bring similar bloodshed and ultimately die by the sword. There are numerous aspects of ancient Rome that are open to critique and condemnation, but it is folly to refuse to learn from the good because of the bad. Rome used its power and influence to bring peace and prosperity to the ancient world. What caused its growth? What were its greatest successes? Are of these successes worth repeating? How did it fail? What can be done to prevent a fall? These are questions worth asking.

These questions are especially worthwhile for us because America's Founding Fathers pondered the same questions about ancient Rome. They consciously imitated the political systems of Ancient Rome so as to replicate their success. They also took steps to modify Rome's weaknesses in the hope of avoiding its fall.

Before answering the question of whether America will fall like Rome, it is important to ask a clarifying question. When did Rome fall? It might come as a shock to learn that scholars don't actually agree about when Rome fell. Most people have heard about the Fall of Rome discussed in very vague terms, but the actual when, where, and how is always missing.

The Fall of Rome is difficult to pin down. There are at least five good candidates for the actual date of the Fall of Rome. Understanding the reasons for each date and the differences between them will be important if we wish to draw parallels and connections with America.

Option #1:
A.D. 476—Romulus Augustus Deposed

Most books usually date the fall of Rome to A.D. 476. This date is a useful fiction. In 476, the last Roman emperor ruling from Rome, Romulus Augustus, was deposed by the Germanic general Odoacer who, instead of crowing himself the new Roman emperor, decided he would rather call himself the King of Italy.

This date puts a nice neat bow on the Roman Empire. It seems both poetic and ironic that the last Roman emperor (Romulus Augustus) was named after both the founder of the city of Rome—Romulus—and the founder of the Roman Empire—Augustus. The truth is that by this point the western Roman emperor had largely ceased to matter in Roman politics. About 200 years earlier, the much-maligned last persecutor of the Church, the emperor Diocletian, had realized that the Roman Empire was too unwieldy for one man to rule alone. To solve the administrative nightmare, he divided the empire into two halves: eastern and western.

The eastern half of the empire, centered in modern-day Turkey, was far more prosperous and peaceful. The western half, ruled from Italy, sank slowly into instability and economic obscurity as wave after wave of Germanic invaders attacked, looted, and destroyed. By A.D. 476, Rome was an unimportant city even in the Western Roman Empire. It wasn't even the administrative capital of Italy. Most decisions were made in Ravenna, a new outpost founded on the Adriatic Sea, south of modern-day Vienna.

When Odoacer decided that he would rule in the West, and not be some figurehead in Rome, it's doubtful if anyone noticed. If they did notice, they probably didn't care. The Germanic tribes that had invaded in the previous century held the real power in Italy and in the Western Roman Empire. This act simply formalized what was already the case. And after all, a Roman emperor still ruled in the East in Constantinople.

Option #2:

A.D. *410—Rome Sacked by Alaric the Visigoth*

If A.D. 476 isn't when Rome fell, perhaps it was a generation earlier. Starting in the late 3rd century, Germanic tribes began migrating into the Roman Empire. They came looking to participate in the health and prosperity of the Roman Empire. Some came peacefully, but most brought bloodshed with them. The Gothic ruler who did the most damage to the Roman Empire was Alaric the Visigoth.

In A.D. 410, Alaric did something that shocked the entire Roman world. He sacked the city of Rome itself. Roman territory had suffered invasion and even some defeats at the hands of the Germans and other enemies, but no foreign army had been able to conquer the city of Rome itself since the Gauls sacked Rome in 390 B.C.

In 390 B.C., a group of Gauls had invaded Italy. After defeating the Roman Army at the Battle of Allia, they sacked Rome. The devastation was so bad that Romans briefly considered relocating to a nearby city which, though recently conquered, was in much better shape than Rome. The Gallic Sack of Rome was the event that thrust Rome onto the world stage. It forced the city to reexamine who it was and what it wanted. Traumatized by the events of 390 B.C., the Romans determined never to let Rome be sacked again. So deeply ingrained was this sentiment that hundreds of years later, any band of Gauls even approaching the borders of the Roman Empire was cause for alarm. Rome began by making defensive alliances with neighboring towns and gradually grew from a crossroads river town perched atop seven hills into a city-state ruling first Latium, then Italy, the Mediterranean, and eventually much of Europe. So successful were Rome's efforts to secure her own peace that Rome herself wasn't sacked again for 800 years until Alaric the Visigoth did it in A.D. 410.

Unfortunately, A.D. 410 doesn't serve as a useful date for the fall of Rome either. The A.D. 410 sack of Rome was more symbolic than serious. Rome had ceased to matter. It had been replaced first by Milan and then by Ravenna. Rome was now a decaying relic—loved and revered but unimportant to the commerce and politics of the Roman Empire.

Option #3:
A.D. 330—Constantine Moves the Capital

It is hard for us to imagine, but pre-Columbus Europe faced east. The Eastern Mediterranean, with its proximity to the wealth of Persia, was the place to be. Rome, on the west coast of Italy was out of the way and far from the action. In A.D. 325, Emperor Constantine rebuilt Byzantium, a city situated on the Bosphorus, the narrow strait of water that connects the Mediterranean Sea with the Black Sea and divides Europe. He named it New Rome, but most people called it Constantinople, the City of Constantine.

In A.D. 330, Constantine moved the administrative center of the Roman Empire from Rome to this eastern city. This shift marked the parting of ways for the two halves. What gradually emerged was two separate and distinct cultures. The Western Roman Empire was ruled from Italy, and spoke Latin. The Eastern Roman Empire was ruled from Constantinople and spoke Greek.

As the Western Roman Empire crumbled, the Eastern Empire continued for another thousand years. So different were the fates of the two halves of the empire that scholars separate them into two different entities calling the western half the Roman Empire, and the eastern half the Byzantine Empire, after the original name of Constantinople. Given the different trajectories of the two halves of the Roman Empire, some argue that when Constantine moved the capital he ended the Roman Empire and created something entirely new.

It's important to realize, though, that the term "Byzantine" is a later designation. The rulers in Constantinople considered themselves Roman emperors. Several took it upon themselves to attempt to reconquer the portions of the Western Roman Empire that had been lost to the Gothic Invasions. But whatever was lost, the heart of Rome continued to beat in the East.

Option #4:
A.D. *1453—Constantinople Falls*

If there is continuity between the Latin-speaking Roman Empire and what we have come to call the Byzantine Empire, then another possible date for the fall of Rome is when the last emperor of Rome was conquered. This happened in 1453 when Mehmet II, the Sultan of the Ottoman Turkish Empire, conquered Constantinople. It's staggering to contemplate that less than a generation before Columbus, there was still a man calling himself the Roman Emperor ruling in a city built by Constantine the Great.

Some might argue that the Byzantine Empire was too different to still be reasonably considered the Roman Empire. The truth is, though, that more than just calling themselves the Romans, they were actively engaged in preserving and defending the legacy of Rome.

Constantinople, though in the East, preserved and continued the Roman legal tradition. The Justinian Code, published around A.D. 530, was an encyclopedia that codified and standardized Roman law. When Roman law was lost in the West with the coming of the Germanic Tribes, the East kept it alive though the Justinian Code and eventually reintroduced it to the West around A.D. 1000.

Constantinople also preserved a tremendous amount of classical Greek and Roman learning. The best example of this is the Byzantine encyclopedia called the Suda. Written in the 10th century A.D., the Suda contains over 30,000 entries on topics ranging from ancient writers and ancient history to ancient religion, both Pagan and Christian. The Suda is just one example of the way in which a tremendous amount of ancient learning from Rome survived, thanks to the Byzantines. The reason they did this: they saw themselves as the guardians of that legacy.

Option #5:
World War I—The Last Gasp of the Roman Empire
It is possible to move the final fall of Rome even closer to modern times. World War I was the last gasp of the Roman Empire. Three of the major belligerents in the Great War all claimed to be the direct heirs of the power and authority of the Roman Empire. As discussed above, the Turkish Ottoman Empire laid claim to the legacy of Rome as the conqueror of Constantinople and through the absorption of the territory of the Eastern Empire.

Russia also considered itself an heir to the Roman Empire. Shortly after the fall of Constantinople, Sophia Palaiologina, the niece of the last Byzantine Roman Emperor, Constantine XI Palaiologos, married Ivan III, a Russian prince who went on to unite all Russian lands and expand Russian dominance over central Asia. His heirs interpreted his marriage as transferring the power of the fallen Byzantine Roman Empire to Russia as a "Third Rome." Towards this end, they adopted the title "Tsar" or "Czar" (a Russian translation of "Caesar") to acknowledge their belief that they were the legitimate heirs to the Roman legacy.

Germany also entered World War I with a ruler whose title, Kaiser, marked their belief that they were the continuers of the Roman Legacy. This is where the stream of the Roman legacy that passed from the Western Roman Empire reemerges. After the Gothic invasions left the Western Empire weak and fragmented, the Roman Catholic Church stepped into the vacuum and began to perform many of the secular responsibilities of civil government. In A.D. 800, the pope bestowed the title "Emperor of the Romans" on Charlemagne, the King of the Franks. This move led to the eventual creation of a new center of power, roughly in modern-day Germany, called the Holy Roman Empire, claiming continuity with the Roman Empire through the Roman Catholic Church.

When the guns of World War I fell silent on November 11, 1918, three empires that claimed descent from the Roman Empire lay in ruins: the Ottoman Empire was replaced by the secular Republic of Turkey; Russian Tsars were replaced by the Bolsheviks; and the German Kaiser found himself replaced by the doomed Weimar Republic and eventually by Hitler claiming to build another German Empire or Reich, as he called it.

Rome and the American Republic

The Roman Republic lasted from 509 B.C. to 27 B.C., and this period saw the creation of a new form of government and the rise of a small city to a place of prominence on the world stage. Eventually the political systems created to administer a city proved incapable of adapting to the demands of a far-flung empire. The last hundred years of the Republic saw cracks emerge and strong men find ways to take control of the state by force. Finally, after several generations of civil war, the Republic collapsed back into the one-man rule from which it had risen.

The Roman Empire was a system of government that emerged from the ashes of the Republic. Augustus, the first emperor, figured out a way to govern as sole ruler without incurring the wrath of the Senate as his adoptive father Julius Caesar had done. From about 27 B.C. until the empire's eventual collapse, whenever you date it, one-man rule would be the norm.

As fascinating as the story is, it might surprise you to learn that our Founding Fathers were not really all that concerned with the fall of the Roman Empire. **Our Founders were concerned with understanding why the Roman Republic rose and fell rather than the history of the subsequent Roman Empire.** The fall of the Empire was merely the sad coda to the more important story of the Republic. It was the Roman Republic that the Founding Fathers desired to imitate. It was the fall of this same Republic that they were trying to avoid. They were trying to create a new government in response to tyranny, so they looked to a government established on principals of liberty. They were interested primarily in the preservation of liberty, not the promulgation of power.

Perhaps the question emerges then: Why discuss the five falls of the Roman Empire if none of them were important to our Founding Fathers? The reason is to help us understand what the eventual fall of Rome civilization actually looked like. It wasn't a single event that led to instantaneous societal collapse. It was a long process that began with the loss of liberty and ended not in cataclysmic destruction but in continual and repeated reorganization. The lesson to be learned from the Fall of Rome is not that bad political or ethical choices lead to immediate societal collapse, but rather that a people and civilization can slowly be transformed by the unsuspecting loss of liberty in ways that seem harmless at that time.

RECOMMENDED READING

Livy, *The Early History of Rome*

David Potter, *Ancient Rome: A New History*
(Thames & Hudson, 2018)

Carl J. Richard, *Greeks & Romans Bearing Gifts:*
How the Ancient Inspire the Founding Fathers
(Rowman & Littlefield, 2009).

THE
MEDIEVAL PERIOD

By David J. Davis, PhD, FRHistS
PROFESSOR OF BRITISH HISTORY

The period known as the Middle Ages, or the medieval period, often gets a bad rap. People sometimes call the centuries following the collapse of the Western Roman Empire in 476 the Dark Ages. Historians like the renowned Jacob Burckhardt in his book *The Civilization of the Renaissance in Italy* described it as a period in which:

> both sides of human consciousness—that which was turned within as that which was turned without—lay dreaming or half-awake beneath a common veil. The veil was woven of faith, illusion, childish prepossession, through which the world and history were seen clad in strange hues. Man was conscious of himself only as a member of a race, people, party, family, or corporation—only through some general category.

Those who imagine the Dark Ages paint a picture of a scientifically backward, economically depressed, and religiously intolerant society. We conjure images of knights and wizards battling monsters, of illiterate bar-barians plundering the innocent, of Catholic Inquisitors persecuting the heterodox, of peasants scraping by on next to nothing, and of crusaders fighting the infidel. If this was what life was like during the Middle Ages, one would hardly look for evidence of political freedom, constitutional government, or any sense of a liberal society.

One problem with looking at medieval politics is that the Middle Ages is far too large to be considered a single, historical period. Politics in the Middle Ages was a complicated variety of local, regional, and national forms of government, which varied quite markedly in time and place. For example, the political history of medieval Italy has little in common with that of England, Scandinavia, France, or the Holy Roman Empire. Not only did these territories follow different historical trajectories, their political institutions could be quite distinct from one another.

Monarchs tended to rule in most places (except the republics of Italy), but the powers of monarchy, its limits and responsibilities, were hardly ever set in stone. Absolute monarchs didn't exist in the Middle Ages, and the amount of power a monarch might wield depended upon several factors, many of which were not under his or her control. The monarchy in France under the Capetian dynasty relied heavily upon its nobles and clergy, who had a wide range of powers across duchies, principalities, counties, and bar-onies. The Holy Roman Empire had an even greater diffusion of power across a federation of mostly autonomous territories, whose rulers swore allegiance to a single emperor, elected by the leading rulers of the empire. Smaller kingdoms like England, Denmark, Aragon, and Sicily enjoyed more centralization of government, but each of these organized themselves around different systems of offices, appointments, laws, and nobility.

The truth is that the image of the Dark Ages created by scholars like Burkhardt holds very little semblance to actual reality. Over the past century, historians and other scholars have identified a variety of areas where the negative view of the Middle Ages distorts reality. From science and technology to religious tolerance and cultural sophistication, the medieval world continues to challenge our modern perceptions, offering not only continuity with the classical tradition but also a level of innovation that we do not expect of them.

In the political sphere, the Middle Ages provided some of the most fundamental ideals to the formation of the American Republic. Despite the messiness of medieval politics, several important ideas about human society and governance emerged and began to solidify. Beginning in the 12th century, notions about the body politic, rooted in the philosophy of Cicero, as well as ideas about individual property ownership, the separation of church and state, and the sovereignty of the people became key features of medieval politics.

The Body Politic

The *Federalist Papers* remain some of the most poignant commentary upon the establishment of the U.S. Constitution. Written by John Jay, Alexander Hamilton, and James Madison they describe in detail the reasoning, motivations, and purposes behind the structure of our government. Throughout the *Federalist*, the authors refer to the American people as "the great body of the people" and "the body politic." And since these terms have become such an essential part of our politics, it is easy to overlook the metaphor about American society that they intend. In *Federalist #28*, Hamilton says, "Seditions and insurrections are, unhappily, maladies as inseparable from the body politic as tumors and eruptions from the natural body." Again and again, the Founding Fathers described society in terms of a living organism, as complex as the human body, with a variety of parts that serve different roles, relying upon one another, and suffering corruptions from within and infections from without. This is not simply a pretty metaphor; it sets out a poignant image of human society that is something more than a social contract, something that is noble and self-sufficient but also fragile and temporal.

Roman writers like Cicero and Livy used the metaphor of the body politic, but medieval England developed the idea when the Norman kings worked to establish their rule of the island. In the 12th century, England was transitioning from a relatively stable island of independent Anglo-Saxon kingdoms to a single Norman kingdom because of William the Conqueror's successful invasion in 1066. The early part of the century had witnessed a civil war (1135–1153) between William's grandchildren over the succession to the English throne. When Henry II became king of England in 1154, he ruled England along with his other territories on the European continent, as his forefathers had done. England after 1066 was one of several territories under Norman dominion, and Norman kingship was part of the larger family business, which was built upon the profits from landholdings, revenues from conquest, marriage alliances with other powerful families, associations with the Church, and the loyalty of their sworn nobles. These were the pillars of successful governance in Norman England.

Interestingly, what emerges in England under this rudimentary monarchical government is one of the most profound works of political philosophy in the Middle Ages: John of Salisbury's *Policraticus*. John (1115–1180) was Anglo-Saxon by birth, and although his family was of modest means, he was educated in France at the prestigious School of Chartres, which emphasized the learning of the classical world. In 1148, John worked for the Archbishop of Canterbury, Theobald, as his secretary, and John remained attached to the archbishopric when the next archbishop Thomas Becket took office. Eventually John rose to the position of Bishop of Chartres, but it was during his years as Theobald's secretary that he set out his political philosophy, which was modeled closely on the writings of Cicero.

Like most political treatises of the Middle Ages, John's *Policraticus* was a guidebook for rulers, a mirror for princes in which they could look and see themselves (as they are and as they should be). In the book, John created a picture of political society in which the monarch is divinely appointed, echoing the Apostle Paul in Romans 13, "The authorities that exist have been established by God." However, John did not believe that this divine appointment meant that the monarch was an absolute ruler or reigned without impunity. In fact, John provides justification for the removal of a monarch who becomes a tyrant by flouting the natural law and setting himself against God.

Part of John's reasoning behind both the divine right of kings and his theory of legitimate tyrannicide (the removal or execution of a tyrant) rests in the image of human society as a human body, a body politic, which he found in the classical tradition. Drawing upon Plato, Aristotle, Plutarch, and Cicero, John developed perhaps the most elaborate version of this metaphor:

> The position of the head in the republic is occupied, however, by a prince subject only to God and to those who act in His place on earth, inasmuch as in the human body the head is stimulated and ruled by the soul. The place of the heart is occupied by the Senate, from which proceeds the beginning of good and bad works. The duties of the ears, eyes, and mouth are claimed by the judges and governors of provinces. The hands coincide with officials and soldiers. Those who always assist the prince are comparable to the flanks. Treasurers and record keepers (I speak not of those who supervise prisoners, but of the counts of the Exchequer) resemble the shape of the stomach and intestines;

these, if they accumulate with great avidity and tenaciously pre-serve their accumulation, engender innumerable and incurable diseases so that their infection threatens to ruin the whole body. Furthermore, the feet coincide with peasants perpetually bound to the soil, for whom it is all the more necessary that the head take precautions, in that they more often meet with accidents while they walk on the earth in bodily subservience; and those who erect, sustain and move forward the mass of the whole body are justly owed shelter and support. Remove from the fit-test body the aid of the feet; it does not proceed under its own power, but either crawls shamefully, uselessly and offensively on its hands or else is moved with assistance of brute animals.

In John's society, the head holds supremacy and authority over the rest of the body and, at the same time, relies upon the other parts, which in turn rely upon the head. Even the feet, if they are abused, corrupted, or removed would humiliate the rest of society, forcing it to crawl on hands and knees. Essential in this image of human society are social values that are integral to modern constitutional democracies.

First, John believed that this image reflected the natural law created by God. Political society was a natural state, a larger version of the community of family that human beings are born into. In this sense, human society is not arbitrary. It is a necessity because we are creatures created by God.

Secondly, John believed liberty was absolutely necessary for the correct functioning of the political society. The individual parts of the body play an active role in the success of society, so they must be at liberty in order to exercise their role (what he calls "virtue") to their fullest capacity. For John, liberty and virtue are inextricably linked: "to all right-thinking men it is clear that true liberty issues from no other source [than virtue] … But virtue can never be fully attained without liberty, and the absence of liberty proves that virtue in its full perfection is wanting." However, when John speaks of liberty, he does not mean "license"—the desire to do whatever one wants. Liberty provides a person with the freedom to do what is right and just, to fulfill their role in society. License sacrifices the needs and desires of everyone else in order to satisfy one's own selfishness.

Finally, John believes that the balance between the liberty of the individual on the one hand and the order needed for the proper functioning of the body on the other can be found in the rule of law. Drawing on the ancient Athenian orator Demosthenes, he explained that human laws should mirror the natural laws of God, which are both just and equitable. If they are created appropriately, laws are "the corrector of excesses of the will, the bond which knits together the fabric of the state, and the banisher of crime." Laws serve not only to restrict wrongdoing but also to promote liberty.

Property and the Separation of Church and State

Medieval politics also contributed to our ideas about democratic liberty with particular freedoms that began to take shape in the 13th and 14th centuries. Today, we don't normally associate property rights with religious freedom, even though they are both recognized in the Bill of Rights.

These rights were essential elements in the political philosophy of John Locke whose thinking heavily influenced the Founding Fathers. In his *Two Treatises on Government*, Locke wrote that "the state of nature has a law to govern it, which obliges everyone: and reason, which is that law, teaches all mankind, who will but consult it, that being all equal and independent, no one ought to harm another in his life, health, liberty, or possessions." This final phrase becomes refashioned in the Declaration of Independence to "life, liberty, and the pursuit of happiness," and yet the idea of property ownership remained essential to the American founding.

At the same time, Locke spent a great deal of his career advocating for religious tolerance, based upon the principle of a separation of ecclesiastical and civil authority. In 1689, the same year that the English Parliament issued the Act of Toleration granting the freedom of worship to a variety of non-Anglican groups in the kingdom, Locke published *A Letter Concerning Toleration*. Locke wrote, "The Church itself is a thing absolutely separate and distinct from the commonwealth," and he argued that the two institutions should not interfere with the other's sphere of authority. The Church should have no authority to direct or govern civil matters; and the civil authorities should not impede or prescribe the sphere of spiritual matters. Locke concludes that the "last and utmost force of ecclesiastical authority" is not the ability to execute heretics, as it had been doing for centuries but simply to remove a person from the Church. He even includes Native Americans. They were "subjected unto a Christian prince" but should not "be punished either in body or goods for not embracing our faith and worship. If they are persuaded that they please God in observing the rites of their own country, and that they shall obtain happiness by that means, they are to be left unto God and themselves."

These two fundamental rights—property and religious liberty—seem distinct from one another, but they appeared in the Middle Ages as two parts of the same debate over the power of the Roman Catholic Church. The question of whether or not the Catholic Church should own property dominated the religious and political conversation of the 14th century. And if the Church could own property, should the Church govern that property in the same manner as a secular landlord? Although there were a variety of positions on these questions that varied between "yes" and "no," the debate was not fully resolved.

The issue eventually reached a boiling point in the 14th century after the papacy moved its capital from Rome to the French city of Avignon, in 1309, aligning itself with the French monarchy against the princes of the Holy Roman Empire. In the 1310s and 1320s, the issue of ecclesiastical property became wrapped up with the succession of the emperor. When Louis, the duke of Bavaria, crowned himself Emperor Louis IV against the will of Pope John XXII, the emperor quickly pronounced the pope to be a heretic, replacing him with Antipope Nicholas V, a Spiritual Franciscan, who condemned the wealth and property of the Church. The Spirituals, with their theology of property ownership and a separation of ecclesiastical and civil authority, found a champion in the imperial throne.

One of the most important voices in this debate between church and state was the English Franciscan theologian William of Occam (or Ockham). Occam is normally recognized for his contributions to the study of logic, particularly the philosophical system known as nominalism, along with his logical dictum known as Occam's Razor. However, in the 14th century, it was his commentary the *Eight Questions on the Power of the Pope* that had the most immediate impact. After Occam's studies at the University of Oxford, Michael Cesena, the Franciscan Minister General, invited Occam to Avignon. Cesena wanted Occam to harmonize property ownership with Apostolic poverty, which the Church continued to profess, and relate them to ecclesiastical power and discipline.

Occam researched the question for several years, and his conclusions sent shockwaves throughout the Catholic world. He argued that it was not appropriate for any ecclesiastical authority to possess material wealth in the same manner as a secular institution or individual. Occam also said that although the papacy was the supreme spiritual authority on Earth, neither the Church nor the civil authorities had the right to interfere in the other's sphere of authority. He wrote:

> For this reason, the head of Christians does not, as a rule, have power to punish secular wrongs with a capital penalty and other

bodily penalties and it is for thus punishing such wrongs that temporal power and riches are chiefly necessary; such punishment is granted chiefly to the secular power. The pope therefore, can, as a rule, correct wrongdoers only with a spiritual penalty. It is not, therefore, necessary that he should excel in temporal power or abound in temporal riches, but it is enough that Christians should willingly obey him.

Occam conceived of property rights as something that God introduced after the Fall, after sin was introduced into the world, as a means of protection for the individual. Anticipating the philosophies of Thomas Hobbes and John Locke, Occam concluded that property ownership belonged in the civil sphere of human society. Not only did the Church have no say in matters of property, Occam believed that it was a violation of the Church's role on earth for it to own property. Since the role of the clergy was to reestablish the pre-Fall state of human society, at least to a certain degree, property ownership ran counter to the Church's purpose. Occam did not condemn property ownership, but it seems to be a necessary liberty in a world of corruption and sin.

After announcing his findings in the 1320s, Occam had to flee Avignon, seeking refuge with Emperor Louis. Occam's later career, as the scholar Brian Tierney has demonstrated, was occupied with developing his ideas more generally about what was slowly becoming a more universal notion of human liberties and rights. Tierney writes, "Ockham had argued that the power to acquire property came from 'nature,' that is corrupt human nature, and from a 'dictate of reason' … he asserted that this power was instituted by divine law."

Occam's treatise did not settle the issue of religion and property, but his influence upon later thinkers was significant. Echoes of Occam's thinking can be heard in key philosophers like Thomas Hobbes and John Locke, as well as theologians closer to Occam's own time like Nicholas of Cusa. Moreover, both Occam and John of Salisbury looked to a natural law, which could be understood through the application of human reason. Natural law could help people understand the fundamental political principles that help construct a more stable and more godly human society.

The Sovereignty of the People

Perhaps the most important contribution that the Middle Ages made to the ideas that shaped the Founding Fathers was that of the sovereignty of the people, or what the Declaration of Independence terms, "the consent of the governed."

The topic of sovereignty began to occupy a central position in Western political thought during the Renaissance. Many 16th- and 17th-century thinkers like Jean Bodin and Thomas Hobbes conceived of sovereignty as an indivisible power, which only could be exercised effectively by a single individual or entity. Absolute monarchy became the Renaissance's answer to this knotty problem of sovereignty. In the Renaissance, not the Middle Ages, a variety of thinkers from Bodin and Hobbes to King James I and King Louis XIV came to believe that absolute monarchy was the best hope for political and social order.

The sovereignty of the people was an idea that medieval thinkers proposed, building upon examples of classical politics—the Athenian democracy and the Roman Republic. Only at the end of the 17th century, when the English Parliament seized certain executive authorities from the monarchy, did the idea of popular sovereignty once again begin to set down roots in the political culture of the West.

When the Founding Fathers of the United States announced their independence from the United Kingdom, they described power and authority so that they were associated with the people. As the Declaration of Independence stated:

> When in the course of human events it becomes necessary for one people to dissolve the political bands which have connected them with another and to assume among the powers of the earth, the separate and equal station to which the Laws and Nature and Nature's God entitle them ... it is their right, it is their duty, to throw off such Government, and to provide new Guards for their future security.

That a people have the right, and even obligation ("their duty"), to dissolve one form of governance and establish another in its place was radical by the standards of the day.

The 18th century thought the language of the Declaration was radical, but several leading thinkers at the end of the Middle Ages would not have seen it as bizarre. One of William of Occam's associates was an Italian scholar named Marsilius of Padua (1275–1342). After serving in the imperial army, Nicholas studied medicine at the Universities of Padua before transferring to the University of Paris, where he embraced the Aristotelianism that was popular among the faculty. Aristotle's writings on civil society influenced much of Marsilius's career. Around 1312, Marsilius's talents and popularity were recognized when he was named rector of the university. However, a decade later during the conflicts between Pope John XXII and Emperor Louis IV, Marsilius sided with the emperor, becoming one of the emperor's most important defenders.

Marsilius's most important work on political philosophy was the *Defensor pacis* ("Defender of the Peace"). In it, Marsilius denounced the idea of a theocratic society—a society governed by the Church. Marsilius was not alone on this point. The Spiritual Franciscans along with others, like the poet Dante Alighieri, voiced similar criticisms about a society governed by the papacy. Moreover, Marsilius suggested that civil authorities should limit papal authority. He even advocated bishops be stripped of the power to excommunicate and impose interdicts. Perhaps more startlingly, Marsilius disagreed with Occam by questioning whether the pope was the supreme ecclesiastical authority. He advocated conciliarism—that is, the entire body of bishops in council together should govern the Catholic Church.

The pope condemned *Defensor pacis* as heresy, and the faculty at the University of Paris burned the book. But Marsilius's writings became some of the more popular political treatises of the period. His theories about conciliarism influenced the pivotal Council of Constance (1415) that ended a schism between rival popes. In the *Defensor*, Marsilius relied upon Aristotle's *Politics*, but he did not slavishly follow the Greek philosopher. At key points, Marsilius forged his own ideas about human society—for example, Aristotle believed the difference between good and bad forms of government rested in the virtue of the ruler, but Marsilius believed that the consent of the ruled was essential in establishing just rule. Elected leaders, among whom he would include the pope and the emperor, possessed a secondary form of sovereignty to that of the people. For Marsilius, "The absolutely primary human authority to make or establish human laws belongs only to those men from whom alone the best laws can emerge." And who are these men? Rather than advocating philosopher-kings, as Plato's *Republic* did, or a wise oligarchic senate like the Romans had, Marsilius insisted that sovereignty must be found in:

> the whole body of the citizens, or the weightier part thereof, which represents that whole body; since it is difficult or impossible for all persons to agree upon one decision, because some men have a deformed nature.... The common benefit should not, however, be impeded or neglected because of the unreasonable

protests or opposition of these men. The authority to make or establish laws, therefore, belongs only to the whole body of the citizens or to the weightier part thereof.

This popular sovereignty even extends to the establishment of rulers. Is it better for a people to elect individual rulers or to select a ruler and his posterity to rule? Marsilius sides with the former in order to preserve not only the virtue of each individual ruler but also to preserve the sovereignty of the people's ability to choose who governed them. Marsilius wrote:

> the monarch who is elected individually will be in conformity both with his virtuous predecessor and with the primary being or ruler of all beings, to a greater degree and with greater frequency than will the hereditary monarch who rules only because he belongs to a family in which someone else was once elected to rule.

Marsilius's ideal society remained theoretical more than actual, but his political theory pointed toward a society governed by and for the people.

Nicholas of Cusa followed Marsilius's innovations, and in the 15th century he became the greatest voice of conciliarism and governance by consent. He was a German humanist and theologian, born in 1411 to a ferryman and his wife. Nicholas studied at the Universities of Heidelberg and Padua before becoming a secretary to the Archbishop of Trier, and over a 30-year career, he wrote on a wide gamut of intellectual interest, from science and contemplative devotion to philosophy and politics. In the politics of ecclesiastical government, Cusa made his first mark on Western thought.

Cusa became well known during a particularly contentious Council of Basel in 1431. The council had been called by Pope Martin V, shortly before his death, but his successor, Eugene IV, quickly showed himself as no fan of conciliarism by abruptly dissolving the council before many of the bishops had a chance to turn up. Cusa and many other bishops openly, but peacefully, defied the papal order and continued to meet from 1431 to 1439. Cusa's role at the council became one of diplomacy and peacemaking, earning him a reputation for his ingenious legal mind. Although Cusa continually asserted the conciliar principle of consent, he also stressed the natural hierarchy within the Church, which appealed to more traditional voices at the council. In 1433, Cusa decided to set down some of his ideas in what would become one of his most important books, *De concordantia catholica*. The *De concordantia* attempted to harmonize the powers of the pope and the emperor in light of natural law and what Cusa referred to as the "consent of the people." In one of the most important passages in the book, he wrote:

> Since natural law is naturally based on reason, all law is rooted by nature in the reason of man.... For since all are by nature free, every governance whether it consists in a written law or is a living law in the person of a prince—by which subjects are compelled to abstain from evil deeds and their freedom directed towards the good through fear of punishment can only come from the agreement and consent of the subjects. For if by nature men are equal in power and equally free, the true properly ordered authority of one common ruler who is their equal in power cannot be naturally established except by the election and consent of the others and law is also established by consent.

The *De concordantia* envisioned consent serving as a glue that held the social body together, in an ordered hierarchy that worked together. The people should consent through the election of local clergy. The clergy should elect bishops, bishops elect cardinals, and cardinals elect popes. By consent, those elected become the representatives of the people that elected them. In this, Cusa criticizes arbitrary authority, regardless of whether it was wielded by the pope or the emperor. Civil and ecclesiastical authorities were subject to the laws, because the laws sprung from the divinely established natural law: "the canons are based on natural law. Even the ruler has no power to violate natural law, and therefore he also has no power over a canon based on, or incidentally following from, natural law." Chosen by consent of the people, the elected officials of whatever role and rank had no power to usurp the sovereign authority that had invested them with their authority.

That being said, we must pay attention to a few differences between our modern notions of the consent of the people and that of Cusa's. First, Cusa was not attempting, like John Locke would be 200 years later, to establish a rational, ahistorical justification for the liberties of the individual. Although Nicholas does point to election as an expression of consent, he also assumed consent within the ecclesiastical hierarchy, unless there was a reasonable expression of dissent. In other words, consent could be given silently. Second, the goal for Nicholas was primarily the harmony of the political or ecclesiastical body. Consent was a natural and legitimate means to securing that harmony. Consent was not an end in itself, but it was the chief mechanism to achieve political peace.

That being said, the *De concordantia* points toward political ideals that would shape America's Founding Fathers. Cusa roots his writings in the traditions of classical and medieval politics, and they point forward to new ways of understanding the relationship between the ruler and the ruled, the government and the people. He, like the others we have discussed, assumed the standard of natural law that should guide all human laws. However, he introduced a sense of equality that had not been apparent in other works of medieval politics. Cusa believed that "by nature" men are "equal in power and equally free," and as such enter into the political society on equal terms with one another.

Far from the Dark Ages that Jacob Burckhardt and others have described it, the Middle Ages offer us many of the essential building blocks of modern political liberty. Over the course of a few centuries, medieval theologians and philosophers developed some of the most essential principles of constitutional government in the West. **These ideas would not be assembled completely and successfully until the 18th century, but medieval thinkers built upon the ideas they had preserved from the classical world.**

* *

RECOMMENDED READING

James M. Blythe, *Ideal Government and the Mixed Constitution in the Middle Ages* (Princeton University Press, 1992)

Brian Tierney, *The Idea of Natural Rights* (Eerdmans, 1997)

THE
ENGLISH CIVIL WAR
AND THE
GLORIOUS
REVOLUTION

By David J. Davis, PhD, FRHistS
PROFESSOR OF BRITISH HISTORY

The early 1640s were tumultuous years for the Somerset countryside near John Locke's family home outside the market town of Pensford. Royalist troops led by Lord George Goring intermittently raided and burned the homes and towns of those who supported Parliament. Locke's father, a well-known puritan attorney in the county, even joined the Parliamentary Army. Locke's home was spared the more destructive aspects of the war, but the young boy would have heard first-hand accounts of the violence, if not seen it with his own eyes. John waited out the war at home, before entering Oxford University in 1652, but his political ideas sprang from the chaos of these formative events. John Locke's key works *A Letter Concerning Toleration, Two Treatises of Government,* and *An Essay Concerning Human Understanding* are shot through with the ideology of the English Civil War and the Glorious Revolution.

In many respects this was as true for every English man and woman. The English Civil War (1642–1653) began a train of events in 17th-century England that led to the overthrow of two kings, Charles I and James II, at the hands of Parliament and the establishment of the English constitutional monarchy in 1689. The Glorious Revolution, crowning William the Duke of Orange and Mary Stuart as the new English monarchs, was the final step in Parliament's assertion of its rights as the representative body of the people to determine the government of the kingdom.

Not only did the English Civil War help form John Locke's thought and life, it also influenced the future English and American constitutions. Later British thinkers like David Hume saw the war as the beginning of modern British politics, and members of Parliament who executed King Charles I were hailed as American heroes (the town of New Haven named streets after them). John Adams considered key battlefields of the English Civil War as holy ground. **The events in England between 1642 and 1689 served as inspiration and models for the American Revolution a century later.**

The English Civil War

No single cause sparked the English Civil War, neither among the leaders in Church and government nor among the men who fought the battles. For many members of Parliament, this was a war about the abuses of power committed by the government of King Charles I and the rectifying of those abuses. For others inside and outside of Parliament, it was a war about good governance, and whether or not the monarchy should have absolute sovereignty over the kingdom. Many, like the Parliamentary cavalry lieutenant Oliver Cromwell, fought for religious liberties and, perhaps more importantly, against the idea that religion should be established by the state.

People in Scotland and Ireland fought against perceived abuses committed upon them by the government in London, some going back to the reign of Henry VIII. Many others who defended the political status quo feared that to fight against the king was to fight for radicalism or anarchy in both politics and religion. War might ultimately dismantle English society.

One example of this final group was Edward Hyde, Earl of Clarendon, who was a Member of Parliament in 1640 and an early critic of the king. However, when it came to war, Hyde ultimately sided with the monarchy, fearing as he wrote in his *The History of the Rebellion*:

> All the folly, and madness, and wickedness of those secret contrivances, and open violences, whereby the nation, as well as the crown was brought to desolation; and see how falsely and weakly those great and busy disturbers of peace pretended reformation and religion, and to be seeking God in every one of their rebellious and sinful actions.

When did momentum for the English Civil War begin to gather speed? In 1628, many of the necessary ingredients were already stirring in the political cauldron. The young King Charles I had made several missteps in his first three years as monarch, including marrying the French Catholic princess Henrietta-Maria, ignoring Parliament's complaints against his favorite adviser the Duke of Buckingham, compelling a tax without Parliament's consent, and then imprisoning, without trial, those people who refused to pay.

Taken together these circumstances prodded Parliament into action. They submitted to the king a document called the Petition of Right, which set out a list of liberties that Parliament claimed were theirs, "according to the laws and statutes of this realm." These liberties included prohibiting the king to establish new taxes without Parliament's approval and ensuring the rights of *habeas corpus* and land ownership. One member of Parliament, John Eliot, who championed the Petition of Right, described what was happening in England under Charles's rule as "the oppression of the subject," and the petition was intended to secure the liberty of the people.

When the king approved the Petition under pressure from both houses of Parliament, it was seen as a watershed victory of popular sovereignty over and against the threat of absolute monarchy. Then, in the next year, Charles dissolved Parliament and arrested 10 members, including John Eliot, who protested the king's actions. Parliament had won the immediate battle with the king, but Charles knew that only the king could summon Parliament. He allowed almost 12 years to pass before doing so again.

This period without Parliament, known as the Personal Rule of Charles I, provided the ammunition that Parliament needed when it reconvened. Between 1629 and 1640, Charles employed policies in finance and religion that appeared tyrannical to many. He resurrected antiquated fines and penalties. He imposed feudal levies known as ship monies, prosecuting those who refused to pay. He granted lucrative monopolies to companies that were willing to pay gifts into the royal coffers. Despite these measures, Charles was still on the verge of bankruptcy by 1640, and he attempted to seize funds held by the City of London and the East India Company, which his government described as "loans" to the royal treasury.

On the religious front, the Archbishop of Canterbury William Laud cracked down on non-conformity with the Anglican confession, paying particular attention to the more radical forms of Protestantism. Laud used the courts to censor religious publications and to prosecute those who refused to conform to the Anglican communion and Book of Common Prayer. Also, Laud attempted to compel the Scottish Presbyterian Churches to embrace the Anglican prayer book, an act that ignited both a nation-wide protest known as the National Covenant and two military conflicts called the Bishops' Wars. All the while, Laud promoted a more traditional liturgy in English Churches, which for many people too closely resembled the Roman Catholic Mass. Also, the king permitted the queen to practice her Catholic faith relatively unhindered.

Financially strapped, a Church in crisis, and Scotland in disarray at the perceived threat to their religious independence—Charles succumbed to pressure and recalled Parliament.

The Long Parliament, as it came to be known because it did not dissolve for over a decade, assembled on November 3, 1640, with the purpose of dismantling many of the Personal Rule policies and prosecuting the king's counsellors, like Laud, who had been instrumental in the Rule. For more radical MPs like John Pym, the Long Parliament was meant to reprimand the king for his abuses of power. And on many points, Charles reluctantly acceded to Parliament's will. He granted the Triennial Act, which guaranteed the formation of Parliament every three years. He allowed Parliament to abolish the Star Chamber, a court presided over by the king's Privy Council and responsible for many of the abuses during the Personal Rule. And Charles permitted the prosecution and execution of his closest adviser Thomas Wentworth, 1ˢᵗ Earl of Strafford, for high treason.

If things had continued in this direction, it is possible that full-scale violence could have been avoided. However, in October 1641, Ireland erupted in one of the bloodiest rebellions in British history. The native Gaelic lords, who had been oppressed by England for over a century, saw an opportunity with events in England to seize the city of Dublin. What began as a political coup, however, spiraled into a series of riotous massacres in the county of Ulster, where Irish Catholics attacked Protestants, killing several thousand and turning tens of thousands out of their homes.

The cheap print media of London exaggerated the stories coming out of Ulster. England read hearsay stories of the butchering of children and the raping of women, with deaths speculated in the hundreds of thousands. Believing that an international Catholic conspiracy was at work to overthrow the English government, Parliament acted swiftly, issuing the Grand Remonstrance and pointing to Ireland as the best example of a long-term plot to undermine English religion and sovereignty. The Remonstrance was a list of 204 grievances that Parliament had with Charles's foreign, domestic, financial, and religious practices, which Parliament insisted must be addressed before they could allow money for an army to crush the Irish rebellion.

The vote on the Remonstrance divided the House of Commons and was severely criticized in the House of Lords. However, the Commons narrowly approved it, and its passage in many respects set England on the course toward civil war.

The Irish rebellion and the Remonstrance deepened suspicions between Parliament and the king. The next six months saw suspicion and rumor lead to recrimination and finally violence. In June 1642, the last legislative effort to avoid open war was sent to Charles. It was called the Nineteen Propositions: a list of demands upon the king's authority that was unrelenting in its intent and purpose. The Propositions included requiring Parliamentary approval for the appointment of the king's Privy Council as well as for royal marriages. It demanded that anti-Catholic laws be strictly enforced (endangering the queen). And it gave Parliament control of the army. The Nineteen Propositions established in all but name a complete reformulation of the English Constitution, restricting the traditional powers and prerogative of the monarchy. For obvious reasons, the king refused to sign it.

The first stage of the English Civil War began in the summer of 1642 with both sides raising armies. King Charles was based in the city of Oxford, and Parliament was based in London. For all of the division and differences between them politically, the armies looked very similar. The war cry of the king's army, the Cavaliers, was "For the King," whereas Parliament's forces, the Roundheads, cried "For the King and Parliament." Both armies had a mix of religious affiliations. Anglicans and puritans, Catholics and Presbyterians fought on both sides. Approximately one-third of the nobles sided with Parliament, including some of the best military minds like Thomas Fairfax, 3rd Lord Fairfax of Cameron, who was appointed general of the army. The gentry were divided almost in half, and of the middle class, two-thirds fought for Parliament and one-third for the king. In other words, this was not a war of class or religious differences. The English populace could not be so neatly divided. Such differences certainly played a role in why people fought, but neither religion nor class were the primary axis upon which the two sides were determined.

In the earliest stages of the war, the king's forces gained the upper hand with several key victories, at Powick Bridge, Stratton, and Newark. Many of Parliament's commanders were hesitant to commit their full force to meet the king in a decisive battle. The king had almost nothing to lose, having already been ousted from power, but Parliament needed to bring the king to heel without chancing utter defeat. The Earl of Manchester said as much to a frustrated Oliver Cromwell after the Second Battle of Newbury in November 1644, when Manchester refused to capitalize on the victory by pursuing the Royalist retreat. When Cromwell demanded to know why Manchester was so reluctant, the earl explained, "if we beat the king 99 times, he would be king still, and his posterity, and we his subjects still, but if he beat us but once we should be hang'd, and our posterity be undone." Interestingly, two years into the war, neither Manchester nor, more surprisingly, Cromwell could envision a political scenario wherein England did not have a monarch. The position of the monarchy, even among those who warred against it, was still a permanent fixture in the kingdom's constitution.

Nevertheless, the military tide turned in 1644 and 1645. First, the king's best commander and nephew Prince Rupert suffered his first, and most important, defeat at the Battle of Marston Moor in 1644. After the battle, the Royalist forces surrendered much of their territory in northern England. Then, in 1645, Parliament formed a national army, which was not tied to any particular garrison or region, and appointed Lord Fairfax and Oliver Cromwell as its commanders. This New Model Army proved to be a highly disciplined and well-trained force, quickly dispatching the king's troops at Naseby and Langport in 1645. It was also an ideologically minded army, composed of puritans and other non-conformists who fought against the usurpation of their religious rights. These men, in Cromwell's mind, were the ideal soldiers. In a letter dating from 1643, he wrote that, "I had rather have a plain russet-coated captain that knows what he fights for, and loves what he knows than that which you call a gentleman, who is nothing else."

After Charles was captured in 1646, this New Model Army, filled with Cromwell's russet-coated men, would become a key player in the increasingly uncertain political future of the kingdom. The various factions that had made up the Parliamentary side of the conflict began to contend amongst themselves for what the English Constitution would come to be. Presbyterians in Parliament disagreed with Anglicans over matters of religious liberty. Moderate voices like Fairfax found themselves at odds with radical factions within the army. Extreme political groups like the Levellers and the Diggers had developed a following during the first period of the war, and they advocated radical social and political changes. Many of these radical changes crystalized in the publication of the *Agreement of the People* (1647), which pressed for the dissolution of the current Parliament with new elections based upon the population and the establishment of Parliament as the supreme authority in England. Furthermore, Parliament's authority should be restricted, so that the institution could not interfere with freedom of religion and could not compel men into military service.

These internal disputes in the army and in Parliament almost saw the words of the Royalist officer Sir Allen Appsly come to pass. After his defeat at the Battle of Barnstable, Appsly was said to have mocked the Roundhead victors: "Well done boys, you've done your work. Now you can go and play. Unless you will now fall out amongst yourselves."

One glimmer of hope in popular sovereignty and the democratic process came in the autumn of 1647 at the Putney Debates. By August 1647, the army was based in the town of Putney, and the commanders convened a debate to discuss the *Agreement of the People*. Most importantly at this relatively democratic debate of England's first national army, there was a general division of opinion between the officers and the common soldiers. The officers agreed with General Henry Ireton, Cromwell's son-in-law, that while all men should enjoy liberty, only those who owned property should be given the right to vote. The common soldiers heartily disagreed. Many of these common soldiers advocated the consent of the people in forming a new government, and even raised questions about the right place of the monarchy in such a government. Most of the officers found such talk too radical.

Although Oliver Cromwell said very little at the debates, he was, at the time, a more moderate voice, fearing the outcome of the more radical course that the Levellers and others would take the kingdom. The danger that he and many other officers saw in what they were doing was in the potential chaos that it could unleash upon England. His response to the *Agreement* was:

> Truly this paper does contain in it very great alterations of the very government of the kingdom.... And what the consequences of such an alteration as this would be, if there were nothing else to be considered, wise men and godly men out to consider.... How do we know if, whilst we are disputing these

things, another company of men shall not gather together, and put out papers plausible as this? I do not know why it might not be done by that time you have agreed upon this, or got hands to it if that be the way. And not only another, and another, but many of this kind. And if so, what do you think the consequence of that would be? Would it not be confusion?

Putney resolved very few of the differences among the various factions of the army, but the differences were set aside when, on November 11, the king escaped from his captivity at Hampton Court Palace and fled to the Isle of Wight. While Parliament and the army had been bickering about the future of the nation, Charles had struck a bargain with Scotland, offering up the English Church, which would adopt Presbyterianism, if the Scottish Army would side with the king in an invasion of England.

The invasion of Scottish Covenanters along with Royalist revolts in South Wales, Kent, Lincoln, Northampton, and northern England absorbed English politics in 1648, in what is often called the Second English Civil War. Although the New Model Army proved indefatigable once again, the hope for compromise with the king that was evident at Putney had completely evaporated after these new conflicts.

After the king was recaptured by the army, events moved swiftly. The hope of reestablishing the ancient constitution of England, underneath the monarchy, had been destroyed for men like Cromwell and Ireton. At the end of 1648, they barred and bullied members of Parliament who refused to prosecute the king for treason. The trial (and subsequent execution) of Charles was something of a box-checking exercise with the outcome never in doubt.

The Interregnum and the Restoration of the Monarchy

Of course, the problems that England had before the execution of Charles—unrest in Ireland, a rebellious Scotland, a politically divided England, and a rise in radical religious factions—still existed. Moreover, not everyone was satisfied with the execution. Royalists continued to plot and plan. One cheaply printed broadside ballad mocked the Parliament's actions:

> To sit and consult forever and a day
> To countenance treason in a parliamentary way
> To quiet the land by tumultuous fray
> New plots to devise, then them to betray.
>
> …
>
> God send these zealots to heaven in a string
>
> …
>
> Who say the lord's prayer is a popish thing
> Who pray for themselves yet leave out the king.
> This is the new order of the land
> And the land's new order.

Leaders in Parliament, like Fairfax, who refused to participate as a judge in the trial, believed executing the king was itself an illegal act, regardless of Charles's crimes. And the question of England's future constitution remained unanswered. From 1652 until 1660, England experimented with several forms of government. It attempted representative democracy with parliaments like the Barebones Parliament. It attempted a military dictatorship. It finally settled, for the legislative powers of Parliament elected on a regular basis and a military dictator with absolute executive authority, on the Lord Protector Oliver Cromwell. In the end, Cromwell was the one man who could control the army and the Parliament. And he found himself at the end of his life being asked to take up the monarchical powers that he himself had fought so hard to overcome.

The death of Cromwell, however, steered England into another constitutional crisis, with the question of his successor. Some advocated for Cromwell's son Richard to take his place, as it would be in a traditional monarchy (even though Cromwell denounced any effort to make him a king). But Richard lacked his father's ability to command, and cooler heads recognized the disaster he would be as Lord Protector.

The crisis of 1659 nearly led England into another civil war as military and Parliamentary leaders squabbled over what should be done. Eventually, Parliament agreed to invite Prince Charles, the executed king's son, to restore the monarchy, after he made several concessions and promises to Parliament about his potential future reign. In some respects, the Restoration of the monarchy was like erasing the last 19 years from a chalkboard. King Charles II insisted upon punishing those who had executed his father, but he pardoned all others who sided with Parliament during the war. The Church of England was restored, and Charles assumed a throne that had the powers and privileges that his father and grandfather had wielded. At the same time, Restoration England was a very different place than England before the war. Parliament divided into two factions, the Whigs who stressed the authority and importance of Parliament in matters of state, and the Tories, who tended to side with the authority of the monarchy. It was also a fragile state, which was rebuilding itself in the minds of the English people. Most importantly, the fragility of the Restoration was centered around the place of religion in public affairs. The fear of Catholic rebellion was never far from the surface of the English Protestant conscious. Since the defeat of the Spanish Armada in 1588 and the discovery of the Gunpowder Plot in 1605, English culture contained an anti-Catholic prejudice that never seemed to be fully eradicated.

This prejudice sent England into its final constitutional crisis of the 17th century. In the 1670s, the old rumors of a Catholic plot to overthrow

Charles's government resurfaced. They were only compounded by the fact that Charles had no male heir, and his brother James (who was next in line to the throne) was a Catholic. Parliament's fears were so strong that they pleaded with the king to name another heir, even issuing three bills of exclusion for Charles to sign that would bar any Catholic heir from assuming the throne.

Then, in 1678, an Anglican priest named Titus Oates successfully convinced much of the government that there was a plot to assassinate the king. Oates fabricated documents and testimony in order to ensure his claims about a "Popish Plot" were taken seriously. When, on October 12, Edmund Godfrey, the magistrate investigating Oates's claims, turned up dead in a London ditch, the suspicions of many Protestants seemed to be confirmed. Oates made the most of Godfrey's death, publicly denouncing the queen and members of her household as conspirators in the plot against Charles. The result was widespread civil unrest. The simmering prejudice of London exploded into public violence. People were attacked in the streets for being suspected of Catholic sympathies. Catholic tradesmen and property owners were banished from the city. The courts took action, executing nine Jesuit priests and putting five noble lords on trial for high treason.

The Popish Plot was eventually uncovered, but in 1683, when a Whig conspiracy was uncovered known as the Rye House Plot, the pendulum swung the other way. Supposedly, the plot was intended to assassinate both the king and his brother James, although scholars question whether or not this was not another hoax intended to gain political leverage in the tension between monarchy and Parliament. Nevertheless, anyone associated with the exclusion bills during the Popish Plot was immediately suspect, including John Locke and his patron Lord Shaftesbury. In the end, 12 people would be executed including Lord Russell; Algernon Sidney, the Lord

Warden of the Cinque Ports; and Sir Thomas Armstrong, a Member of Parliament. Another 13 people were imprisoned and many more (including Locke) fled the country.

The Glorious Revolution

Almost 70 years after the Glorious Revolution, in 1757, as the American colonies slowly moved toward independence, a young lawyer and future parliamentarian named Edmund Burke was engaged by a London publisher to write *An Abridgment of English History*. Unfortunately, Burke only managed to write 90,000 words describing the ancient British world, the Roman period, the Saxon conquest, and concluding with the Magna Carta. The complete project was never achieved, as it seems that married life and his professional career overtook this ambitious project. Burke never wrote about the critical events of the 17th century. As someone who defended the cause of American liberty in the British Parliament, it would be interesting to know Burke's thoughts on the reign of James II and his removal from power during the Glorious Revolution of 1688.

Perhaps we can get a sense of what Burke might have written, when he mentions that, "It has been observed that the reigns of weak princes are times favorable to liberty." Although Burke stressed the importance of the rule of law and the long tradition of a people in establishing good governance, he also recognized that strong and weak leaders could provide essential pivot points. It would seem that James II was just such a leader.

Having failed to secure the line of succession for Protestants, the Whigs' worst fears were realized almost immediately upon James's ascension. In just a few years, James had remodeled the royal court and large portions of the military command to his own Catholic leanings. He appointed Catholics to the highest positions in government and gave preferential treatment to Catholic officers. Also, he began expanding the size of the army without Parliament's support, and he undermined the authority of the Anglican Church, even threatening to have his heir raised as a Catholic.

Charles II was skilled in political pragmatism, but his younger brother was more bold than wise. An English Parliament that had strained for almost three decades to avoid open conflict with the monarchy was once again on the brink of crisis when challenged with James's reign. The historian Tim Harris summarizes the general scholarly confusion surrounding James:

> The jury will doubtless remain out on James for a long time.... Was he an egotistical bigot ... a tyrant who rode roughshod over the will of the vast majority of his subjects ... simply naïve, or even perhaps plain stupid, unable to appreciate the realities of political power.

For the past 50 years, Parliament and the monarchy had been in fundamental disagreement with each other about the extent and nature of monarchical power, the established branches of English governance, the control over the judiciary, the right to tax, and the control over the treasury. While the Whigs had disagreed with Charles, as they did with James, Charles was willing to compromise. By 1688, Whigs in Parliament feared James to be an absolute monarch in the fashion of Louis XIV of France. Tories feared James was intent upon disassembling the traditional authority of the Church. It didn't help that James had spent much of his 20s, while in exile, fighting alongside the French Army under the Viscount of Turenne, in a historical moment when France, under Louis, was increasingly viewed as a threat to England.

Parliament issued the Declaration of Right, detailing James's abuses of power, including: the suspension of the rule of law, the usurpation of Parliament authority, the infringement upon the electoral process, and the corruption of the courts. It also contained 13 provisions that would become the backbone of the new Bill of Rights (1689) when it was signed by the new monarchs King William III and Queen Mary II. These included popular sovereignty through a representative assembly, the right to bear arms for defense, the rule of law, freedom of speech, and trial by jury.

John Locke had accompanied Queen Mary, daughter of James II, to England before her crowning, and many of Locke's notions about political society were infused into the Bill of Rights and the Act of Toleration (1689), which granted religious liberties to all sects and confessions, excepting atheists, nontrinitarians, and Roman Catholics. Although it was not an entirely bloodless revolution, the Glorious Revolution successfully established a permanent constitutional monarchy with the representative assembly as a permanent fixture of the government.

The establishment of popular sovereignty in England did not happen in a few short years. Like all successful government founded on the people, by the people, and for the people, it germinated over several generations. In 1782, Edmund Burke reminded his fellow members of Parliament of this reality, that government is not established in an atemporal vortex of philosophy but is instead rooted in a particular time and place. In his "Speech on the Reforms of the Representation of the Commons in Parliament," he reverberated one of the most important lessons of this history of England's Constitution:

> Because a nation is not an idea only of local extent, and individual momentary aggregation, but it is an idea of continuity, which extends in time as well as in numbers and in space. And this is a choice not of one day, or one set of people, not a tumultuary and giddy choice; it is a deliberate election of ages and of generations; it is a Constitution made by what is ten thousand times better than choice—it is made by the peculiar circumstances,

occasions, tempers, dispositions, and moral, civil, and social habitudes of the people, which disclose themselves only in a long space of time. It is a vestment, which accommodates itself to the body. Nor is prescription of government formed upon blind, unmeaning prejudices—for man is a most unwise, and a most wise being. The individual is foolish. The multitude, for the moment, are foolish, when they act without deliberation; but the species is wise, and when time is given to it, as a species it almost always acts right.

So important was the 17ᵗʰ-century history of England that our Founding Fathers, fighting a century later for their own liberty, would refer back to this period as "*the* Revolution." The lessons of liberty, limited government, and the rule of law would provide the basis for their own revolution to come.

* *

RECOMMENDED READING

Mark Kishlansky, *A Monarchy Transformed: Britain, 1603–1715,*
6ᵗʰ edition (Penguin, 1997)

Kevin Sharpe, *The Personal Rule of Charles I*
(Yale University Press, 1996)

Divine Right and Democracy:
An Anthology of Political Writings in Stuart England,
ed. David Wootton (Hackett, 2003)

CONSTITUTIONS
AND THE
AMERICAN
REVOLUTION

By Anthony M. Joseph, PhD
PROFESSOR OF EARLY AMERICAN HISTORY

Without the American Revolution, there would be no U.S. Constitution. The Revolution propelled Americans on a course of constitution-making that began with grievances against Parliament in the 1760s and ended with the drafting and ratification of the U.S. Constitution in the late 1780s. No one at the time could have predicted this sequence of events; the ultimate outcome would have appeared far-fetched had anyone dared to predict it. Americans were members of a flourishing empire, and the British Constitution was their revered and cherished political inheritance. It was, by their reckoning, the human source and the guarantor of their rights. In declaring independence in 1776, Americans tossed aside this treasured inheritance. What began as a conservative attempt to preserve rights under the British Constitution ended in the radical rejection of that Constitution and its replacement with a new one.

And yet the U.S. Constitution that emerged from the Revolution incorporated many familiar elements of the British Constitution. The Founding Fathers created a new political order by brilliantly rearranging those elements, giving them new philosophical underpinnings, and directing them toward a new end. The U.S. Constitution is like a new musical composition that contains familiar notes and chords but nonetheless strikes the ear as highly original and fresh. The American Revolution itself, for all its radically destructive powers, provided the creative impulse for this new arrangement of old materials.

The British Constitution

Let's look first at those old materials in all their glory. The British Constitution was the body of principles and customary practices that defined the powers of the British government and the rights of the British people. British subjects on both sides of the Atlantic revered this Constitution for several features that they believed were unique to it or powerfully expressed in it.

The British Constitution was *unwritten*, but large portions of it were indeed found in writing—in the Magna Carta of 1215, in the English Bill of Rights of 1689, in P'arliamentary statutes and judicial decisions. However, these texts were held to be *expressive* of the Constitution, not a complete statement of it. The British Constitution did not depend on these written expressions of its principles. The written expressions were proofs of constitutional principles without being the Constitution itself. This unwritten quality of the British Constitution bothers Americans today, but 18th-century British subjects didn't mind. The very word "constitution," after all, implied not a set of written rules but rather the fundamental shape and function of a thing, particularly a living thing. Why would a constitution need to be written down? A human body had a "constitution" regardless of what was or was not described in the anatomy books. The British Constitution was the political body of the British people rather than a set of principles inscribed on parchment. Acts that contradicted the well-being of that body were "unconstitutional"—whether or not the particular harm had ever been identified in writing. Britons believed in this unwritten constitution long before Americans determined that a constitution was best placed in a single written, definitive text.

The British Constitution was also *mixed*. It contained elements of the three forms of government: monarchy, aristocracy, and democracy. The king represented monarchy; the House of Lords, aristocracy; and the House of Commons, democracy. And because none of these elements ruled alone, the British Constitution was a *balanced* constitution. Being both mixed and balanced, the British Constitution achieved stability. That stability had been severely disrupted twice in the 1600s—both times from aggressive power plays by kings. First, King Charles I attempted to govern without Parliament—by monarchy alone—eliminating the mix and therefore the balance. Later, King James II attempted to govern by controlling the Parliamentary elections—corrupting the mix and again imperiling the balance. But in the 1700s the British state regained its stability, for the most part. Stability in this era, it is true, was accompanied by a particularly intense sort of mixing. Perhaps one-fifth of the House of Commons consisted of "placemen." These were members of the House of Commons who also held administrative appointments under the king. The placemen in Commons were reliable supporters of the king's interests and could be expected to vote as he wished on controversial legislation. From 1707 to the era of the American Revolution, no British monarch vetoed a bill because no bill ever passed Parliament that the monarch objected to. Some Englishmen vilified the placemen for compromising the independence of Parliament. Others saw the placemen as part of the well-oiled, balanced machine that was the British Constitution.

But to speak of the British Constitution as a "machine" is in fact a misleading metaphor. For the British Constitution was meant to reflect a human society, not a machine. King, Lords, and Commons reflected not simply generic forms of government but the actual structure of classes or "estates" in British society. The king represented not only monarchy abstractly; he represented the interests of the royal family in the deliberations of government. The House of Lords, a hereditary body of some 200 noblemen, represented the interests not just of aristocracy as a form of government but of the actual British aristocracy. The House of Commons, consisting of 558 elected members, represented not simply democracy but the British people at large, the commoners, who comprised the overwhelming majority of British subjects.

Social mobility among these three estates was minimal. The great propertied families of England rarely conveyed their lands to outsiders. According to historian Lawrence Stone, less than 10 percent of England's elite ever put their landholdings up for sale in the three-and-a-half centuries spanning from 1540 to 1880. The three estates of British society were persistently unequal in wealth, power, and status. The British envisioned a government whose structure substantially echoed the unchanging structure of the society as a whole. They could not easily envision one that did not.

The vision of an unchanging social order matched a vision of an unchanging constitution. British history occasionally included dramatic constitutional change, but such convulsions were interpreted as conservative events. In the Glorious Revolution of 1688, the English deposed James II and invited a new king and queen, William and Mary, to replace him. English philosopher John Locke defended the move, arguing that a people had the right to overthrow a government that failed to protect their rights. Locke noted a change of leadership did not imply a change of government. In the years that followed, Englishmen clung to the belief that the

Glorious Revolution was a restorative change—a change that affirmed the Constitution and did not alter it. England had merely replaced a bad king, not changed a good Constitution. The British Constitution might be clarified over time—through court decisions, statutes, decrees—but it did not change. Particular laws expressed or conformed to the Constitution. They did not create or change it.

Finally, the British Constitution was *protective*. The Constitution incorporated and affirmed the common law of England and protected rights from violations by government. Those rights were grounded in the natural law, the moral rule of right and wrong originating with God. Common-law rights took their particular expression from the life and culture of the British people. These rights included the rights to trial by jury, to representation, and to a free press, among many others. Natural law, common law, and Constitution intertwined in a sturdy rope that secured the liberty of the people against government encroachment. Americans used much of that rope later for a new constitution of their own.

The British Constitution in Colonial America

How did this British Constitution fare among colonial Americans, before the American Revolution? Colonial Americans considered the British Constitution their own. They had their own version of mixed and balanced government. In each colony a governor, council, and assembly acted as a kind of small-scale replica of Britain's King, Lords, and Commons. This American imitation of the British Constitution was far from exact. Americans quarreled with their governors, ignored their councils, and preferred their elected assemblies above both.

That preference reflected the social reality, which also diverged from Britain's. As the historian Gordon Wood puts it, colonial America was a "truncated" version of British society—with the top and bottom classes, the social and economic extremes, lopped off. No royal family lived in America, no royal court attracted the upper classes by its power, culture, and intrigue. Americans celebrated the succession of a new monarch to the throne or the current monarch's birthday as keenly as other British subjects, but their governors lacked the social support necessary to fully exert their powers as royal appointees.

America also didn't possess any real aristocracy. The colonies certainly contained plenty of aristocratic wannabes, but the wealthiest families of colonial America appeared quite modest compared to the great aristocratic families of England. For example, George Washington's estate generated perhaps £300 income per year. Compare that to the fictional estate of *Pride and Prejudice*'s great Mr. Darcy, whose lands pulled in £10,000 per year. Darcy was merely a creation of Jane Austen, of course, but this kind of income gap was no fiction. Charles Carroll, future signer of the Declaration of Independence and one of the wealthiest landowners in the southern colonies, earned £1,800 per year. The Earl of Derby in England, however, enjoyed an annual income of more than £40,000. Slaveholders were the wealthiest men in the Thirteen Colonies, but even they paled in wealth compared to the landed elite of England. Wealthy American landowners filled up the seats on America's colonial councils, but these men were a weak imitation of true aristocracy.

In the colonies, the great mass of lesser landholders exercised much of the social and political influence asserted by the aristocracy in England. Landownership in America was much more widespread than in England. Two-thirds of white male colonists owned land; only one-fifth of English men did. More widespread landowning translated into a much broader right to vote, which in both England and America was based on property holding. In England, perhaps 25 percent of adult males had the right to vote. In America, more than half did. America's democratic estate thus possessed too much wealth and power to be part of a carefully balanced mixed constitution of monarchy, aristocracy, and democracy. Not surprisingly, the elective assemblies, as representatives of the democratic estate, acquired and held the most power in colonial government. They wrested the power of the purse from the governors and made the councils weaker brothers in governing.

Colonial America's truncated society thus resulted in a government that, even allowing for the difference of scale, diverged from the British model of a mixed and balanced constitution. But America did not differ from Britain only by subtraction: it differed also by addition. African slavery became a novel appendage on the American body politic. Only 4 percent of the population of the northern colonies consisted of African-American slaves, but every northern colony contributed to that total. In the southern colonies, slaves were much more numerous, comprising a third of the population in the upper southern colonies and more than half in the lower ones. In England, even the lowest levels of society were part of the social order and possessed legal rights. Americans did not make a similar place for slaves—an omission that would vex America for the next century and beyond.

All of these variations from the British constitutional model rendered the Americans ripe for a shift in their own constitutional order—a shift that would adjust American politics to American society. Even so, Americans were not a constitutionally separate people. They belonged to the British Empire and they celebrated the British Constitution. **Americans considered themselves Englishmen and claimed all the "rights of Englishmen" that the British Constitution protected. Perhaps no group of people in the British Empire believed more in the British Constitution than the Americans did.**

As the 1700s wore on, another important divergence between America and Britain developed. British politicians began to embrace Parliamentary supremacy—the belief that, whatever the Constitution may be, Parliament had the authority to change it. An English lawyer in 1774 argued that Parliament was "perpetually altering …[the] constitution" and that it would be "the highest absurdity" to say that Parliament had no right to do so. By the time of the American Revolution, this view was on its way to becoming the majority view in England, and it became settled law after the Revolution. Americans, by contrast, clung to the good old Constitution as a body of unchanging principles to which all were subject—King, Parliament, and people alike.

This divergence in constitutional outlook fueled the conflict between the colonies and Parliament that ultimately led to the Revolutionary War. Beginning in the 1760s, Parliament began to tax the colonists and to pass laws for them in unprecedented, intrusive ways. First came the Sugar Act (1764) and the Stamp Act (1765), then the Townshend Duties (1767) and the Tea Act (1773). Parliament enacted all these taxes without the consent of the colonists' own representative assemblies. Radicals resisted the tea tax in the Boston Tea Party (1773), and Parliament responded with the Coercive Acts (1774) which not only pressured Bostonians to pay for the dumped tea but also asserted Parliament's right to alter the government of any colony. All along the way Americans cried foul—or more accurately, "Unconstitutional!"

Americans claimed the rights of Englishmen. They wanted to be treated as the English living in England were treated. They feared the British government would view them as it viewed the Irish—as a conquered people, a nation of inferiors with whom Parliament could do as it wished. The colonists believed their ancestors had moved to America as full English subjects who had left behind none of their constitutional rights when they crossed the Atlantic. Americans argued that those first settlers would not have come at all if their coming had required a loss of rights.

When Massachusetts governor Thomas Hutchinson wrote that some diminishment of rights in America was to be expected given its distance from the mother country, opinion in the colony became inflamed, and Hutchinson became one of the most hated men in all of North America. Americans believed the rights held by those first settlers were subsequently bequeathed *undiminished* to their descendants. The British Constitution guarded these rights, stretching its protective mantle across continents and oceans, wherever men and women breathed the free air of British liberty. "I have looked for [our rights] in the Constitution ... and there found them," said the American Joseph Galloway.

Revolution and Constitution-Making

The American Revolution began as a British Revolution—a revolution on behalf of the British Constitution—a movement to restore the British constitutional order against the unconstitutional acts of Parliament. Earlier British revolutionaries—in the English Civil War and Glorious Revolution—had challenged kings and taken the side of Parliament. The British revolutionaries living in America challenged Parliament and took the side of the Constitution.

But something happened during the fight. The king sent his troops. The king sent his ships. He hired German mercenaries. He refused to even hear the colonists' request for his intervention in their dispute with Parliament. He declared all the colonists in rebellion, outside his protection. After a year of fighting, the Americans declared independence. Invoking John Locke's case for revolt against failed government, they rejected the Constitution for which they had begun the fight. These true believers gave up their long held constitutional creed with a sudden, stunning destructive force. Hell hath no fury like an American scorned. No wonder that some twenty percent of the American population—the

Loyalists—opposed the Declaration as an insane act of forfeiture—a willful loss of the best thing America had.

Almost immediately, however—before the ink on the Declaration was even dry—the constitutional energies of the Americans were redirected from destructive to creative ends. A war for the redress of grievances became, in 1776, a war for independence, and, at the same time, a war for republican independence. British authority was thrown off in every colony, and every colony claimed to be an independent state. Each new state established a republican government, secured with a republican constitution. These constitutions reflected the heritage of the British Constitution including bills of rights. But the constitutions also created some very un-British imbalances in political power. Revolutionaries tossed out the glorious British model of a mixed and balanced constitution and concentrated power in their assemblies. The biggest loser in this process was the office of governor. State after state clipped the wings of the governor. Governors would now be elected, either by the people or the assemblies. Their power of appointment was curtailed: in some states the assemblies began appointing judges. Most states made the governor subject to annual election and to term limits, or "rotation in office," as it was then called. In every state but New York the governor was denied the power to veto legislation.

In no state was British constitutional balance more dramatically upset than in Pennsylvania. Pennsylvania's Constitution of 1776 gave government power into the hands of the state's assembly. The Pennsylvania Constitution did not merely diminish the powers of the governor; it eliminated the governor. Pennsylvania opted instead for a twelve-member elective "supreme executive council" that lacked veto power over the assembly's legislation. Pennsylvania's radical concentration of power in the assembly proved objectionable both outside Pennsylvania and within it. In

Massachusetts, John Adams predicted that the Pennsylvania Constitution would produce tyrannical government and lead Pennsylvanians to return to British rule. No state, said Pennsylvania's own James Wilson, had so embraced "the policy of fettering power"—and by that he meant the fettering of *executive* power. In other states, the Pennsylvania Constitution became a negative reference point for constitution-makers who consciously sought ways to prevent a similar result. Even so, Pennsylvania's radical constitution showed how far revolutionary America could depart from the British Constitution that all Americans had given up. It removed any doubt that Americans would recast their political life on a new basis.

After a few years a reaction to this radical first wave of state constitutions set in. Americans who had been excluded from the constitution-making process, or who had voluntarily withdrawn, began to re-enter the politics of their states. In a second wave of state constitution-making, states introduced constitutions that were more balanced. The Massachusetts Constitution of 1780 became the model for other state constitutions in this second wave. Massachusetts adopted a constitution that included both a house and a senate as well as a governor with veto power. Ultimately, the Massachusetts Constitution of 1780—which today is the world's oldest functioning written constitution—heavily influenced the framing of the federal Constitution of 1787.

In the midst of these dramatic changes, the states approved in 1781 the Articles of Confederation. Had the Articles established a full-fledged national government, they might have been the endpoint of American constitution-making in the revolutionary era. But the Articles did not establish such a government. Instead, they concentrated executive and legislative power entirely in the Congress and made no provision for a national judiciary, and the powers invested in Congress lacked their usual vigor. The most important example was Congress's insufficient power to raise revenue. The Articles empowered Congress to requisition funds from the state governments and required the state governments to comply. Congress exercised its requisitioning power, but the states did not comply, at least not fully. By the mid-1780s the states had paid to Congress only about one-third of all the money Congress had asked for. The result: Congress faced bankruptcy. The national treasury contained a mere $663—not enough money to run a small mercantile business much less a nation. In addition, Congress owed some $25 million to creditors both domestic and foreign. This "requisition system" failed partly because of the economic depression the country was going through at the time, but opponents of the Articles pointed to Congress's lack of the power to tax as the main problem.

This deficiency pointed to a larger truth: Americans were accustomed to a national government. Even in their dispute with Parliament they had acknowledged that Parliament possessed a "superintending" authority to regulate relations between the colonies and the rest of the British Empire and the world. The Articles did not provide such a government, and that general omission, which the revenue troubles highlighted, inspired the movement to replace the Articles with a more truly national constitution. The Articles of Confederation resembled neither the British Constitution that had been left behind nor the U.S. Constitution that was to come. They reflected the immediate concrete reality of the American Revolution: the powers of the British government had passed to the state governments. This transfer reflected American fears about centralized power and esteem for state sovereignty, but it did not constitute a final position for the American constitutional order.

The Constitution of 1787

When 55 delegates drafted the U.S. Constitution in Philadelphia during the summer of 1787, the example of the British Constitution seemed to recede as much as the Articles of Confederation did. The state constitutions produced since 1776 became brighter, closer lights by which to work. No one was particularly keen on openly identifying the British Constitution as the basic starting point for producing a new national constitution for America. John Adams had remarked that the British Constitution had been betrayed by the British themselves; Americans had no wish to return to the "mire" they had left behind. The Framers of the U.S. Constitution did create a true national government, with national legislative, executive, and judicial institutions. The new Constitution gave this new government numerous powers such as the power to tax, to print paper money, to declare war, to make peace. The list went on and on. Some of these powers would be shared with state governments; others would be held by the national government exclusively. But in crafting this powerful national government, had the Framers in effect created another British Constitution?

In the debate over ratification of the U.S. Constitution, Anti-Federalist opponents of the new text warned that it smelled of monarchy and aristocracy. Federalists defended the Constitution by flatly denying that it was like the British Constitution. They insisted, for example, that the president under this new American Constitution would not be at all like the king under the old British one. "There is a total dissimilitude between *him* and a King of Great-Britain," wrote Alexander Hamilton in *The Federalist #49*. Both the president and the king had a veto power over legislation, but the president's veto could be overridden whereas the king's could not. Both would be commander-in-chief of the nation's armed forces, but the king had the power to declare war, a power which the president would lack, it having been lodged with Congress instead. The king held the throne as a hereditary possession, transferrable "to his heirs forever;" the president, by contrast, was to be elected to a four-year term. In fact, Hamilton saw a "close analogy" not between the president and the

British king but between the president and the governor of New York, who served a three-year term. Here as elsewhere, the Framers looked to state constitutions rather than the British Constitution for parallels to the document they had crafted. Of course, many of the powers of the president were indeed carried over—copied—from the British monarchy. The president's veto power, his pardoning power, his treaty-making power, and his immense power of appointment were all powers held by the king. But the very substantial differences between president and king enabled Federalists to argue that formerly *royal* executive powers had been poured into a quite different *presidential* vessel.

The Senate seemed to anti-Federalists to resemble Britain's aristocratic House of Lords. George Mason warned that the Senate's aristocratic character would work to "destroy any balance in the government." Patrick Henry claimed that the Senate would actually be worse than Lords. For the Senate would constitute an "aristocracy of ambition" that lacked the restraint of economic self-interest that the real aristocrats of the House of Lords had. As with the presidency, Federalists responded to such criticisms by sharply distinguishing the Senate from its British antecedent. The Senate, not being hereditary, would actually better secure "knowledge, wisdom and virtue" in its members than Lords had, "for by these qualities alone are [the Senators] to obtain their offices." The Lords held their seats for life, "wholly independent" of the people; senators served for six years only. The House of Lords was Britain's highest judicial court; the Senate, by contrast, would have no judicial powers. Federalists also claimed that, there being no American aristocracy, the American Senate could not be aristocratic. James Wilson of Pennsylvania considered the American imitation of the British Constitution impossible: "We have no materials for a similar one."

Behind such arguments lay a reality about the relationship between the two constitutions that was not always acknowledged in the 1780s. The

U.S. Constitution did contain important similarities to the British one but, as the Federalists argued, it offered striking points of divergence and was set in a very different framework. Both constitutions were, for example, supreme laws, and both found expression in written law. But the American Constitution was truly a "written" one, embodied in a single text; the British Constitution, as we have seen, was unwritten, with only *evidences* of its principles dispersed in writing across the English legal landscape. Both Constitutions were in some sense mixed. But the American separation of powers between the legislative, executive, and judicial branches was a mix very different from Britain's King, Lords, and Commons. In Britain, both executive and judicial power were thought to lay with the king, who enforced law as well as appointed judges. The House of Lords exercised both legislative and judicial power. In Britain, the mix was primarily a mix of the social orders—the royal family, the aristocracy, and the commoners—not a mix of governmental powers. Americans balanced powers; the British balanced estates.

Each balance represented a radically different vision not only of the form of government—one being a monarchy, the other a republic—but of the relationship between government and society. The British Constitution was imitative of British society. It reflected *and was meant to reflect* the actual arrangement of society into estates with their respective interests and points of view. The balance of the British Constitution came from bringing these social classes *as they were* into the political realm. One's social status was not left at the door but carried into the government. In the United States, the branches of government echoed in some degree King, Lords, and Commons, but did not reflect estates or classes in American society, nor were they meant to. The U.S. Constitution did not take class into account. Americans did not exactly believe the United States was a classless society. They recognized differences in occupation, income, and social status, but none of these distinctions amounted to the broad, sweeping divide between royalty, aristocracy, and commoners in England. American had no precedent for creating a mixed and balanced government on the class difference between, say, the wealthy farmers and the modest craftsmen. Class differences, ever-changing, would play themselves out in American politics, but they were given no recognition in the constitutional order. The American Constitution was detached from the social order—in stark contrast to the British Constitution.

We really have no idea how American history would have developed had our Constitution incorporated social classes as the British Constitution did. We do know that in the years before America's next great war, the Civil War, northerners accused southerners of trying to do that very thing—of trying to convert the American democracy into a slavocracy—a government of slaveholders—making that social class into the controlling center of the American Constitution. For all of our history since 1787 we have viewed our true Constitution as a thing detached from social class. Americans have generally been dismayed by any indication that social class has penetrated the wall that separates the government from the society.

The U.S. Constitution reflected in one respect the American social order. Just as American classes were held to be changeable, the American Constitution was held to be amendable. It was not designed to be an unchanging text. Its provisions were not grounded in a remote and untouchable past. The amendability of the U.S. Constitution owed much to the American revolutionary experience. The Declaration of Independence announced the right of a people to alter a government, which implied that the people could amend their constitution. By 1787, state constitutions had already been amended and even replaced. The Articles of Confederation were amendable, though that required unanimous consent of the states. Revolutionary Americans grew accustomed to the idea that their most fundamental instruments of government could be altered.

The amendability of the Constitution was clearly a departure from the sort of reverence in which Americans had held the unchanging British Constitution. In spite of its amendability, we have been a people reluctant to change our Constitution. Since 1789 more than 11,000 Amendments to the Constitution have been proposed. Only twenty-seven have been approved. The 27th Amendment, which delays changes in congressional salaries until after the next election, took 202 years to be ratified. We are a people divided in mind. The Revolution gave us an amendable Constitution, but we retain an old-fashioned British constitutional reluctance to actually amend it. Indeed, most changes to our Constitution occur under cover of Supreme Court decisions rather than by explicit constitutional amendment.

We can get some further idea of the role of the Revolution in creating a new American constitutional order by looking at the part of British North America that did not revolt against British rule in the late 1700s: Canada. In the aftermath of the Revolutionary War, Parliament promised not to tax the Canadians, and kept its promise. Canadian government as a result was heavily subsidized by the British treasury, but Canada paid a constitutional cost for its freedom from Parliamentary taxation. The British government made absolutely sure that Canada's government reflected the essential shape of government back in England. Canada remained under the king. It was divided into two provinces each of which had a governor appointed by the king. The legislatures of these provinces were filled with the governor's supporters who reliably voted the way the king's governors wanted. The home government went to great lengths to ensure that the British Constitution—particularly the government's understanding of it—remained firmly in place in Canada. The rejection of constitutional creativity in the case of Canada marks a path that the American colonies might have travelled had there been no Revolution.

But we traveled the path of Revolution. **The experience of the Revolution led to a U.S. Constitution that contained old principles in a quite new arrangement.** The musical analogy mentioned earlier seems especially apt for this point. The Constitution was a new song, new to the ear. You can hear the strains of ancient ideas of power, the themes of constitutional balance, the tones of rights. The song, in a sense, depended on these for its very substance. And yet the composition heard as a single whole differed radically from all of these. It served a republic, not a monarchy. It was an instrument for governing society and not a reflection of society. Its provisions, whatever their constitutional antecedents, were unique and in any case amendable. The U.S. Constitution was more than a reprise of the British Constitution. It was the fruit of the American revolutionary experience and, so far as we can tell, could not have come about in any other way.

★ ★

RECOMMENDED READING

Jack Rakove, *Original Meanings:*
Politics and Ideas In the Making of the Constitution
(Knopf, 1996)

John Phillip Reid, *A Constitutional History of the American Revolution,*
4 vols. (University of Wisconsin Press, 1986–1993)

Gordon Wood, *The Radicalism of the American Revolution*
(Vintage, 1993)

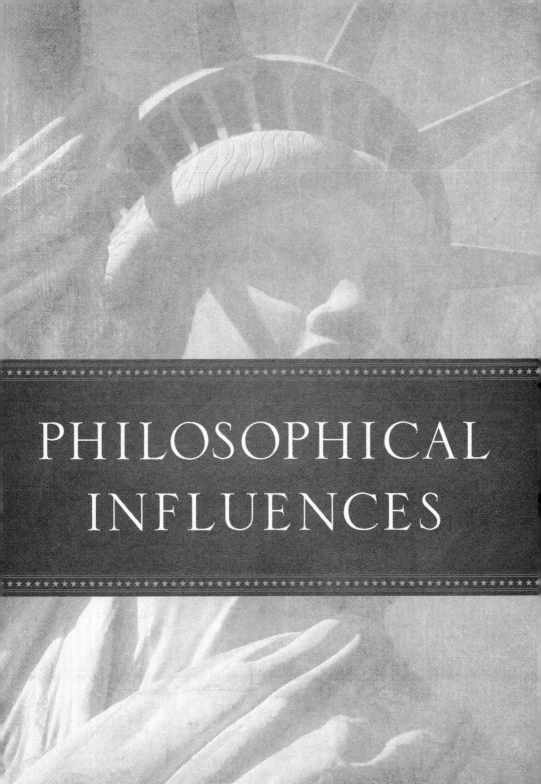

PHILOSOPHICAL
INFLUENCES

NATURAL LAW
AND THE
AMERICAN
FOUNDING

By John O. Tyler, Jr. JD, PhD
PROFESSOR OF LAW & JURISPRUDENCE

Natural law dominates America's founding principles. Natural law maintains that human conduct is subject to eternal and unchanging moral laws. These moral laws originate, not in human legislation, but in nature or a divine lawgiver. These moral laws govern all people, at all times, and in all circumstances. These moral laws are unwritten, but man can discover their content by intuition, careful reason, or divine revelation. Human happiness depends on obeying these moral laws and pursuing justice.

In politics, natural law prevents tyranny by establishing individual rights that limit government power. These rights are inalienable, and they exist prior to the formation of the state. State actions that violate these natural rights are tyrannical and citizens may resist them. John Locke's *Second Treatise of Government* (1689) provides the natural law foundation for our Constitution and political institutions.

In jurisprudence, natural law prevents injustice by establishing a standard of legal validity that invalidates unjust laws. Man-made laws that violate the moral precepts of natural law are unenforceable and citizens have no duty to obey them. Sir William Blackstone's *Commentaries on the Laws of England* (1765–1769) provides the natural law foundation of our legal system.

Natural law developed in response to tyrannical governments and unjust laws, and a page of history is worth a volume of logic in understanding its precepts. Natural law began in Athens. Plato and Aristotle wrote in the political and legal chaos that followed Athens's defeat in the Peloponnesian War, including the judicial murder of Socrates in 399 B.C. Plato gives the first statement of natural law precepts in the *Crito*, the dialogue in which Socrates refuses an opportunity to escape his unjust execution. Aristotle presents his theory of natural law in his *Politics*, *Rhetoric*, and *Nicomachean Ethics*.

Natural law continued its development in Rome. Cicero wrote his theory of natural law in hopes of saving and restoring the constitution of the Roman Republic. Cicero presents his theory of natural law in his *De Legibus* (*The Laws*), *De Officis* (*On Duties*), and *De Re Publica* (*The Republic*). Justinian I commissioned the *Corpus Juris Civilis* to preserve the Roman natural law tradition when the Western Roman Empire fell.

Natural law reached its full flowering in England. John Locke wrote in response to the tyrannical Stuart kings and the judicial murders of Lord William Russell and Colonel Algernon Sidney in 1683. Locke presents his theory of natural law and natural rights in his *Essay Concerning Human Understanding*, *Second Treatise of Government*, and *A Letter Concerning Toleration*. Sir William Blackstone synthesizes the work of all these writers in his *Commentaries on the Laws of England*. Blackstone establishes a necessary connection between law and morality. Unjust laws are not *bad* laws. They are not laws at all.

Natural law theory must answer three important questions. First, what are the moral precepts of natural law? Second, what is the source of these precepts? Third, how can man know these precepts? The following traces the answers given by the thinkers who most influenced our political and legal institutions.

Natural Law Begins in Athens

Plato was born to an aristocratic Athenian family in 427 B.C. Two events shaped Plato's philosophy. The first was the Peloponnesian War with Sparta from 431–404 B.C. Plato grew up during a period of economic, political, and moral dissolution. Athens suffered five regime changes between 413 B.C. and 403 B.C., and its inept democracy grossly mismanaged the war. Defeat came in 404 B.C., and the Thirty Tyrants imposed a bloody reign of terror.

The second event that shaped Plato's philosophy was the trial and execution of Plato's mentor Socrates in 399 B.C. The democratic party under Anytus prosecuted Socrates to silence its most formidable critic of Athens's radical democracy. Plato described Socrates as "the bravest, wisest, and most upright man of his time." (Plato, *Phaedo*, 115b–118b). Plato had planned a career in politics but "withdrew in disgust" after observing how Athenian courts "corrupted the written laws and customs." (Plato, *Letter VII*, 325a–c).

These experiences led Plato to three conclusions. First, a bad state breeds only bad men. Second, a good man cannot live in such a state. Third, a state ruled by the many is inevitably bad. The many are ignorant, emotionally unstable, and stupidly self-centered.

Plato sought the basis for a good state in which good men can find happiness and peace. Plato provides the foundation for natural law with three claims. First, universal moral principles exist. Second, human reason can discover these principles. Third, living in accord with these principles makes us better and happier.

The Sophist philosopher Protagoras opposed Plato and denied the existence of universal moral principles. Protagoras argued that all knowledge comes from sense perception. Each man's sense perceptions are private and subjective. It is impossible to know, for example, if others perceive the color red the same as we do. Since all knowledge comes from perception, all knowledge is private and subjective as well. Therefore, all knowledge claims are equally true. Since morality is merely a specialized type of knowledge, all moral claims are equally true. If all moral claims are equally true, then there are no universal moral principles. (Plato, *Protagoras*, 323a–328d).

The Sophist Callicles agreed with Protagoras. There are no universal moral principles. Instead, might makes right. (Plato, Gorgias, 483b–d, 490a). The Sophist Thrasymachus denied any duty to obey the law. Obedience to law is a form of slavery. Disobedience is "a stronger, freer, and more masterful thing" than obedience. (Plato, *Republic*, 338c–344c).

Plato refutes Protagoras's moral relativism in the *Theaetetus*. First, Plato denies that knowledge is perception. If knowledge were perception, we would understand anyone speaking to us in a foreign tongue. This is clearly not the case. Second, remembered knowledge involves no perception, but it is knowledge nonetheless.

Third, moral relativism is incoherent. Assume one man claims, "All beliefs are true." Assume another man claims, "Not all beliefs are true." If Protagoras is correct, both claims are true, but the claims contradict each other. Moral relativism is thus incoherent. (Plato, *Theaetetus*, 160e–177b).

Plato refutes Thrasymachus and establishes a qualified duty to obey the law in the *Crito*. Plato's *Crito* provides the two main elements of natural law jurisprudence. The first is a set of moral precepts. The second is the principle that laws violating these precepts are unjust and unenforceable. There is no duty to obey unjust laws.

The *Crito* finds Socrates imprisoned awaiting execution. Crito urges Socrates to escape and avoid his unjust execution. Socrates refuses, replying that the soul is more precious than the body. Good actions benefit our souls, but wrong actions mutilate them. Circumstances, no matter how dire, never justify wrong action.

Socrates utilizes three principles in determining whether to escape. First, the important thing in life is not living, but living well. This means living honorably. Second, one should not injure others, even when they injure you. Third, one "ought to honor one's agreements, provided they are just." (Plato, *Crito*, 47e–49e).

The Roman jurist Ulpian (*c.* A.D. 170–223) adopts Socrates's principles as the three precepts of natural law. *Honeste vivere, alterum non laedere, suum cuique tribuere.* Live honestly; harm no one, and render every one their due. Justinian's *Digest* (A.D. 533) adopts these precepts into Roman law (Justinian, *Digest*, 1.1.10), and Blackstone's *Commentaries on the Laws of England* (1765) adopts these precepts into our common law tradition. (Blackstone, *Commentaries*, § 40).

Plato next refutes Thrasymachus's claim that disobeying the law "is a stronger, freer, and more masterful thing" than obeying the law. The Laws of Athens present two arguments for obedience. The first is the "argument from consent." Socrates consented to obey Athens's laws by choosing to live in Athens. Socrates was always free to leave, but he chose to stay with full knowledge of how the laws functioned. The duty to obey the Laws, however, is not absolute. Their orders are "proposals, not savage commands." Socrates can either obey the Laws *or* persuade them that they are at fault.

The Laws' second argument is the "argument from injury." Disobedience destroys both the Laws and the city. The city cannot exist if its citizens ignore the Laws. Socrates must either obey the Laws or "persuade them in accordance with universal justice" that they are at fault.

Laws must comply with principles of "universal justice" to command obedience. (Plato, *Crito*, 51e–52d). Men should obey just laws, but there is no duty to obey unjust laws. Unjust laws are invalid and unenforceable. Plato's *Crito* thus provides the two main elements of natural law jurisprudence: the three moral precepts of natural law, and a moral standard of legal validity.

Aristotle designs his political and legal philosophy to avoid the political catastrophes suffered by Athens from 632 B.C. to 329 B.C. Aristotle describes these events in *The Athenian Constitution* (325 B.C.). Aristotle concludes that laws must be just. They must also foster virtue. Justice is required to prevent revolution, and virtue is required for human happiness. Man separated from justice is "the worst of animals," and man without virtue "is the most unholy and the most savage of animals." (Aristotle, *Politics* 1253a).

The state's most important function is establishing justice. Governments must rule justly to endure. Unjust rule and unequal treatment of similarly situated citizens provoke revolution. Establishing justice, however, preserves the state by forming a bond between its citizens. (Aristotle, *Politics,* 1328b, 1332b, 1253a).

Justice is lawfulness concerned with the common advantage and happiness of the political community. Aristotle distinguishes *legal* justice from *natural* justice. *Legal justice* involves positive (human) laws and customs enacted by man, such as measures for grain and wine. These "are just not by nature but by human enactment" and vary from place to place. Aristotle secures *legal justice* by granting law sovereignty over political rulers, and by utilizing custom to encourage obedience. (Aristotle, *Nicomachean Ethics*, 1134b–1135a).

Natural justice, on the other hand, involves principles of natural law. These principles originate in nature rather than the minds of men. Natural law principles provide immutable standards of justice that apply everywhere, just as fire burns the same in Greece as in Persia. "There is in nature a common principle of the just and unjust that all people in some way divine." (Aristotle, *Rhetoric*, 1373b).

Aristotle secures *natural justice* in two ways. First, Aristotle secures natural justice by invalidating human laws that violate the moral precepts of natural law. (Aristotle, *Nicomachean Ethics*, 1134b; *Rhetoric*, 1373b). There is no duty to obey unjust laws. Antigone rightly disobeyed Creon's decree denying funeral rites to her brother Polyneices. Juries rightly nullify human laws that violate natural law precepts. (Aristotle, *Rhetoric*, 1373b, 1375a–b).

Second, Aristotle secures *natural justice* by fostering virtue. Human happiness depends on virtue more than liberty. Government is therefore responsible for producing a virtuous state. Although virtue requires more than obeying the law, virtue will only flourish in a state that enforces virtue through law. The laws must conform to natural law precepts, and the state must use its laws as a moral schoolteacher to make its citizens just and good. Failing to do so undermines the state's political system and harms its citizens. (Aristotle, *Nicomachean Ethics*, 1179b; *Politics*, 1280b, 1310a, 1337a).

Natural Law Develops in Rome

Cicero admired Plato, and like Plato, Cicero lived in turbulent times. Rome was ignoring its constitution and losing its Republic. The histories of Herodotus, Thucydides, Xenophon, and Polybius persuaded Cicero that natural law imposes justice on human events. Cicero hoped his writings would restore the Republic by reviving virtue in the ruling class. He then hoped the ruling class would impose virtue on the people through legislation. Mark Antony had Cicero murdered in 43 B.C. Although Cicero's *De Legibus (The Laws)*, *De Officis (On Duties)*, and *De Re Publica (The Republic)* failed to restore the Republic, they greatly influence the natural law tradition, particularly the political philosophy of John Locke.

Cicero was not a Stoic, but Cicero's great contribution to natural law is adopting Stoicism's divine Nature as the source of natural law. Nature is the omnipotent ruler of the universe, the common master of all people, and the omnipresent observer of every individual's intentions and actions. Law and justice originate in Nature as a divinely ordained set of universal moral principles. Belief in divine Nature stabilizes society by encouraging individual virtue and obedience to law. (Cicero, *De Legibus*, 2.15–16).

Natural law dominates Cicero's jurisprudence. Cicero defines natural law as perfect reason in commanding and prohibiting. These principles are the sole source of justice and provide the sole standard of legal validity. "True law is right reason in agreement with Nature." (Cicero, *De Re Publica*, 3.33).

Natural law precepts are eternal and immutable. They apply at all places, at all times, and to all people. Natural law summons to duty by its commands, and averts from wrongdoing by its prohibitions. Nature serves as the enforcing judge of natural law precepts, and Nature's punishment for violating natural law precepts is inescapable. (Cicero, *De Re Publica*, 3.33).

Natural law provides the *naturae norma*, the standard of legal validity for human laws and customs. Justice requires that laws and customs comply with the *naturae norma* and preserve the peace, happiness, and safety of the state and its citizens. Human laws and customs that violate the *naturae norma* are not truly laws at all. (Cicero, *De Legibus*, 1.44, 2.11–2.14).

Cicero establishes three important limits on the power of magistrates. First, like Plato, Cicero limits the power of magistrates by establishing the sovereignty of law over magistrates. The magistrate's limited role is to govern according to existing law. Although the magistrate has some control of the people, the laws have full control of the magistrate. An official is the speaking law, and the law is a nonspeaking official. (Cicero, *De Legibus*, 3.2). Political rulers cannot alter, repeal, or abolish natural law precepts. Their commands must conform to natural law precepts. Political rulers have no role in interpreting or explaining natural law precepts. Every man can discern the precepts of natural law for himself through reason. (Cicero, *De Re Publica*, 3.33).

Second, like Aristotle, Cicero limits the power of magistrates by rotating political offices. Rotation of political offices encourages evenhanded administration by magistrates who know they will soon be subject to the power of others. Magistrates may not serve successive terms, and ten years must pass before the magistrate becomes eligible for the same office. Every magistrate leaving office must submit an account of his official acts to the censors. Misconduct is subject to prosecution. No magistrate may give or receive any gifts while seeking or holding office, or after the conclusion of his term. (Cicero, *De Legibus*, 3.9–3.11).

Third, like Locke, Cicero limits the power of magistrates by emphasizing the rights of individuals. Laws must protect individuals against unjust coercion. Rulers may use sanctions to enforce legitimate commands, but every subject has the right to appeal to the people before any sanction is enforced. Furthermore, no ruler can issue commands concerning single individuals. Only the highest assembly of the people can order any significant sanction against an individual, such as execution or loss of citizenship. As a further protection, the censors must officially record all laws. (Cicero, *De Re Publica*, 2.53–2.54; *De Legibus*, 3.10–3.47).

Lastly, Cicero agrees with Aristotle that custom maintains social stability by encouraging obedience to law. Custom can even achieve immortality for the commonwealth. The commonwealth will be eternal if citizens conduct their lives in accordance with ancestral laws and customs. (Cicero, *De Re Publica*, 3.41).

The Roman Republic fell in 27 B.C., and the Western Roman Empire fell in A.D. 476 Emperor Justinian I of the Eastern Roman Empire ordered the preservation of Roman law and jurisprudence in A.D. 529. The project required seven years to complete, and the resulting four books of the *Corpus Juris Civilis* (A.D. 535) became the sole legal authorities in the Eastern Roman Empire. The *Institutes* was a law school text. The *Codex* contained statutes dating from A.D. 76. The *Digest* contained commentaries by leading jurists, and jurists updated the *New Laws* as new laws became necessary.

The *Corpus* is the direct ancestor of continental Europe's civil law systems. Although English common law jurisprudence never accepted the *Corpus* as binding authority, the rediscovery and revival of the *Corpus* in the 12th century profoundly influenced the structure and formation of common law jurisprudence through the works of the "father of the common law," Henry de Bracton (*c.* 1210–1268).

The *Corpus* divides law into two branches. Public law governs state interests, and private law governs persons, things, and actions. Natural law is the primary source of private law in the *Corpus*. The *Corpus* establishes a severe hierarchy of authority in law. Natural law, which originates in a divine lawgiver, holds the highest position. Custom, which originates in popular consent, holds the middle position. Municipal (positive) law, which originates in magistrates, holds the lowest position.

Like Cicero, the *Corpus* relies on a divine lawgiver as the source of natural law precepts. "The laws of nature, which are observed by all nations alike, are established by divine providence." Natural law precepts are universal, eternal, and immutable. (Justinian, *Institutes*, 1.2.11; *Digest*, 1.3.2).

Natural law governs all land, air, and sea creatures, including man. "The law of nature is that which she has taught all animals; a law not peculiar to the human race, but shared by all living creatures." The *Corpus* extends natural law to "all living creatures" to repudiate the Sophist arguments that law is merely a human convention with no basis in nature, justice does not exist, and there is no duty to obey the law. The *Corpus* rebuts these Sophist arguments by emphasizing the highly socialized behavior of such animal species as ants, bees, and birds. Although animals cannot legislate or form social conventions, they nevertheless follow norms of behavior. These norms affirm the existence of natural law. (Justinian, *Institutes*, 1.1.3, 2.1.11).

The *Institutes* and the *Digest* adopt the Roman jurist Ulpian's three precepts of natural law: "*Honeste vivere, alterum non laedere, suum cuique tribuere.*" *Live honestly, injure no one, and give every man his due.* (Justinian, *Institutes*, 1.1.3; *Digest*, 1.1.10). These precepts track Socrates's commands in the *Crito* to live honorably, harm no one, and honor agreements so long as they are just. (Plato, *Crito*, 47e–49e). Blackstone's *Commentaries* adopts these precise natural law precepts from Justinian. (Blackstone, *Commentaries*, § 2).

The law of nations is the portion of natural law that governs relations between human beings. (Justinian, *Digest*, 1.4). Its rules are "prescribed by natural reason for all men" and "observed by all peoples alike." The law of nations is the source of duties to God, to one's parents, and to one's country. It recognizes human rights to life, liberty, self-defense, and property. Property rights enable contracts and commerce between peoples. Locke's *Second Treatise* adopts these precise natural rights from Justinian. (Locke, *Second Treatise*, § 6).

The precepts of natural law provide the standard for legal validity. This standard voids any right or duty violating natural law precepts. The *Institutes* provides illustrative examples. Contracts created for immoral purposes, such as carrying out a homicide or a sacrilege, are not enforceable. (Justinian, *Institutes*, 3.19.24). Immorality invalidates wrongful profits. Anyone profiting from wrongful dominion over another's property must disgorge those profits. (Justinian, *Digest*, 5.3.52).

Immorality invalidates agency relationships. Agents are not obliged to carry out immoral instructions from their principals. If they do, they are not entitled to indemnity from their principals for any liability they incur. (Justinian, *Institutes*, 3.26.7). Immorality even invalidates bequests and legacies if the bequest is contingent upon immoral conduct. (Justinian, *Institutes*, 2.20.36).

Justinian's *Corpus*, like Locke's *Second Treatise*, emphasizes the importance of consent by recognizing custom as the second highest source of enforceable law. The *Corpus* defines legal custom as the tacit consent of a people established by long-continued habit. Since custom evidences the consent of the people, it is a higher source of law than positive or statutory law.

Custom binds judges. Statutory provisions, if customarily ignored, are equivalent to repealed legislation. (Justinian, *Digest*, 1.1.3). Legal custom even controls statutory interpretation. "Custom is the best interpreter of statutes." (Justinian, *Institutes*, 4.17; *Digest*, 1.1.37).

Municipal or positive law is the least authoritative source of law. The *Corpus'* political dimension resides in its six categories of Roman municipal law, the "statutes, plebiscites, senatusconsults, enactments of the Emperors, edicts of the magistrates, and answers of those learned in the law." In contrast to natural law and the law of nations, Roman municipal law applied only to Rome. Its provisions were also "subject to frequent change, either by the tacit consent of the people, or by the subsequent enactment of another statute." (Justinian, *Institutes*, 1.2.3, 1.2.11).

Lastly, following Plato and Cicero, the *Corpus* establishes the sovereignty of law over magistrates. A judge's first duty is "to not judge contrary to statutes, the imperial laws, and custom." (Justinian, *Institutes*, 4.17; *Digest*, 1.1.37). Blackstone's "declaratory theory of law," explained below, adopts this limit on the power of judges. (Blackstone, *Commentaries*, §§ 69–70, 142).

Natural Law Matures in England

England endured a bitter constitutional struggle, including three civil wars, between the ascension of James I in 1603 and the Glorious Revolution in 1688. This bitter struggle profoundly influenced American political institutions through the work of John Locke, particularly Locke's *Essay concerning Human Understanding* (1689), *Second Treatise of Government* (1689), and *Letter Concerning Toleration* (1689). This struggle profoundly influenced American legal institutions as well through Sir William Blackstone's *Commentaries on the Laws of England* (1765–1769), the most influential work in the history of common law jurisprudence.

Locke is the philosopher of liberty. Locke describes "the pursuit of happiness" as the greatest good, and stresses the "necessity of ... pursuing true happiness" as "the foundation of our liberty." Man obtains happiness by following God's law, the law of nature. (Locke, *Essay concerning Human Understanding*, 2.21.51; 2.28.8).

Thomas Jefferson adopted the most famous ideas in the Declaration of Independence from Locke's *Second Treatise of Government* (1689). These ideas include the claims that God created all men equal; that God endows all men with inalienable rights; that men institute governments to protect these rights; and that the people have the right to alter or abolish governments that fail to protect these rights.

Locke revolutionized natural law by providing a solution to one of its fundamental problems, the problem of obtaining *certain* knowledge of natural law precepts. Since these precepts are unwritten, we can only find them in the minds of men. Men, however, are subject to passion and self interest, and there is no authority to correct our mistakes if we misstate or misapply natural law precepts. (Locke, *Second Treatise*, § 136).

Earlier thinkers gloss over this issue. Most argue that human reason is sufficient to gain knowledge of natural law precepts. Locke explains in *The Reasonableness of Christianity* (1695), however, that human reason alone has never fully deduced natural law precepts. Other thinkers, like Thomas Aquinas, argue that God inscribes natural law precepts in the hearts of men. Locke rejects inscription in *An Essay concerning Human Understanding* (1689), arguing that man is born a *tabula rasa*, a blank slate.

Locke realized that he could not solve this problem of natural law, or any other philosophical problem, unless he first established a basis for *certain* knowledge. He told a meeting of his friends in 1671 that the project should take him several weeks. It required 18 years. Locke's "new way of ideas" provides the basis for certain knowledge in *An Essay concerning Human Understanding* (1689). Locke's *Essay* is one of the most important works of all philosophy, and Locke's "new way of ideas" empowered Locke's natural law theory to transform the world.

Locke's "new way of ideas" presents five principles for establishing certain knowledge. First, there are no innate ideas. Man is born a *tabula rasa*, a "blank slate." (Locke, *Essay*, 2.1.2). We have no innate ideas of God's existence or natural law precepts. (Locke, *Essay*, 1.3.1; 1.4.8–11, 17). Second, all ideas come from experience, either the experience of sense perception or the experience of reflecting on our sense perceptions. (Locke, *Essay*, 2.1.2).

Third, words represent only the ideas of things, not the real essences of things. Definitions alone, therefore, are unable to give us knowledge. (Locke, *Essay*, 3.4.4–11). Fourth, reliable knowledge requires certainty. (Locke, *Essay*, 4.2.1–2). Science cannot provide certain knowledge because it seeks to know the real essences of things. The real essences of things, however, are beyond human faculties. (Locke, *Essay*, 4.3.26).

Locke's fifth principle explains that man can nevertheless obtain certain knowledge of God's existence and God's moral laws using "intuition" and "demonstration." Intuition gives us certain knowledge of undoubtable truths, such as our own existence. Intuition, however, cannot give us certain knowledge of God's existence. God is never directly in our mind. Only the idea of God is in our mind. Nevertheless, we can still obtain certain knowledge of God's existence by building on our intuitions using a process of "demonstration." "Demonstration" carefully connects intuitive truths, one step at a time, to reach a conclusion. (Locke, *Essay*, 4.9.2).

Locke's "cosmological argument" utilizes intuition and demonstration to establish certain knowledge of God's existence. The argument has six steps. First, intuition gives us certain knowledge of our own existence. Second, intuition gives us certain knowledge that no being can be produced from nothing. Third, we know from demonstration that some being has existed since eternity past. Unless a being is eternal, some other being must have produced it. Since the chain of producing beings reaches back into eternity, there must be an eternal being.

Fourth, we know by intuition that no being can have more power than the being that produced it. The eternal being must therefore be the most powerful being. Fifth, we know by intuition that no being can be more knowing than the being that produced it. The eternal being must therefore be the most knowing being. Sixth, we know from the previous steps that God exists as the eternal, most powerful, and most knowing being. (Locke, *Essay*, 4.10.1–19).

Locke maintained this argument proved the certain existence of God. (Locke, *Essay*, 4.11.13, 4.17.2). Certain knowledge of God's existence permits certain knowledge of God's moral law. Natural law is part of God's moral law, and God publishes natural law to man in two ways. First, God gives man "the light of nature," a special faculty that illuminates truth and falsity for man. Second, God reveals the precepts of natural law in Scripture. (Locke, *Essay*, 2.28.8).

Justinian reduces natural law to three precepts. *Live honorably, injure no one, and give every man his due.* (Justinian, *Institutes*, 1.1.3; *Digest*, 1.1.10). Locke reduces natural law to a single law. No person should violate another person's natural rights to life, health, liberty, or property. (Locke, *Second Treatise*, § 6). God is the author of natural law. Natural law is part of God's divine law, which God establishes to govern man. Divine law is "the only true touchstone of moral rectitude." Divine law provides the moral standard for man. It also provides the validity standard for human laws and government. Like Cicero, Locke says the divine law is inescapable. Like Cicero, Locke says that obeying the duties established by divine law brings happiness, but sinning against them brings misery. (Locke, *Essay*, 2.28.8).

Natural law regulates human laws. Human laws are "only so far right, as they are founded on the law of nature." Human laws that violate the moral precepts of natural law are invalid. (Locke, *Second Treatise*, § 12). The problem of politics is establishing a state that brings civil law into conformity with divine law.

Locke uses a hypothetical state of nature to explain his political philosophy. The state of nature is man's original condition prior to the formation of a government. Men in the state of nature are free, equal, and independent. They have no political ruler. They have moral ties but no civil or state-originated ties. (Locke, *Second Treatise*, § 4).

Unlike Thomas Hobbes's *Leviathan* (1661), which describes the state of nature as a state of war of every man against every other man, Locke's *Second Treatise* (1689) describes the state of nature as generally peaceful. Man in the state of nature has certain inalienable rights bestowed upon him by an eternally valid moral law. These natural rights are life, health, liberty, and property. (Locke, *Second Treatise*, § 6, *adopting* Justinian, *Digest*, 1.4). The right to liberty includes freedom from government without one's consent. (Locke, *Second Treatise*, § 22). As explained in Locke's *Letter Concerning Toleration* (1689), the right to liberty includes freedom from state coercion in religious belief and worship.

The state of nature is a state of liberty, but it is not a state of license. The state of nature has a law to govern it. This law is absolutely binding, and it has a single provision: "No one ought to harm another in his life, health, liberty, or possessions." (Locke, *Second Treatise*, § 6). If all individuals obey this law, they will maintain peace and harmony and avoid a state of war. (Locke, *Second Treatise*, § 7).

Since all men are born morally equal in the state of nature, all men have a duty not to interfere with the natural rights of other men. Every person in the state of nature has the right to punish any man who breaches this duty. (Locke, *Second Treatise*, § 7). Additionally, every injured party has an individual, private right to retribution. (Locke, *Second Treatise*, § 10). These rights of punishment and retribution are the only instances in which another's natural rights to life, health, liberty, and property are subject to interference in the state of nature.

Locke places special emphasis on private property rights. The great and chief end for which men join into societies is the protection of their property. (Locke, *Second Treatise*, § 124). Locke's justification for private property is one of the most famous aspects of his thought. (Locke, *Second Treatise*, §§ 25–32). To avoid royal claims to all property, Locke argues that the earth belongs to everyone in common and no one man in particular. To avoid socialism, Locke argues that every man has a "property" in his own person. No one has a right to one's person except the individual himself. The labor of the body and the work of his hands are properly his. If someone takes something from nature and improves it through his labor, then the product becomes his private property. (Locke, *Second Treatise*, § 34). For example, if a man takes wood from the forest and fashions it into a table, the table belongs to him.

Because the world belongs to everyone in common and no one man in particular, every individual must comply with two requirements when appropriating resources. First, he must not waste resources. Second, he must leave "enough, and as good, in common for others." (Locke, *Second Treatise*, § 33).

The state of nature, although generally peaceable, has three defects that make it difficult to protect private property. First, there is no consent to a common law in the state of nature. Second, there is no impartial judge of disputes. Third, individuals do not possess the power required to execute just sentences. (Locke, *Second Treatise*, §§ 124–126).

The introduction of money exacerbated the three defects in the state of nature. All men had relative economic equality in hunter-gatherer and agricultural societies. The introduction of money, however, led to the development of economic inequality. This led to increased violations of the laws of nature. The difficulties of protecting property under such conditions led to the introduction of civil government. (Locke, *Second Treatise*, §§ 36–50).

Men correct the defects in the state of nature by entering a social contract to create a state. (Locke, *Second Treatise*, § 21). Every man in the state of nature has the right to personally exact retribution for themselves for crimes committed against them. Under the social contract, each man gives up this right to private retribution in return for impartial justice backed by overwhelming force. (Locke, *Second Treatise*, §§ 128–131).

Locke also places special emphasis on the consent of the governed. The moral legitimacy of government requires the consent of the governed. The people always remain sovereign. Every man has the right to be free from any government without his consent. (Locke, *Second Treatise*, § 22). No one can be compelled to enter a society without his consent. (Locke, *Second Treatise*, § 95). After one consents to form a government, however, he consents to government by majority rule. Majority rule is morally justified and made binding by the consent of the governed. (Locke, *Second Treatise*, § 99).

Locke places strict limits on the power of government. Political power is the right to make laws and enforce them under penalty of death. (Locke, *Second Treatise*, § 3). Government may never exercise power beyond that needed for the peace, safety, and public good of the people. Political power is therefore limited to the power necessary to accomplish two ends. First, government must cure the three defects of the state of nature to secure every person's property. Second, government must protect the community from foreign attack. In accomplishing these ends, government must respect the sovereignty of law and govern according to known and established laws. (Locke, *Second Treatise*, § 131).

The governed have the right and duty to resist tyrannical government. "Wherever law ends, tyranny begins." Government acts tyrannically when it fails to govern according to known and established laws. Governments exist by the consent of the people to protect the rights of the people and to promote the public good. The people should resist and replace governments that violate these duties. (Locke, *Second Treatise*, § 202).

The illegitimate exercise of power by a government, the use of force without right, systematically violates the rights of subjects and seeks to enslave them. Such acts are a breach of trust that forfeits the powers entrusted to the government by the people. (Locke, *Second Treatise*, § 232).

Such acts by the government void the social contract, place the government in the state of nature, and create a state of war against its subjects. This reversion to the state of nature cancels all ties between the government and the governed, and every person has the right to defend himself and resist the aggressor. (Locke, *Second Treatise*, § 232).

Locke's *Letter Concerning Toleration* (1688) argues for religious liberty. Government should not use coercion to bring people to the true religion. The care of men's souls has not been committed to the state, either by God or by the consent of men. Neither the New Testament nor the example of Jesus Christ supports coercion as a means to salvation. The selection of beliefs by the state offers no assurance of a correct selection.

Furthermore, coercion cannot compel belief. Man believes what he thinks is true, not what he is compelled to do. Lastly, religious organizations are voluntary organizations. They have no right to coerce their members or any one outside their group.

Sir William Blackstone's *Commentaries on the Laws of England* (1765–1769) is the most influential work in the history of common law jurisprudence.

It is unique in the history of the Western legal tradition because it is the only system of jurisprudence to impose *two* standards of legal validity on positive law. The first is an *historical* standard based on legal custom and tradition. The second is a *moral* standard based on natural law precepts.

No law is valid or enforceable unless it satisfies both standards. Consequently, no system of jurisprudence has ever surpassed the power of Blackstone's jurisprudence to ensure liberty and establish justice. The following discussion explains Blackstone's application of natural law theory to jurisprudence.

Blackstone is heir to two legal traditions, the English common law tradition and the Roman civil law tradition. Blackstone lived under English common law. In common law, the primary source of law is legal custom and tradition. Common law is unwritten, but its enforcement depends on its compliance with historical custom, tradition, and precedent. This *historical* standard of legal validity, developed by Sir Edward Coke (1522–1634), John Selden (1584–1654), and Sir Matthew Hale (1609–1676), maintained liberty by preventing rulers, including judges, from utilizing law as an instrument of tyranny.

Although Blackstone practiced law and wrote in the common law tradition, his training was in the Roman civil law of Justinian's *Corpus Juris Civilis* (535–539). In Roman civil law, the primary source of law is the civil code. The civil code is written, but its enforcement depends on its compliance with natural law precepts.

Common law jurisprudence before Blackstone only imposed the *historical* standard of legal validity. Blackstone's *Commentaries* adds a second, *moral* standard of validity to common law based on natural law precepts. Human laws are invalid and unenforceable if they violate natural law precepts. The natural law standard prevents magistrates and judges from imposing unjust laws. Justice is required for human happiness, and just acts comply with natural law to produce human happiness.

The source of natural law precepts in Blackstone's *Commentaries* is the omnipotent, omnipresent, and omniscient God of Christianity. Natural law is the will of man's maker, and its moral precepts are eternal and unchanging. (Blackstone, *Commentaries*, § 39). Man obtains knowledge of natural law precepts through reason and divine revelation in Scripture. Before Adam's fall, man's reason was sufficient to guide him to knowledge of natural law precepts. After the fall, however, man's reason is corrupted. Man now requires revelation of natural law precepts, which God's "compassionate Providence" provides in Scripture. (Blackstone, *Commentaries*, § 42).

The pursuit of happiness provides the foundation of natural law. "Man should pursue his own true and substantial happiness." Natural law permits actions that promote man's real happiness, and forbids actions that destroy it. (Blackstone, *Commentaries*, § 41). Man is a created being subject to the laws of his Creator. The Creator established immutable laws of human nature that govern man and restrain his free will. Man's happiness depends on conforming to these laws. (Blackstone, *Commentaries*, § 39).

The Creator made justice and happiness mutually interdependent. Man obtains happiness by pursuing justice, and man obtains misery by pursuing injustice. Man pursues justice and obtains happiness by following the three moral precepts of natural law. Blackstone adopts the same precepts originated in Plato's *Crito*, formulated in Ulpian's *Rules*, and codified in Justinian's *Institutes*: "Such, among others, are these principles: *that we should live honestly, should hurt nobody, and should render to every one his due*; to which three general precepts Justinian has reduced the whole doctrine of law." (Blackstone, *Commentaries*, § 40). Blackstone explains that the precept "that we should live honestly" has a richer meaning than merely avoiding dishonest conduct. Instead, it requires one to live honorably and avoid vices that ultimately prove detrimental to society.

Blackstone divides jurisprudence into natural law and positive (human) law, distinguishing the rights and duties arising under each. Substantively, natural law consists of eternal immutable laws of good and evil. Natural law is the will of man's maker, and its moral precepts are eternal and unchanging. Natural law binds all men, "in all countries, and at all times." (Blackstone, *Commentaries*, § 41). God applies natural law precepts throughout human history, and these precepts are necessary for conducting human activities. God providentially enables us to discover these laws through reason and divine revelation.

Natural law does not determine every legal issue. On most issues, man is at liberty to adopt positive laws that benefit society. Natural law is indifferent, for example, as to whether positive law permits the export of wool. (Blackstone, *Commentaries*, § 43).

Positive laws, however, must meet the moral requirements of natural law. God's natural law trumps man's positive law. "No human law should be suffered to contradict" natural law. (Blackstone, *Commentaries*, § 42). All such positive laws are unenforceable, because positive law derives its validity and force from natural law. Furthermore, individuals are morally bound to disobey positive laws that violate natural law, such as a law requiring us to commit murder. (Blackstone, *Commentaries*, § 43).

Blackstone divides rights into two types, *absolute* rights and *relative* rights. The "immutable laws of nature" vest *absolute* rights in individuals. Blackstone names the same *absolute* rights as Locke: personal security, personal liberty, and private property. Individuals enjoy *absolute* rights in the state of nature, prior to the formation of society. (Blackstone, *Commentaries*, § 120).

The *absolute* right of personal security consists of "the legal enjoyment of life, limb, body, health, and reputation." (Blackstone, *Commentaries*, §§ 125–130). The *absolute* right of personal liberty consists of the free "power of locomotion, of changing situation, a moving of one's person to whatsoever place one's own inclination may direct, without an imprisonment or restraint, unless by due course of law." (Blackstone, *Commentaries*, §§

131–134). The *absolute* right of property consists of "every man's free use and disposal of his own lawful acquisitions, without injury or illegal diminution." (Blackstone, *Commentaries*, §§ 135–136).

Relative rights, in contrast to *absolute* rights, exist only in society. The purpose of *relative* rights is "to serve as outworks or barriers to protect and maintain inviolate the three great and primary rights, personal security, personal liberty, and private property." Unlike *absolute* rights, which are "few and simple," *relative* rights "are far more numerous and more complicated." (Blackstone, *Commentaries*, §§ 136–140).

Blackstone protects the sovereignty of law by strictly limiting the power of judges. One of Blackstone's most important doctrines is the declaratory theory of law. The declaratory theory provides that judges may never make new law. They simply discover and declare what the law has always been. Blackstone forbids judges from making new law because doing so unites the power to *make* and *enforce* law in one body, and this invites tyranny. (Blackstone, *Commentaries*, §§ 142). In applying the common law, the judge should determine the law "not according to his own private judgment, but according to the known laws and customs of the land." The judge is not empowered "to pronounce a new law," but only "to maintain and expand on the old one."

Nevertheless, since all law is subject to the standard of reason, judges may set aside common law precedents that are "manifestly absurd or unjust" and contrary to reason. (Blackstone, *Commentaries*, §§ 69–70). Setting aside manifestly absurd or unjust precedents, however, does not create new law. Instead, it "vindicates the law from misrepresentation." Blackstone sees the common law as the embodiment of reason itself. Manifestly absurd or unjust precedents are not set aside because they are *bad law*, but because they are *not law*. *Unreasonable* rules of common law, by definition, are not law. (Blackstone, *Commentaries*, § 70).

Blackstone also prohibits the power of judicial review. In applying statutory law, the judge may never exercise his discretion to set aside the will of Parliament. The judge's role is to "interpret and obey" the clear mandates of the legislature. Judges may not act as legislatures in miniature. "In a democracy," writes Blackstone, "the right of making laws resides in the people at large." (Blackstone, *Commentaries*, § 49). The only authority that can declare an act of Parliament void is Parliament itself.

Conclusion

Natural law developed in response to tyrannical governments and unjust laws. Natural law maintains that human conduct is subject to eternal and unchanging moral laws. These moral laws originate, not in human legislation, but in nature or a divine lawgiver. These moral laws govern all people, at all times, and in all circumstances. These moral laws are unwritten, but man can discover their content by intuition, careful reason, or divine revelation. Human happiness depends on obeying these moral laws and pursuing justice, and government must permit all men the necessary liberty to pursue their happiness. Natural law dominates our founding principles because those principles establish one nation, under God, with liberty and justice for all.

Natural law began in Athens as a reaction to Sophist claims that moral principles do not exist, justice does not exist, the laws have nothing to do with morality, and the only real authority in the world is force. Might makes right, and power is all that matters. The English philosophers Jeremy Bentham (1748–1832), John Austin (1790–1859), and H.L.A. Hart (1907–1992) resurrected these claims in a philosophy known as legal positivism.

Legal positivists claim there is no necessary connection between law and morality. Bentham writes that natural law is "nonsense," and inalienable natural rights are "nonsense walking on stilts." Positivists reduce law to the will of the political ruler. The power of the ruler, and nothing else, determines the validity of a law. Hart recognizes the validity of "morally iniquitous" laws having "no moral justification or force whatsoever." Rulers may utilize "any necessary means" to force obedience to their laws.

Legal positivism rejects Blackstone's declaratory theory of law. Hart's "penumbra doctrine" argues instead that judges should make new law in almost every case because legal terms have "a penumbra of uncertainty at the outer fringe of their meaning." The U.S. Supreme Court adopted Hart's penumbra doctrine in *Griswold v. Connecticut* (1965) to "imply" a right of privacy. Admitting that no right of privacy was contained in the Constitution, the Supreme Court nevertheless used this implied right of privacy to overturn a Connecticut statute governing birth control. The Supreme Court now utilizes this "implied" right of privacy to violate the consent of the governed and overturn state statutes it dislikes, such as the Texas abortion statute in *Roe v. Wade* (1973) and the Texas sodomy statute in *Lawrence v. Texas* (2003).

Only two legal systems in the history of the Western legal tradition have intentionally purged natural law precepts from their jurisprudence. The first was the Soviet system under Lenin and Stalin. The second was the Nazi legal system under Hitler. Stalin's legal positivism authorized the death of more than 22 million innocents. Hitler's legal positivism authorized the death of 11 million innocents. Their examples confirm the observation by natural law theorists from Plato to Blackstone that moral laws preserve society, and in Plato's words, secure for society every blessing heaven can provide. Unjust laws, however, lead to destruction and ruin.

The German philosopher Hegel observed in 1837 that "experience and history teaches us that people and governments have never learned anything from history, or acted on principles deduced from it." If America abandons its natural law tradition to embrace legal positivism, then America will confirm Hegel's observation.

RECOMMENDED READING

Aristotle, *The Politics of Aristotle,*
trans. Ernest Barker (Oxford University Press, 1946)

Sir William Blackstone, *Commentaries on the Laws of England,*
ed. Wilfrid Prest, vol. 1 (Oxford University Press, 2016)

Cicero, *De Re Publica (On the Republic) and De Legibus (On the Laws)*
trans. C.W. Keyes, ed. Jeffrey Henderson
(St. Edmundsbury, 2000)

John Locke, *The Second Treatise on Government and
A Letter Concerning Toleration* (Dover, 2002)

Plato, *Crito,* in *The Collected Dialogues of Plato, including the Letters,*
trans. Lane Cooper, ed. Edith Hamilton and Huntington Cairns
(Princeton University Press, 1961)

LIBERTY
AND
LIMITED
GOVERNMENT

By Scott Robinson, PhD

PROFESSOR OF POLITICAL SCIENCE

The founding era resistance against tyrannical "taxation without representation" substantiated the American idea that liberty means that government power should be constrained or limited by the consent of the governed. This fundamental American idea was not only an important philosophical position during our founding era, but was enshrined in our Constitution and remains an important principle in American politics to this day.

This idea did not grow out of thin air, and our proclivity for liberty is only partly due to our geographic and historical circumstances—the wilderness, the farming and cowboy lifestyles, and the distance from the European power centers that hallmarked our nation's formative years. American views on freedom also developed as a result of the interest of the American Founders in the great philosophical texts of western civilization.

These ideas developed into the religious and political discourse of western European and American societies. The notion of freedom as individual responsibility was integral to the development of classical and Christian political philosophy and was revitalized and deepened by the English and Americans in light of tyrannical monarchs in the 17th and 18th centuries.

Philosophical Roots of Liberty and Limited Government

The classical and Christian thinkers who form the backbone of today's arguments for limited government did not necessarily defend the notion of limited government, though they did defend the ancillary idea of liberty and the individual responsibility that liberty implies. We commonly attribute the birth of political science to the 4th-century-B.C. Greek philosopher Plato and to his student Aristotle. These thinkers recognized that various forms of government existed: monarchy, aristocracy, and democracy. They also recognized that each could have its faults. A self-interested monarch is a tyrant, while an aristocracy (this word technically means "rule by the best") that seeks to enrich itself instead of providing for the entire city is an oligarchy (a regime that is characterized by "rule by the wealthy"). Democracy could easily devolve into mob rule. Classical thinkers struggled with the propriety of these various regimes for centuries, with the question of which way of life was most proper for man.

Aristotle understood that naturally growing things, including human beings, had a proper purpose, or *telos*, which they should reach upon its maturity. For instance, the *telos* of an acorn is a tall and mighty oak tree. The *telos* of a human being consists of maturing to a rational person capable of sorting through life's choices and doing so in a way that benefits himself, his family, and his community. In his *Ethics*, for instance, Aristotle argues that such a person understands that it is never proper to engage in adultery. He is also capable of discerning when it is proper to engage in an emotion such as anger—in the right manner, at the right time, directed at the right persons, and for reasons which are just. In *Politics*, his sequel to *Ethics*, Aristotle demonstrates how this mature individual would intelligently amass resources and relationships within his community, and would be eager to use them, as the accoutrements of his virtue, to better his city.

Generally, classical thinkers believed that aristocracy (rule by the best), would be the best form of government. But achieving a lasting aristocracy is not easy. Plato recognized that the form of government a city adopts will reflect the characters of the citizens in that society. Aristocracy is hard to maintain, because society would need to be composed of angels: people who intelligently analyze their actions in life and do the right thing for themselves and their community at all times, simply because they understand doing so is what a human being properly does. The individuals in such a city must be capable of maintaining an excellent way of life in order to abide by the laws in such a city. If anything less than excellent citizens takes root, the city cannot maintain itself as an aristocracy and will change into whatever deviant form is fashionable.

Unfortunately, the deviant varieties are many, and aristocracy then becomes only one of many appealing ways of life for the next generation to pursue. The temptations of money, fame, power, and fun times can easily pull humans and societies from the straight and narrow path of virtue that is required of aristocracy.

For the classical thinkers the dilemma was fairly straightforward. An ideal way of life for human beings exists, but not all humans follow it, and some societies don't even tout it as the best way of life. In fact, most societies at most times laud some other way of life. Human nature inclines us to behave badly—for self-interest instead of communal interest or for fun instead of for virtue. The Greeks and Christians understood this element of human nature. The Greeks understood that Utopia was not a real city. The word

Utopia actually means both "best place" and "no place" to the Greek ear. Christians teach that sin is inevitable and heaven was not of this world. Here exists the perennial human problem of being imperfect creatures.

Aristotle understood the obvious solution to this problem—separating the power inherent to various factions within a city would keep one faction from tyrannizing the others. The Romans attempted a mixed regime to promote this ideal, but wild swings of democracy and oligarchy persistently plagued them until their republic caved-in and became a monarchy. It was this chronic danger of human nature in human history that inspired Ben Franklin to famously caution, "We have a Republic, madam, if you can keep it."

Despite the temptation to live differently, this best way of life was also seen by classical and Christian political philosophers to be the natural way of life for human beings. This "best way" is often articulated as the "natural" way, and this argument was made at the time by referring to a "natural law" that should serve as model for human laws.

It was the 17th-century English philosopher John Locke, writing and thinking in a time of profound upheaval, in the wakes of the Reformation, Thirty Years War, and English Civil War and Restoration, who made the greatest strides in the modern era to revitalize the classical notion of Natural Law. Locke found a way to transform the old notion of natural "law" into the notion of natural "rights." The difference may be subtle, but the implications from this transition from law to right are profound.

Natural law was often used as way of describing the laws one must follow to successfully reach the maturity and self-sufficiency that a human should properly fulfill, but it was also used to demonstrate the deference owed to political rulers. Aquinas famously argued that if a king's laws were in accord with the natural law, they would also then be consistent with divine law. They would be consistent with that which God would sanction, and therefore his decrees would be just. In this way, the emphasis upon "law" in "natural law" from Cicero through the Middle Ages allowed political rulers to maintain power through the guise of being naturally sanctioned by God.

The shift from "law" to "rights" facilitated by Locke allowed a fundamental change in the structure of government. **Natural rights would serve to justify limiting the power of government for the sake of individuals claiming for themselves the God-given right to mature into the *telos* designed by God for humans—mature men capable of governing their own affairs and for their own welfare.**

Locke developed this argument amidst the Exclusion Crisis, which played out in England throughout the 1680s. The culmination of this fight was the Glorious Revolution of 1688, which removed the Stuart dynasty and established William of Orange as the new, limited monarch, but the fight for power earlier in the 1680s had a lasting impact on the nature of democracy in not only England but also America. Buttressed by the tradition of kings and nobles working together as established by the Magna Carta, Locke and his employer, the Earl of Shaftsbury, the leading political opponent of the king in Parliament, worked fervently to develop an argument which would justify limiting the prerogatives of King Charles II.

All of this occurred during very tumultuous times in England, when many individuals pursued religious freedom by dissenting from the Anglican Church. Charles came to power during the Restoration—his father had been beheaded in 1649, and one of Charles's main goals upon regaining the throne in 1660 was to consolidate his tenuous grasp on power. Charles attempted to do this by granting to dissenters the right to worship as they pleased. This ploy riled his Anglican allies. Charles then rescinded those religious freedoms and persecuted the dissenters in order to both crush his opposition and to satisfy his allies. One of the main arguments made by dissenters at this time, which would be worked into Locke's political arguments, was that all individuals had the capacity to judge human affairs through their consciences, and they did not owe outright deference to the king to decide such matters for the entire realm.

Locke worked his arguments for religious freedom into a scheme for greater political participation by the masses. This argument wove the classical position on the natural maturity of individuals together with the religious, economic, and political circumstances of 1680s England. This argument not only proved to be quite persuasive within his own society, but it would form the modern basis for the notion of limited government.

From Christianity, Locke establishes that individuals are the workmanship of God. In other words, we are created by God for the uses intended by God. We may not, therefore, commit suicide, as this would infringe upon God's work. We may also not allow ourselves to be enslaved to another human being for the same reason.

From the classics, Locke establishes that a "natural law" would assert that individuals should collect private property and use it for the betterment of their communities. Natural law is basically that which most men would do in the absence of human law. He pointed out that if we imagined a primitive society living at the beginning of time, in the wilderness, they would all abide by this principle. Locke calls this the "state of nature." In such a state, he argues, few of us would wish to harm or steal for others for private gain. The reason is simple and grounded in common sense: there is no good reason to steal or harm. The things that we would need in this primitive state, such as acorns or venison, need not be hoarded because they would spoil long before you could consume them all. These things would exist in abundance. It would be very foolish to harm another individual for the sake of stealing his acorns. It is less risky to collect your own, and you do not need an abundance of them anyway.

Locke thereby demonstrated that the proper owner of property should be the individual who labored to produce or collect it. If one individual, say, collected an apple from an apple tree, the others would not be inclined to fight for or to steal that apple. It would be easier and safer—avoiding the dangers of theft and fighting—if one simply procured one of the many apples that we might imagine existing in this primitive place.

One of the benefits of this natural system in which individuals retain that which they have produced or worked for is that the natural resources tend to become improved upon over time. Men learn how to farm wilderness so that more produce can be grown. Animals are domesticated so that less effort and land may produce more food than through hunting. Population increases as a result of these basic agricultural advances and even more is produced on even less land. Trade develops. Money is created, and commodities are invented and then improved. Locke sees the greatest part of the technological advancements throughout time to have been made feasible through the spontaneous, natural, inherent productivity of mature individuals pursuing their own welfare.

The picture isn't all roses, however. At some point in time, Locke argued, this law of nature broke down. Money and the temptations of power meant that the reasons for theft and other harms now existed. People created governments to protect them from those who would do them harm. The essence of civilized society, Locke argues, lies in the inherent ability of individuals to provide for themselves in life. Any power ceded to this government by individuals is inherently limited to that which is necessary to preserve the welfare of the members of the society. If a king does not allow individuals in society to build lives for themselves with that for which they had labored, he no longer serves as government should and must be replaced for the sake of the community's welfare. **The basic idea of revolution as Locke presents it is fairly simple: government exists** to protect the "lives, liberties, and properties" of the members of a society, and when it doesn't, a new one must be created that does.

These arguments were easily applicable to 1680s England. In the midst of the religious tensions between Anglicans and dissenters arose a clamoring for political power among English nobility. The king's opposition cohered into the Whig party and relied upon the tactic of attempting to expand suffrage to the rabble in England, many of whom were members of the dissenting religious movement and, as mentioned earlier, had become targets of persecution by the king. Their goal in doing so was to win majorities in Parliament which would allow them to introduce legislation to exclude the king's brother from succeeding him to the throne. The king thwarted them, for a time, by employing tactics ranging from persecution and torture to the proroguing of legislatures and the corrupting of legislators. Locke's famous text was written during the height of these machinations to justify a rebellion to overthrow him, most likely in 1683. It would be another five years before the Glorious Revolution would peacefully unseat the Stuart dynasty and establish new limits on the monarchy in England and another six years before the conditions in England were safe enough for Locke' manuscript to be published anonymously. He did not claim credit for it until he was near death in 1704.

The Colonial Experience and Limited Government

The American colonists applied Locke's arguments amidst the Great Squeeze and ensuing Coercive Acts to depict the British as tyrants infringing on the Americans' natural ability to provide for themselves in what was essentially a wilderness, thousands of miles from home. Locke's expression of the most fundamental natural rights, "life, liberty, and property," was easily morphed into Jefferson's famous "life, liberty, and the pursuit of happiness."

The experience of the English colonies in North America in the 1760s and 1770s was greatly affected by England and France's wars for empire. This conflict spilled over into North America as the French and Indian War, in which the British successfully defended their northern and western territorial boundaries in North America from French conquest. Wars are expensive undertakings, and this one was no exception. The British national debt nearly doubled as a result of it. Feeling as though they had provided a service to the American colonists for which they were due compensation, the British government attempted to increase the revenue generated from their colonies through a series of tax laws and regulatory measures.

The colonists viewed these taxes and regulations as increasingly harmful because many of them infringed on their ability to provide for basic necessities in a hostile wilderness setting. Taxes on glass and paint, part of the Townsend Acts of 1767, as well as regulations prohibiting the production of nails in the colonies, greatly increased the cost and time needed to construct buildings. The famous Tea Act of 1773, passed after these more cumbersome acts, actually reduced taxes on British tea in an attempt to undercut the demand for tea smuggled from the Dutch. The Tea Act infuriated the colonists because it gave the impression that petty and arbitrary measures were being taken to enrich the British at the colonial expense. Following the Boston Tea Party in December of 1773, Parliament passed the Coercive Acts to punish the colonists for the destruction of the king's tea. These acts further angered many colonists.

The Coercive Acts greatly restricted freedom in and around Boston. The British Navy closed the port, and armed soldiers guarded the city's one bridge to the mainland. The British also began confiscating arms from the Bostonians. For all intents and purposes, martial law existed in Boston, and the average citizens became fearful. In September of 1774, during the dead of night, the British Army confiscated all of the munitions from a powder house outside of Boston—a warehouse where the colonists stored their gun powder. Now, not only were basic provisions for life difficult to procure, but a distant government imposed arbitrary limits on everyday actions. By the following Spring, the colonists were prepared to defend themselves from tyranny.

In April of 1775, Paul Revere warned local militiamen that the British were preparing for another night-time mission to seize more munitions from another powder house in Concord, outside of Boston. The Revolutionary War began at dawn the next morning, when a small group of militiamen confronted the British Army on the Lexington parade grounds, in between Boston and the British destination in Concord. Although the battles of Lexington and Concord occurred on April 19, 1775, it would be more than a year before the Continental Congress would approve a motion on independence on July 2, 1776 (a written Declaration was approved on July 4, the date we now celebrate).

The debates surrounding the decision to declare independence in the years prior to 1776 demonstrate that the American founding generation was deeply indebted to the philosophical ideas articulated by the British during the debates of the Glorious Revolution. First, many writers developed the argument that the American colonies were essentially in a state of nature—it was, after all, an undeveloped wilderness, replete with excellent natural resources which could be used to develop a successful society. Thomas Paine argued that America contained all the wood and rope-making materials necessary to build a navy that could compete with the British. Many focused on the fact that the Americans had no voice in the British Parliament. They found themselves in a condition in which the arbitrariness of the British taxes was especially painful and onerous. The idea that government exists to provide for the welfare of the society was particularly relevant in these conditions, but the reality was that the British government was not limiting its actions based upon the welfare of the colonies.

The decision to declare independence was vehemently contested in the colonies for some time. It was an unpopular position throughout the 1760s (Americans still referred to themselves as "Englishmen" at that time), but as the 1770s progressed the onerous nature of the British government grew more intense. More and more colonists became persuaded of the viability of independence. The Founders cited and mimicked Locke's work more than any other source when they were crafting arguments designed to justify resistance against the British.

Liberty and Limited Government in the U.S. Constitution and American Political History

Constitutions usually explain what governments may do—in many ways they are designed to empower rather than limit power. It is a notable feat of our Founders that they enshrined limits to governmental power in a document designed to do precisely the opposite. These limits are important because they help to animate the philosophical spirit of individual responsibility that is connected to our moral character, economic success, and national identity.

The Anti-Federalists, the group who opposed the ratification of the Constitution, feared that the proposed government would possess too much power. At their behest the most important limits to our government were included in the Constitution, the Bill of Rights. Many of the specific grievances held by colonists against the British are addressed in the first four Amendments: the right to peaceably assemble, to keep and bear arms, to not be forced to quarter soldiers, and to be free from unreasonable searches and seizures. Many of the judicial protections provided in Amendments six through eight can be traced to the practices of Charles II to limit Whig opposition during Locke's day.

The Constitution also contains a number of limits on legislative power, most importantly on the types of laws which Congress may make. First, because tax issues are directly tied to the people's ability to retain their property, the Constitution mandates that revenue laws originate in the House of Representatives. Members of this body are elected more frequently and represent far fewer constituents than do Senators, making them much more responsive to the wishes of the people. The Constitution further mandates that revenue may be spent on particular things which are required for the "general welfare" of the nation.

It is often argued that today's rising budgets and deficits reflect an inability for Americans to retain the character of liberty in which the nation was conceived. There may be some merit to these claims. Two specific challenges have diminished the Americans' ability to retain a strict interpretation of the constitutional limits on governmental power.

One challenge concerns the nature of power in politics. The definition of "general welfare" has changed dramatically over time and reflects the basic tension between the parties in our system. Once, this term was taken literally, and if a proposed spending project did not benefit the entire nation, it would either be defeated in Congress or vetoed by presidents. In the early 1800s, for instance, an infrastructure project to dredge the Savannah River in Georgia was defeated because it would only benefit one state, while a project to fund lighthouse development along the Atlantic seaboard was approved, because its benefits would affect multiple states.

Today, the prevailing interpretation of "general welfare" is rather expansive. In the mid-19th century, presidents ceased the practice of vetoing legislation which contained specific benefits for localities, and the practice of including these benefits became increasingly common. Congress has a natural incentive to attach locale-specific benefits (we call this "pork-barrel legislation") to laws, as it often provides incentives for members of congress to vote for bills. Pork provides obvious goods to the congressman's constituents, and this helps him retain his seat over time. Today, the practice is widespread. This trend is one reason why federal budgets and, consequently, tax rates, have risen tremendously throughout American history.

The broadening of "general welfare" suggests that the desire of politicians to expand the purview of government is a natural one. As early as George Washington's administration, tensions between a more expansive federal government erupted between Treasury Secretary Alexander Hamilton and Secretary of State Thomas Jefferson on a number of issues, including the president's discretion in revoking treaties, the administration's powers to promote economic development, and its ability to build a standing army. These divisions grew into fissures by the election of 1800, with the nation clearly divided between the Federalist's proclivity for more expansive governing power and the Democratic-Republican's desire for limited government (as evidenced by their opposition to Hamilton on each of these issues). When Jefferson was elected, he moved to rescind all direct taxes on the American public, instead preferring tariffs to excise taxes. These early examples indicate that there has always been a tension in our political system between individualism and deference to authority; between limiting and empowering government. When today's conservatives lament an expanding bureaucracy and unconstrained governmental spending, they are echoing a position that was taken before them by English Whigs, American colonists, and Jeffersonian partisans.

Accordingly, the principle of limited government, while being a principle inherent to our Constitution, appears also in our day-to-day life as a partisan principle in American politics, and one which is still today countered by a more expansive interpretation of constitutional power.

Once America's two-party system was entrenched through the divisions sowed during the election of 1800, the notion of limited government became the rallying cry of whichever party happened to represent the areas of the nation most distant from the economic and political power centers in D.C. and the Atlantic Coast. Though Jefferson vociferously opposed the growth of the federal government, his successor James Madison used the power inherent in the Spending Clause to establish the national bank. Andrew Jackson established the Democratic Party by appealing to the rural voters who were harmed when the National Bank effectively closed local banks to the economic detriment of those with holdings in them. When the Civil War erupted, the notion of limited government articulated as "states' rights" formed the backbone of the southern Democrat's opposition to Lincoln's aggressive executive actions. When FDR attempted to stack the Supreme Court with justices who would assure a further expansion of executive power during the Great Depression, Republicans balked. Southern Democrats again rejected the aggressive use of governmental resources during Johnson's attempt to create the "Great Society," a program which distributed significant resources to urban areas in attempt to improve those neighborhoods.

Today, the issue of limited government is most prominently displayed in the area of fiscal policy and the resistance to the expansion of the federal government into areas that would have been rejected by the Founders as violating the principle of "general welfare." Federal spending programs that have an explicitly local impact, such as funding for roads and bridges, are regularly funded by Congress.

The other natural challenge to limited government today is the requirement that government do much more than the governments of yesterday.

The world is more developed, industrialized, and complex. Only four federal departments existed in 1800 (Treasury, War, State, and Justice). Today we have some fifteen cabinet-level departments (including areas such Energy, Transportation, Labor, and Homeland Security). Thomas Jefferson employed merely a handful of functionaries in his executive office, but there are now thousands of employees that work in the president's office, and hundreds of thousands stretched across a complex landscape of bureaus and agencies, who oversee and regulate aspects of American life which the Founders could not have fathomed.

Some contemporary political prerogatives have developed due to technological and industrial changes in society, which challenge the concept of limited government. A good example might be the desire to save endangered species. This issue rose to prominence during the 1970s, when Americans attempted to become more environmentally conscious. The Endangered Species Act (ESA) was one of many (like the Clean Air Act and the Clean Water Act) rolled out during this decade. The ESA required that efforts must be undertaken at any expense to protect endangered species. Not surprisingly, this led to many conflicts between individuals who owned various natural resources and the government over the proper extent of its power to limit private activity on privately owned land. For instance, one golf course developer in Oregon had invested some ten million dollars into a project, when it was discovered that an endangered butterfly resided in the sand dunes adjacent to the planned course. Despite the financial investment, the developer was forced to abandon the project, along with his personal investment and his chance for future profit.

Another area where the idea of limited government becomes clearly discernible is in taxing and spending policies. As our bureaucratic needs seem to grow over time with increasing industrial and technological complexity, so too grows the federal budget, and with it the taxation rates. The Founders viewed income taxes as so inconsistent with the principle of liberty that they were unconstitutional until the passage of the Sixteenth Amendment in 1913. This came at a time of immense corporate growth during the Industrial Revolution, and a modest income tax was proposed on corporations only. After the Constitution was amended, the tax statue expanded to include a tax on millionaire individuals. Today, all individuals are subject to income taxes, and at rates much higher than proposed a century ago.

The relationship between liberty and government expanse is clear. The greater the rate at which income is taxed, the less personal possessions an individual will retain. The fewer possessions one retains, the less one may do with oneself—both in the sense of basically enjoying the limited time given to humans by God, but also in the Aristotelian sense of the diminishment of the ability to do great and virtuous things for one's community with one's resources. As taxes rise, it becomes more difficult to save and to retire, and it becomes more difficult to start businesses or undertake philanthropic activity. Although tax rates have risen dramatically over the past century, this trend has occurred despite consistent pleas for fiscal restraint and limited government.

The American political order is blessed to be buttressed by the venerable philosophical ideas which encourage individual responsibility through liberty. The American political order is, however, still a political order composed of imperfect humans. The behaviors of politicians wielding power are not, even in our system, inherently conducive to virtuous behavior. The growth of industry and technology through time has substantially expanded the ground over which politicians will battle. Thus, there is an enduring tension in America's political order between our institutions, which are designed to limit government's power, and our human politicians, who will try to expand government's power. But in this context, the philosophical inspirations behind our political institutions have done much good in preserving the idea of liberty as one of the most important political ideas in American culture.

RECOMMENDED READING

Aristotle, *Nicomachean Ethics* and *The Politics*

John Locke, *The Second Treatise of Government*

Plato, *The Republic*

SEPARATION
OF POWERS

By Scott Robinson, PhD
PROFESSOR OF POLITICAL SCIENCE

The separation of powers created by the U.S. Constitution was both an innovation in government and a dedication to some of the most basic ideas of classical political science. This notion is indeed perhaps one of the most important concepts to grasp when it comes to understanding how American political ideas regarding freedom and equality are practically implemented by the Constitution.

Power in Classical Political Thought

Plato identified the various types of societies and governments that can be categorized by the fundamental attributes of the people who compose the different societies. For instance, he noted that the people of Sparta were different than the people of Athens in some essential characteristics. Spartans were warlike. Training for war was an indelible part of their culture, and you could see this too in the structured nature of their government, where, like a military, deference was given to the commander. The Athenians were different people with a different culture. They were more inclined to study, enjoy theatre, and debate than were the Spartans, and, again, you could see manifestations of this in their democratic government which provided much more room for debate and persuasive argument than did the Spartans'. Plato noted that another city, Phoenicia, was composed of people who cared about making money and were dedicated primarily to trade. Such concerns likewise affected their lifestyles and laws. Political science began with this basic observation about the differences between cities, much as botany begins with elementary distinctions between, say, deciduous trees and conifers.

Aristotle contributed to Plato's categorization of regimes by providing a more organized framework and providing clear names to different regimes. He identified three basic types of regimes, which could be identified by the three different types of citizens wielding power. If one individual ran a city, he was a king. If a few individuals were in power, this was an aristocracy. Many individuals sharing power was a democracy.

Aristotle also noticed that, often times, both aristocrats and democrats existed within a city—both are naturally occurring classes within a city. Aristocrats are few, and tend to be in the elite classes, while democrats are many, and compose the laboring classes. If a city's laws especially benefitted the few and wealthy, it could be said to be an aristocracy; if its laws benefitted the many, it was a democracy. He further noted that it was common for a democracy to change into an aristocracy and vice versa, if, for instance, the laws were structured in a way to benefit the ruling class too much. This tended to upset the other group, leading to a revolution.

Such observations led Plato and Aristotle to grapple with the question of which type of society and regime would be the best type for human beings. This was not an easy to question to answer—indeed, it has in some ways never been answered. Thousands of years after Plato and Aristotle wrote,

Winston Churchill could still only proclaim, "Democracy is the worst form of government except for all those other forms that have been tried from time to time." Plato and Aristotle did not view democracy as particularly effective—Plato writing that "the many do things quite at random." Generally, Plato and Aristotle thought that aristocracy (it literally means in Greek "rule by the best") was superior, though it too was prone to problems. **The true problem with any type of regime lay in human nature. There is an inherent tendency for humans to behave selfishly.**

Christianity affirms this basic view of humanity. The Christian doctrine of original sin teaches that humans are essentially flawed in their very natures. The reality of human fallibility highlights the importance of grace because Christians are redeemed from sin only through God's gift of salvation.

Aristotle posed a limited solution to this problem of potentially self-interested rulers with the idea of a mixed regime. He noticed that if a regime were to empower elements of both an aristocracy and a democracy, then the interests of both parties would be represented in government. This would make it much harder for laws which only benefit one group at the expense of the other group to become implemented.

Cicero and Machiavelli were perhaps the most astute observers of the Roman experience, which had attempted to implement an Aristotelian mixed regime during their Republican era. Cicero's *On the Republic* tells a story of the origin of Rome in which the Senate degenerates from a simple body of humble leaders to an oligarchical body to a tyrannical one, drawing the conclusion that "when everything is in the power of a faction ... [that] cannot be called a commonwealth." His *On the Laws* contains a description of alterations he recommended to Rome's Constitution that he believed would better preserve Rome against factional disintegration. One sees in this work a studied attempt to balance power between the oligarchic and democratic elements of the population. He recommended, for instance, a prominent role for the people in the judicial process, while also providing substantial (instead of advisory) powers in the Senate.

During the Renaissance, Machiavelli studied Roman history. He often addressed the same sort of issues dealing with strife between rich and poor in the struggles for power which characterized Rome. His works, *The Prince* and *Discourses on Livy* explain how many Roman emperors struggled to maintain power due to the difficulties they encountered in trying to appease the disparate interests of the Roman people, the Roman elites, and the Roman military. Because a prince may not appease each of these three factions simultaneously, many emperors had rather short reigns due to civic strife, insurgency, and military coups.

Power in the Modern Era

The idea of separating powers inherent in the government was altered slightly during the modern era. Throughout the era between the classical and modern, in which most societies were ruled by some form of monarchy, it was common for the three basic types of government identified by Aristotle to also exist in some form or another. For instance, Germany's Holy Roman Empire consisted of not only an emperor but also a congressional body called a "Diet." England had a king, but the nobles had their own role, eventually forming Parliament.

In the modern era, the idea of separating the powers inherent in these representative types gradually took hold. A revitalization of the works of Aristotle, Cicero, and Machiavelli during the Enlightenment contributed to the trend of experimentation in government along the lines suggested by these authors. The two most important contributors to this development, prior to the U.S. Constitution and its defense by James Madison in the renowned *Federalist #10* and *#51*, were the English political theorist John Locke and the French aristocrat Baron de Montesquieu.

John Locke worked from within the English constitutional heritage, which had a tradition of division between powers. English monarchs had worked with a bicameral parliament for centuries in the ways limited by the Magna Carta. Locke contributed by explaining the division between legislative and executive powers and by laying out the difference between executive power and federative power (the power to work with other heads of state).

Locke referred to the legislative power as the supreme power within a society. The legislative power need not always meet or be in existence, but when it does exist, Locke argues that it's imperative for it to follow certain rules which comport with the well-being the society. It must dispense justice, cannot act arbitrarily, or otherwise violate the law of nature by confiscating personal property without consent: "A man cannot subject himself to the Arbitrary Power of life, liberty, or possession of another, but only so much as the Law of Nature gave him for the preservation of himself, and the rest of mankind, this is all he can give up to the Commonwealth, and by it the legislative power, so that the legislative can have no more than this." The legislative power is the deliberative body which determines what these standards might mean in particular contexts, and it doesn't matter how large or small that body is (be it one, few, or many individuals doing the deliberating).

The executive power, by contrast, is subordinate to the legislative power, but it does always need to be in existence. Executive power is the type of power in which action occurs. It is the body that implements the laws created by the legislative body. It must always exist so that it may implement the laws whenever a need arises. In simple terms: the legislative body passes a law which prohibits murder, and the executive body then enforces the law by apprehending and punishing murders.

Sometimes, the powers of the executive and the legislative branches may be intertwined. In Locke's era, the monarch could call and dismiss Parliament at will. Locke refers to this power—which could be perverted by kings to produce laws of their particular liking—as a "fiduciary trust." The executive power should be exercised for the public good, and one of the true challenges for kings is to act along these lines, or to face the consequences of a rebellion if they do not.

The tendency for mismanaged monarchies to degenerate into a rebellion had become evident by the 1770s. The old song was being sung again: Parliament was enacting and the king was enforcing tax laws upon the American colonies to which the colonists had not consented. Just as in the English Civil War of the 1640s and Glorious Revolution of 1689, another rebellion would be necessary in order to limit the powers of the king and of Parliament, even though the two executive and legislative powers resided in distinct bodies. **The past two centuries of British history had taught the American revolutionaries that merely placing power in distinct bodies was not enough to protect liberty.**

Charles-Louis De Secondat, Baron de Montesquieu, wrote about sixty years after Locke, and he greatly contributed to the American constitutional scheme with his *Spirit of the Laws* (1750). Montesquieu's more sophisticated analysis of power provided the American Founders with the ideas necessary to provide an alternative other than rebellion to the inevitability of governmental abuse. Montesquieu was a French aristocrat and historian who noticed that in many societies the laws tended to advantage the nobility or the clergy. He lauded the English for their constitutional arrangements which better protect against this tendency through assuaging the fear of others wielding power: "The political liberty of the subject is a tranquility of mind arising from the opinion each person has of his safety. In order to have this liberty, it is requisite the government be so constituted as one man need not be afraid of another." Montesquieu expounded at length on the various ways in which this could be accomplished by carefully arranging the distribution of power within members of society.

He discusses at much greater length than had Locke the specific mechanisms by which the legislative and executive powers could be limited. For instance, he explains, as had Locke, that the executive power should always be in existence and the legislative should not, and that for this reason it would be improper for the legislative to constrain the actions of the executive. But, in an argument which anticipates our Constitution, Montesquieu argues the legislature may still properly "have the means of examining whether its laws have been properly executed." Indeed, in the American Constitution congressional oversight—the ability to call before Congress executive officials who have behaved badly—is from time to time highlighted in our system. The Presidential oath of office and Article II of the Constitution require the president to "faithfully execute" the laws, and Article II further provides Congress with the power to impeach the president if it decides he has abrogated that duty. Montesquieu also argued that the executive should have some power over the legislature, and recommended the power of "rejecting" legislation. This mechanism, of course, also appears in our constitutional system as the veto power.

Montesquieu also included judicial powers in the list of powers which need to be separated. "There is no liberty," he writes, "if the judiciary power be not separated from the legislative and executive. Were it joined with the legislative, the life and liberty of the subject would be exposed to arbitrary control; for the judge would then be the legislator. Were it joined to the executive power, the judge might behave with violence and oppression." He also provides detailed suggestions for how the judiciary may remain separate from the legislative and executive, some of which are practiced in the United States today. For instance, he argues that the jurors in cases should consist of peers from society; otherwise, the monarch or other nobles might too easily use the judiciary to maintain power through the persecution of would-be adversaries.

The U.S. Constitution posed the solution which the British tradition could not find, but which had been suggested by Montesquieu. There are two important ways in which the U.S. Constitution achieves this goal. First, by not only separating powers but by providing some checks and balances between them, and second, by relying on a federal system that divides power between the national government and the states. In achieving the second goal, the Founders provided an even deeper level of security than had been suggested by Montesquieu.

Separation of Power in the United States

James Madison is hailed as the "Father of the Constitution." Not only did he provide a thorough collection of notes recording the debates of the Constitutional Convention, but he penned most of the entries in a series of essays published in American newspapers during the 1780s in order to argue for the ratification of the Constitution. The *Federalist Papers* provide a lucid account of the reasons for the design of the Constitution. Madison acknowledges the classical and Christian worldview in *Federalist #10* by noting that factions—groups of self-interested partisans—are a chronic problem of human nature which no government may eradicate. Working from this basic assumption, he saw the U.S. Constitution as containing the mechanisms whereby naturally self-interested factions could be constrained.

There was, however, a group of Founders who opposed the notion of abandoning the Articles of Confederation. Under that constitution, the states remained sovereign and independent states who joined together merely for the purpose of fighting the British. These Anti-Federalists echoed an argument that Montesquieu had made, that the best size of a government was naturally quite small. They argued that interests in a small political entity would be more consistent. For example, Rhode Islanders, they thought, shared a common identity and interest based upon their proximity to one another and upon shared culture. There was no compelling reason for union, as individuals living in New England would find little in common with individuals living in the mid-Atlantic states or the Deep South.

Madison's response to this proposition is today referred to as the "Madisonian Model." His argument is profoundly important today because he both demonstrates that factional conflict will even occur in relatively small cities (as might occur between the poor and the rich) and that the key element required to prevent factional conflict is to facilitate a sufficient number of factions to complicate the debate. In such a way one faction is not merely fighting against another faction. When numerous factions must join forces to win a political fight, Madison believed that the group whose policy was in the best interest of the greatest majority would prevail. In this way the Madisonian model assures that government by consent is also government for the greater good. The Madisonian Model also paved the way for today's pluralism and globalization, as it encourages political cooperation across large geographic territories and amongst large and diverse populations.

Madison's argument contained two primary points. First, in an argument made in *Federalist #51*, Madison argues that "ambition must be made to counteract ambition." By this, Madison means that humans and perhaps especially politicians are poised to act in a self-interested manner. Merely separating powers as the English had done led to the types of conflicts we saw between Parliament and the king. Parliament had no recourse if the king dismissed them. **Madison saw, by standing on the shoulders of Montesquieu, that not only must the executive power have some check**

over the legislative, but vice versa. In the American system there is always a way for one power to counteract the other in a manner consistent with majority rule. If a president were to veto a law passed by Congress, thereby "checking" their power, they may "balance" out that action, by overriding the presidential veto if a super-majority of two-thirds of both houses agree.

In a subtle example of this, the two houses of Congress can check and balance one another. Because congressmen represent relatively small districts (originally of about 35,000; today they represent about 750,000 people), their interests are local and can change within states and regions. A Democratic congressman may represent an urban district of Texas, while a Republican congressman may represent a nearby rural district. A senator, on the other hand, is almost certain to represent the broader interests of the state (and more likely to vote his conscience, given his lengthier term in office). As a result of the manner in which the two houses are composed, and because 60 votes are generally needed to pass legislation in the Senate, we are much more likely to produce laws which reflect the interests of a diversity of regions, areas, and states. This system is not, however, perfect, and still allows for the possibility that one party in our two party system may retain power. From 1916 to 2015, the Democrats retained control of Congress for 57 years of those 100 years and controlled both Congress and the White House for 35 of those years.

As James Madison famously argued in *Federalist #10*, a "double security" could provide another layer of separation and thereby solve this problem. For this particular innovation Madison receives most of the credit. Inspiration for a large federal scheme of government cannot be found in either Locke or Montesquieu (the latter famously argued for particularly small republics, in which personal relations would assuage the tendency for power to corrupt). In the English case, a single national government existed, and it could work in cahoots with itself (even though its powers had been separated) in order to burden the colonies. The Americans eliminated the ability for the nation as a whole to subjugate some small portion of the nation to the dictates of the majority by making the states a constituent and integral part of a new federal system. The true solution to the problem lied not in creating small republics which would be likeminded (as the Anti-Federalists preferred), but to create a large republic, and to recognize its many different divisions. It would be very difficult for any one faction to create a majority capable of tyrannizing the rest. Features of the Constitution ensured the states retained power in areas that were integral to their welfare. We refer to this as a federal system of government—the national government represents a "federation" of states (or states that have joined together for a common cause).

The debate between the Federalists and Anti-Federalists was a rather heated contest. The votes of merely three delegates swayed New York in favor of ratification. A mere ten votes separated delegates in Virginia. In the end, the Federalist's arguments won the day, and the Constitution was ratified in 1789. However, in order to collect sufficient votes to facilitate ratification, the Federalists acquiesced to the Anti-Federalists' demand that a Bill of Rights be added to the Constitution. Though many of the first 10 Amendments to our Constitution ensure individual protections, the tenth also assures that "powers not delegated to the United States by the Constitution ... are reserved to the states respectively, or to the people." Traditionally, the range of legislative issues which has been reserved for the states has consisted of health, safety, and welfare issues.

The tension between national and state power has erupted many times over the years, from the Civil War to the conflict between Eisenhower and Arkansas Governor Faubus over control of the National Guard during school desegregation in the 1950s to a host of contemporary issues, such as gay marriage and abortion. This tension is yet another reason the American Founders conceived that a hard separation between state and federal power could be beneficial. After John Adams passed the Sedition Act, which prohibited criticism of the president in apparent contradiction to the First Amendment, Thomas Jefferson encouraged states to declare that law null and void. The Territory of Kentucky did precisely that.

Much has changed regarding the division between federal and state powers. Many of the protections granted to the states do not exist today. In 1804, Chief Justice John Marshall penned *Marbury v. Madison*, establishing judicial review and seizing for the federal government the upper hand in the conflict between the federal government and the states. The Civil War further solidified federal power, as the 14th Amendment now allows the federal government to review the legality of many state actions. Many areas of health, safety, and welfare now fall under national control, as our recent debates regarding healthcare indicate.

The legal principle which allows the 14th Amendment's protections for individuals to be applied to state actions is referred to as "selective incorporation." This term means that the Supreme Court selects when an issue has reached a point of national concern and needs to be handled on a national basis. For instance, the 14th Amendment's protections against police performing searches without warrants did not apply to state law until the ruling of *Mapp v. Ohio* in 1961, when the Court expanded this protection against federal actions to state actions as well. Originally the provision only applied to federal police. Prior to that ruling, state police could perform raids without warrants, as the Colorado state police did when they shut down an illegal abortion clinic in the 1940s. Abortion, at that time, was proscribed by many states' laws. The ruling in *Roe v. Wade* (1973) placed significant limits on how states could legislate in that area. A similar trend occurred in the area of gay rights, as a series of court ruling beginning in 2003 removed state authority to legislate in this area.

The effect of selective incorporation on the balance of power between federal and state governments over time has been significant. As each of the issues discussed in this paragraph exemplify, areas of health, safety, and morals which were once regulated by the state governments are now regulated by the federal government.

The reduction of the areas in which states retain sovereign control has diminished the effectiveness of the Madisonian Model. Whereas the states once provided a mechanism for diverse laws to effectively govern a diverse society, today's system encourages so many issues to be handled at the national level. The loss of diversity in laws has the effect of diminishing the sovereignty of the states and particularly those states that would oppose many of these issues on the grounds of religious freedom.

Even so, much of the integrity of the original division between federal and state power remains. There is much merit to such a system. An American may find, spread across the vast continent that is our country, a plethora of lifestyles and ways of life, in a range of climates consisting of a diverse population. The differing laws in places like Texas and Colorado will attract residents who prefer different lifestyles. There is here, as Plato put it, "a bazaar of constitutions." In a nation founded upon the venerable principles of freedom and equality, it is perhaps the greatest blessing of our Constitution that it may provide the necessary conditions for us to freely enjoy the lives of our choosing within some reasonable bounds, and for those who choose diverse lifestyles to enjoy a relative equality of hospitality within our society.

RECOMMENDED READING

Aristotle, *The Politics*

John Locke, *The Second Treatise of Government*

James Madison, Alexander Hamilton, and John Jay,
The Federalist Papers

Machiavelli, *The Prince*

Montesquieu, *The Spirit of the Laws*

Plato, *The Republic*

THE
NECESSITY
OF THE
RULE OF LAW

By John O. Tyler, Jr. JD, PhD
PROFESSOR OF LAW & JURISPRUDENCE

Aristotle, in a famous passage in the *Politics* (c. 330 B.C.), discusses whether the rule of law is preferable to the rule of men. Aristotle chooses the rule of law. "Rightly constituted laws must be the final sovereign." The rule of law is better, so long as the laws meet two requirements.

First, laws must be "rightly constituted." As explained below, rightly constituted laws establish justice, and justice preserves society and protects liberty. Justice is a moral concept, and laws must be moral to be just.

Second, laws must be "the final sovereign." Sovereignty establishes the authority of law. Sovereign laws have three important properties that preserve society and protect liberty. First, sovereign laws wield supremacy over political magistrates. Second, sovereign laws bind magistrates to the same extent that they bind the public at large. Third, magistrates must enforce sovereign laws. Rulers may not suspend enforcement of laws they dislike.

History and the great thinkers of the Western legal tradition confirm Aristotle's requirements for the rule of law. This chapter explains how American jurisprudence established a system of just laws by adopting natural law jurisprudence. It then explains how the U.S. Constitution established a government of sovereign laws. Together, these developments established the rule of law and rejected the rule of men in the United States.

Maintaining the rule of law, however, is a never-ending struggle. Two factors have eroded the rule of law in the United States. The first is the separation of law from morality, which produces unjust laws. The second is judicial activism, which destroys the sovereignty of law. This chapter explains how these factors have eroded the rule of law in the United States. It then concludes by explaining how we can restore the rule of law.

The Necessity of Just Laws

American jurisprudence adopted English common law as described in Sir William Blackstone's *Commentaries on the Laws of England*, published from 1765 to 1769. Blackstone's *Commentaries* dominated American jurisprudence from our founding through the early 20th century. As explained below, Blackstone's jurisprudence ensures just laws by adopting natural law jurisprudence.

Just laws preserve society and protect liberty. Justice is a moral concept, and laws must be moral to be just. Natural law jurisprudence ensures laws are just. If laws are unjust, natural law declares them invalid and unenforceable.

Natural law has three traditional moral precepts. First, one should live honorably. Second, one should harm no one. Third, one should give every man his due. "Positive" laws, those laws "posited" or created by governments, are invalid and unenforceable if they violate these moral precepts.

For example, laws that permit slavery violate these precepts. Such laws are therefore unenforceable under natural law.

Natural law is the oldest tradition in Western jurisprudence. The Greek poet Hesiod describes natural law in his poem "Works and Days" (c. 700 B.C.). Hesiod writes that just actions bring peace and prosperity. Unjust actions, however, bring famine, plague, infertility, and military disaster.

The Greek philosopher Socrates describes natural law in the *Crito* (c. 380 B.C.). One should live honorably. One should harm no one. One should honor their agreements, so long as they are just. Citizens have a duty to obey just laws, but there is no duty to obey unjust laws.

The Byzantine emperor Justinian codified Roman law in the *Institutes* (A.D. 535). The *Institutes* gives the classic statement of natural law precepts. Natural law requires us "to live honestly, to injure no one, and to give every man his due." Divine providence establishes these natural law precepts. These precepts never change, and they apply to all people at all times.

The English jurist Sir John Fortescue adopted natural law jurisprudence into English common law in his treatise *In Praise of the Laws of England* (c. 1470). "Positive" laws, those laws created by governments, are invalid and unenforceable if they violate these moral precepts.

The English philosopher John Locke describes natural law in his *Second Treatise on Civil Government* (1689). Natural law originates in God's will, and God grants every person four natural rights. These natural rights include the right to life, the right to liberty, the right to own property, and the right to be free from physical injury. God granted these natural rights to every person before any government existed. These natural rights are therefore *inalienable*, meaning no government can take them away without our consent.

Like Fortescue, Locke holds that "positive" laws, those laws created by governments, are "only so far right, as they are founded on the law of nature." "Positive" laws are invalid and unenforceable if they violate natural law precepts.

Locke looks to scripture for guidance in discerning the moral precepts of natural law. Locke maintains that human reason is incapable, by itself, of discerning these precepts. God reveals the moral precepts of natural law in scripture.

The great English jurist Sir William Blackstone combines all these elements of the natural law tradition in his *Commentaries on the Laws of England* (1765–1769). Blackstone adopts the Greek poet Hesiod's view that unchangeable laws of human nature govern man. Man's happiness depends on conforming to these laws.

The pursuit of man's "true and substantial happiness" provides the foundation for natural law. God, as both the creator of man and the author of natural law, made human happiness and justice mutually interdependent. Human beings obtain happiness by pursuing justice. Conversely, human beings become unhappy by failing to pursue justice. Natural law permits just actions that promote man's happiness, and it forbids unjust actions that destroy man's happiness.

Blackstone adopts the Byzantine emperor Justinian's three precepts of natural law. "Such, among others, are these principles: that we should live honestly, should hurt nobody, and should render to every one his due; to which three general precepts Justinian has reduced the whole doctrine of law." Blackstone also adopts the English philosopher John Locke's view that "positive" laws, those laws created by governments, derive all their validity and force from natural law. Blackstone lastly adopts the English jurist Sir John Fortescue's view, shared by Locke, that laws created by government are invalid and unenforceable if they violate natural law precepts.

Blackstone's natural law jurisprudence commands us to ignore unjust laws created by government if they violate natural law precepts. True laws are just laws. Unjust laws, by definition, are not laws at all. For example, if government creates an unjust law that permits slavery, then we should ignore that law. We have no duty to obey it, and judges have no power to enforce it.

Blackstone, like the English philosopher John Locke, looks to scripture to discern the moral precepts of natural law. Prior to Adam's fall, human reason was sufficient to discern these precepts. Adam's fall, however, corrupted human reason. Fallen man requires divine revelation to discern the moral precepts of natural law. God's "compassionate providence" provides this revelation in scripture.

The most famous case in the English language, *Ex Parte Somersett*, (1772), illustrates the mechanics of natural law jurisprudence. *Ex Parte Somersett* applied natural law jurisprudence to outlaw slavery in England. The author of the opinion, Lord Mansfield, was Sir William Blackstone's patron and friend. Many jurists consider Lord Mansfield to be the greatest judge in Anglo-American legal history.

England's "positive" or government-created law permitted slavery. Lord Mansfield applied the moral precepts of natural law in *Ex Parte Somersett* and found slavery to be unjust. Lord Mansfield then refused to enforce the unjust law. He ordered the release of the slave James Somersett in this famous passage:

> The state of slavery is of such a nature, that it is incapable of being
> introduced on any reasons, moral or political, but only by positive
> law, which preserves its force long after the reasons, occasion, and

time itself from whence it was created, is erased from memory. *It is so odious, that nothing can be suffered to support it, but positive law.* Whatever inconveniences, therefore, may follow from the decision, I cannot say this case is allowed or approved by the law of England; and therefore the [slave James Somersett] must be discharged. [Emphasis added].

Sir William Blackstone's *Commentaries on the Laws of England* provided the foundation of American law and legal education for more than a century. Published reports of American case decisions did not exist in the decades surrounding the American Revolution, and reports of English decisions were frequently unavailable. In many jurisdictions, the four volumes of Blackstone's *Commentaries* represented all there was of the law.

Carl Sandburg describes Blackstone's influence on the life of Abraham Lincoln. The young Lincoln was advised by a lawyer friend that Blackstone's *Commentaries* was the first book that a prospective lawyer should read. Lincoln fortuitously obtained a copy from a man driving west who needed to lighten the load of his covered wagon. Twenty-five years later, Lincoln wrote a letter advising another young man to "come to the law" as Lincoln had, by reading Blackstone "for himself, without an instructor."

A 1914 Carnegie Foundation study records that "all of the older American law schools started by being so-called lecture schools. Blackstone's *Commentaries*, which, as we know, were used for purposes of instruction earlier and with far more lasting effect in the United States than in England, formed the almost exclusive basis of the work." For more than 100 years, "thousands upon thousands of lawyers and influential laymen on both sides of the Atlantic read Blackstone's *Commentaries* and believed them."

Today, however, judges in the United States increasingly reject Blackstone's natural law jurisprudence and its demand for moral laws. Instead, they prefer "legal positivism," a jurisprudence that intentionally sepa-rates law from morality. Three English philosophers, Jeremy Bentham (1748–1832), John Austin (1790–1859), and H.L.A. Hart (1907–1992), developed legal positivism to oppose Blackstone's jurisprudence. H.L.A. Hart, the most influential of the three philosophers, argues that judges should enforce all "positive" or government-created laws, even if those laws are "morally iniquitous" and "have no moral justification or force whatever."

The legal positivist movement began in the United States at Harvard Law School in 1957 when Oxford philosopher H.L.A. Hart gave a lecture enti-tled "Positivism and the Separation of Law and Morals." Hart made three claims in his lecture. First, "positive" law, the law created by government, is the only real law. Second, natural law is imaginary, not real. Third, there is no necessary connection between law and morality.

Hart's lecture built on the works of English philosophers Jeremy Bentham (1748–1832) and John Austin (1790–1859). Jeremy Bentham rejected the moral precepts of natural law that people should live honorably, injure no one, and give every man his due. Instead, Bentham claimed the only stan-dards for right and wrong are physical pleasure and physical pain. Morality is not determined by the nature of an act, but rather by its consequences. Acts are moral if they produce physical pleasure. Acts are immoral if they produce physical pain.

Jeremy Bentham also rejected the existence of natural law. Bentham claimed that "positive" laws, those laws created by government, are the only real laws. Only "positive" laws, therefore, can create real rights. Natural law is "imaginary," and natural rights are "simple nonsense." *Inalienable* natu-ral rights, the type of rights described by John Locke and the American Declaration of Independence, are "nonsense walking upon stilts."

John Austin (1790–1859) agreed with Bentham that natural law is "stark nonsense." Austin claimed that morality has no role in law. "The existence of law is one thing; its merit and demerit another." Austin rejected Blackstone's claim that true laws are just laws, and unjust laws, by definition, are not laws at all. Instead, Austin argued that an immoral law is still a law, even if "we happen to dislike it." Austin also rejected scripture as a basis of morality in law. Austin wrote in *The Province of Jurisprudence Determined* (1832) that the laws of God are too uncertain and ambiguous to provide a source of law.

Austin lastly attacked Blackstone's "declaratory theory" of law that judges must never make new law. They must find, declare, and apply established law. Austin actually prefers judges to legislatures for making law. "That part of the law of every country which was made by judges," he wrote, "has been far better made then that part which consists of statutes enacted by the legislature."

Austin saw no need to protect against tyranny by separating the power to make law from the power to enforce law. He saw no "danger whatever" in allowing judges to legislate from the bench. Instead, Austin argued that judges *must* legislate from the bench "to make up for the negligence or incapacity" of legislators.

H.L.A. Hart published *The Concept of Law* in 1961, four years after his Harvard Law School lecture entitled "Positivism and the Separation of Law and Morals." *The Concept of Law* is the most influential work on jurisprudence since Blackstone's *Commentaries* on the Laws of England (1765–1769). Hart rejects natural law's refusal to enforce unjust laws. Hart argues that all "positive" laws created by government should be enforced, even "morally iniquitous laws" having "no moral justification or force whatever." Hart's jurisprudence enforces laws establishing slavery, laws facilitating the Holocaust, and laws permitting capital punishment of innocent parties.

Like John Austin, Hart encourages activist judges and rejects Blackstone's "declaratory theory" of law. Hart's "penumbra doctrine" holds that every legal term has a "penumbra of uncertainty at the outer fringe of its meaning." Judges should provide certainty to the meaning of legal terms by legislating from the bench.

Many judges in the United States, including justices of the U.S. Supreme Court, prefer legal positivism to Blackstone's jurisprudence because it increases their power. Blackstone condemns judicial activism. Blackstone's "declaratory theory" of law requires judges to apply the existing law, not their private judgments, in deciding cases. Judges only *find*, *declare*, and *apply* the law; they never *make* the law. Legal positivism, on the other hand, encourages activist judges to "make new law" and legislate from the bench in every case. Legal positivism replaces the rule of law with the rule of men.

Hart's legal positivism entered the mainstream of American jurisprudence in *Griswold v. Connecticut*, 381 U.S. 479 (1965). The U.S. Supreme Court adopted Hart's "penumbra doctrine" in *Griswold* to make new law and "imply" a new right of privacy in the Bill of Rights. Even though the Bill of Rights contains no right of privacy, the Court claimed to find it in the "penumbras" or shadows of other rights.

The Supreme Court then used its judge-made right of privacy to strike down state laws governing contraception, *Griswold v. Connecticut*, 381 U.S. 479 (1965); to strike down state laws governing abortion, *Roe v. Wade*, 410 U.S. 113 (1973); and to strike down state laws governing sodomy, *Lawrence v. Texas*, 539 U.S. 558 (2003).

The German philosopher Georg W.F. Hegel wrote in *The Philosophy of History* (1837) that history is "the slaughter-bench at which the happiness of peoples, the wisdom of States, and the virtue of individuals have been victimized." Soviet Russia and Nazi Germany illustrate the slaughter-bench that results when governments separate law from morality. Both countries adopted legal positivism during the 20th century.

The Soviet Criminal Codes of 1922 and 1926 adopted Italian positivist jurisprudence, particularly the work of Enrico Ferri (1856–1929). These codes expressly permitted the execution and punishment of innocent parties. Article VII of the 1926 Criminal Code authorized punishment, including death, for any person deemed to pose a "social danger." No crime was required for punishment. Article LVII also permitted Soviet authorities to punish the innocent family members and dependents of convicted offenders.

Soviet rulers designed and enforced their legal system to control the population through terror. Stalin utilized the Criminal Codes to execute 3.5 million without trials during the "Great Terror" of 1936–1938. He killed an estimated 7.25 million while forcing peasants off their farms during the "Dekulakization" of 1929–1933. Stalin intentionally starved 12 million Ukrainians to death, half of them children, during the "Holodomor" or "terror-famine" of 1932–1933.

The Nazis adopted Article 1 of the Soviet Civil Code into their own legal system. Article 1 permitted the government, at its discretion, to disregard all civil rights. The Nazis also adopted Article XVI of the 1926 Soviet Criminal Code entitled "Crimes by Analogy." Article XVI permitted punishment, in the absence of any crime, if the defendant committed an act that was "analogous" to a prohibited act. Most of the atrocities of the Holocaust were legal under German positivism.

Stalin's legal positivism authorized the death of more than 22 million innocents. Hitler's legal positivism authorized the death of 11 million innocents. Legal positivism in the United States, exemplified by *Roe v. Wade*

(1973), has authorized the death, so far, of more than 60 million unborn children.

The legal history of Soviet Russia, Nazi Germany, and the United States after *Roe v. Wade* proves the necessity of Aristotle's first requirement for the rule of law. Laws must be moral and establish justice. The following explains Aristotle's second requirement for the rule of law. Laws must be sovereign.

The Necessity of Sovereign Laws

Sovereign laws have three properties that preserve society and protect liberty. First, sovereign laws wield supremacy over political magistrates. Second, sovereign laws bind magistrates to the same extent that they bind the public at large. Third, magistrates must enforce sovereign laws. Rulers may not suspend enforcement of laws they dislike.

As explained below, no government is possible without sovereign laws. Rightly constituted laws must be the final sovereign. Only sovereign laws can establish the rule of law rather than the rule of men, and only the rule of law can preserve society and protect liberty.

Sovereign laws are necessary to preserve society. Plato writes in the *Laws* (c. 360 B.C.) that the preservation or ruin of a society depends on sovereign laws more than any other factor. Sovereign laws are a society's salvation, but their absence brings the society's destruction. (*Laws*, 715d–715e). Plato writes in the *Statesman* (c. 360 B.C.) that sovereign laws are the only means by which governments can govern with true statecraft. Governments must therefore keep strict obedience to established laws and customs. (*Statesman*, 300e–301a). Plato considers the sovereignty of law so important that his primary criterion for selecting magistrates is their obedience to established laws. (*Laws*, 715c–715d).

Aristotle explains in the *Politics* (*c.* 330 B.C.) why rightly constituted laws must be the final sovereign. Laws make better rulers than men. (*Politics*, 1282a). Human beings are susceptible to corruption by passion. Man beset by passion is the worst of all creatures, and passion corrupts even the best of men from time to time. (*Politics*, 1281a).

Law, on the other hand, is reason liberated from passion. The rule of law is therefore preferable to rule by any individual. (*Politics*, 1287a). Personal rule should be limited to contingencies the laws did not foresee. (*Politics*, 1282a). Aristotle concludes in the *Politics* that no government is possible without sovereign laws. (*Politics*, 1292a).

Cicero writes in the *On the Laws* (*c.* 54 B.C.) that no true state can exist without a sovereign set of valid laws. Valid laws distinguish between justice and injustice. (*On the Laws*, 2.13). He agrees with Aristotle that no constitution can exist without a sovereign set of valid or "rightly constituted" laws. Magistrates must respect the sovereignty of valid laws. (*On the Laws*, 2.13). A state without valid laws does not deserve the name of state. (*On the Laws*, 2.12).

Magistrates must be subject to laws, just as people are subject to magistrates. (*On the Laws*, 3.2). For Cicero, "a magistrate is a speaking law, and the law is a silent magistrate." Magistrates who rule contrary to the law become unjust tyrants. Echoing Aristotle, Cicero likens such rulers to beasts in the *Republic* (*c.* 54 B.C.). A tyrant is "the foulest most repellent creature imaginable," "the most abhorrent to god and man alike. Although he has the outward appearance of a man, he outdoes the wildest beasts in the utter savagery of his behavior." (*Republic*, 2.48).

The Byzantine emperor Justinian agrees. Justinian's *Institutes* (A.D. 535) provides that a judge's highest duty is to rule in accord with the established statutes, the Constitution, and legal custom. (*Institutes*, 4.17). Roman judges that violated the sovereignty of law were deported.

Establishing and maintaining the rule of law is a never-ending struggle. Sovereign laws are essential to the rule of law, and English history illustrates the high cost of restoring sovereign laws once they are lost. The Magna Carta (1215) established the rule of law in England by establishing the sovereignty of law over the English king and all his magistrates. The Magna Carta became the first of four pillars of the English Constitution.

Henry de Bracton's treatise *On the Laws and Customs of England* (*c.* 1235) also proclaimed the sovereignty of English law over the king. In England, De Bracton wrote, the laws make the king. The king does not make the laws.

During the 17th century, however, the four Stuart kings persistently violated the sovereignty of English law. The Stuarts sought to replace the rule of law with an absolute monarchy. The bitter struggle to restore the sovereignty of law in England lasted from 1603 until 1689, a period known as the "English Legal Revolution."

The Stuart campaign against sovereign laws began with the ascension of James I in 1603. James I advocated the divine right of kings in a book entitled *The Trew Law of Free Monarchies* (1598) and in a 1609 speech to the Lords and Commons at Parliament. James told Parliament in his speech that "The state of monarchy is the supremest thing upon earth, for kings are not only God's lieutenants upon earth and sit upon God's throne, but even by God himself they are called Gods." "Kings are justly called Gods," James told Parliament, "for that they exercise a manner or resemblance of Divine power upon earth." Subjects may not dispute the king's absolute power. Kings have the same divine power on earth as God himself.

James I claimed, contrary to the Magna Carta, that law wields no sovereignty over kings. Once the king establishes his hereditary right to the throne, the king is elevated above the law and has no obligation to obey the law. The king is "free," wielding absolute supremacy over the law. The king may unilaterally change the law and suspend the law at will. The king is not even obliged to follow the laws he makes himself.

Kings, James claimed, are not accountable to any man. The king, like God, sits in judgment of all men but is himself judged by none. The king wields supremacy over Parliament, the courts, and all his subjects. Subjects may never resist the king, even when the king is wicked. The king may treat his subjects in any manner he pleases, just like pieces in a chess game.

It took almost a century, including the English Civil War and the Glorious Revolution, to restore the sovereignty of law in England. The first great champion of sovereign laws against the Stuarts was Sir Edward Coke. Coke served as Chief Justice of the Court of Common Pleas from 1603 to 1613, and as Chief Justice of the Court of the King's Bench from 1613 to 1616.

Coke authored a series of opinions establishing the sovereignty of the common law over the king and over Parliament. Coke also established the supremacy of the common law courts over other court systems in England. Coke further established the independence of common law judges to decide cases without royal interference.

James I eventually fired Coke from both Chief Justice positions, but the tenacious Coke won election to Parliament and continued his fight for sovereign laws as a Member of Parliament. In 1621, Coke authored a Protestation asserting that English subjects have the right to free speech. The liberties of English subjects were matters of right, not matters dependent on royal toleration.

Charles I, son of James I, came to the throne in 1625. He shared his father's views on the divine right of kings. In 1626, Charles I illegally attempted to collect taxes, without the required consent of Parliament, in the form of forced loans.

Charles I arbitrarily imprisoned subjects, without due process, who refused to make the forced loans. In 1628, Sir Edward Coke authored and obtained passage of the Petition of Right in Parliament to stop this practice. The Petition of Right joined the Magna Carta as the second of four pillars of the English Constitution.

The Petition of Right provided that the king cannot imprison or execute any Englishman without due process of law. If arrested, all Englishmen are entitled to a writ of *habeas corpus* to ensure the king has just cause for their imprisonment. Furthermore, the king and his ministers must enforce the law. The king has no power to tax without Parliament's consent. Lastly, Coke translated and popularized the Magna Carta in the Second Part of his *Institutes on the Lawes of England* (1642).

Charles I consented to the Petition of Right but ignored its terms. He tried to rule without Parliament for 11 years, levying taxes without Parliament's consent. Financial difficulties eventually forced him to summon a Parliament in 1640. On January 3, 1642, Charles entered the House of Commons with 400 armed men to arrest five of its members. This act began the English Civil War that lasted from 1642 until 1651. Parliament executed Charles I for treason on January 30, 1649.

Parliament restored the monarchy in 1660. Charles II, the son of Charles I, became the third Stuart king. Charles II arbitrarily imprisoned his political enemies without due process in violation of the Magna Carta. He wrongfully denied writs of *habeas corpus* by sending prisoners overseas. Parliament passed the Habeas Corpus Act in 1679 to stop this practice. The Habeas Corpus Act became the third pillar of the English Constitution.

James II, the brother of Charles II, came to the throne in 1685. Like the earlier Stuarts, James II disrespected the sovereignty of law. He tried to rule without Parliament, and he levied taxes without Parliament's consent.

James II claimed the "dispensing power" to suspend statutes he disliked. He used this power to violate English laws governing religion and bring Roman Catholics into the Church, the army, and the government. Hoping to drive England back into the Roman Catholic fold, James II raised an illegal standing army and illegally disarmed his subjects. The English refused to tolerate these actions, and the Glorious Revolution of 1688 forced James II's abdication.

Parliament then passed the fourth pillar of the English Constitution, the English Bill of Rights (1689). The first two paragraphs of the English Bill of Rights finally re-established the sovereignty of English law over the king:

> That the pretended power of suspending the laws or the execution of laws by regal authority without consent of Parliament is illegal.

> That the pretended power of dispensing with laws or the execution of laws by regal authority, as it hath been assumed and exercised of late, is illegal.

John Locke fled to Holland in 1683 to avoid judicial persecution by the Stuarts. He returned to England after the Glorious Revolution in 1688 and published his *Second Treatise on Civil Government* (1689). Locke's *Second Treatise* provides that kings who violate the sovereignty of law are tyrants. "Where-ever law ends, tyranny begins." Tyrants, even kings, may be opposed like any other man who uses force to invade the rights of another. (*Second Treatise*, § 202).

The U.S. Constitution establishes the sovereign rule of law. The text of the U.S. Constitution fulfills all three requirements of sovereign laws. The first requirement of sovereign laws is that they wield supremacy over magistrates. The Supremacy Clause of Article VI, Clause 2 fulfills this requirement by establishing the Constitution as "the supreme law of the land":

This Constitution, and the laws of the United States which shall be made in pursuance thereof; and all treaties made, or which shall be made, under the authority of the United States, *shall be the supreme law of the land*; and the judges in every state shall be bound thereby, anything in the Constitution or laws of any State to the contrary notwithstanding. [Emphasis added.]

The second requirement of sovereign laws is that they bind magistrates to the same extent as all other citizens. The Due Process Clause of the Fifth Amendment fulfills this requirement by subjecting all federal officials to the rule of law:

No person shall be ... deprived of life, liberty, or property, without due process of law.

The Due Process Clause and the Equal Protection Clause of the 14th Amendment fulfill this requirement subjecting all state officials to the rule of law:

No state shall make or enforce any law which shall abridge the privileges or immunities of citizens of the United States; nor shall any state deprive any person of life, liberty, or property, without due process of law; nor deny to any person within its jurisdiction the equal protection of the laws.

The third requirement of sovereign laws is that magistrates must enforce the laws. Magistrates may not suspend enforcement of laws they dislike. The Take Care Clause of Article II, § 3 imposes this requirement on the president by requiring the president to enforce the laws. "[The President] shall take care that the laws be faithfully executed." The Supremacy Clause of Article VI, Clause 2 imposes this requirement on judges by requiring all judges to follow the Constitution:

> This Constitution, and the laws of the United States which shall
> be made in pursuance thereof; and all treaties made, or which
> shall be made, under the authority of the United States, *shall be*
> *the supreme law of the land; and the judges in every state shall be*
> *bound thereby, anything in the Constitution or laws of any State to*
> *the contrary notwithstanding.* [Emphasis added.]

In the United States, as in England, establishing and maintaining the rule
of law is a never-ending struggle. As explained below, the great adversaries of sovereign laws in the United States are the very people entrusted
to maintain the rule of law. Activist federal judges, including justices on
the U.S. Supreme Court, have steadily increased their personal power
by increasing the power of the federal courts. The following discussion
explains the legal techniques employed by federal judges to replace the rule
of law with the rule of men.

Western jurists traditionally condemn judicial activism. Plato wrote
that magistrates "must all keep strictly to the laws once they have been
laid down and never transgress the enactments or established national
customs" (*Statesman*, 360 B.C.). The great Roman jurist Ulpian (A.D.
170–223) wrote that a judge's highest duty is to rule in accord with the
statutes, the Constitution, and legal customs. Justinian's *Institutes* (A.D.
535), which codifies Roman law, adopts Ulpian on this point. (*Institutes*,
4.17). Any Roman judge who violated this duty was deported.

Blackstone's *Commentaries on the Laws of England* (1765) explains the
"declaratory theory" of law that judges should only *find, declare, and apply*
existing law; they should never *make* new law. "Judges swear to decide
cases, not by their own private judgement, but according to the known laws
and customs of the land. Judges should not pronounce a new law. They
must maintain and expound the old one." (*Commentaries*, § 70).

The French philosopher Montesquieu explains the reason for this rule in *The Spirit of the Laws* (1748). Giving one magistrate the power to make law *and* the power to enforce law invites tyranny. Any magistrate who enacts a tyrannical law will also enforce it tyrannically (*The Spirit of the Laws*, 11.6). Blackstone agrees (*Commentaries*, § 142).

Controlling judicial activism is essential for maintaining the rule of law. Judge Robert Yates, a delegate to the Constitutional Convention for New York, predicted the judicial activism of federal judges in 1788. Writing as "Brutus" during the ratification debates, Judge Yates warned that the Constitution did not provide adequate checks and balances on the power of the federal judiciary, particularly the power of Supreme Court justices.

"There is no authority that can remove them," wrote Yates, "and they cannot be controlled by the laws of the legislature. In short, they are independent of the people, of the legislature, and of every power under heaven. Men placed in this situation will generally soon feel themselves independent of heaven itself" (*Essay XI, 31 January 1788*).

Judge Yates predicted that federal judges, particularly Supreme Court justices, would exploit the lack of adequate checks and balances on their power and transform the structure of the republic in four steps. *First*, the Supreme Court would evade or ignore the text of the Constitution. In interpreting the Constitution, Supreme Court justices would not confine themselves to the letter of the Constitution or to fixed and established rules of law (*Essay XII, Part I, 7 February 1788*).

Second, the federal courts would expand their jurisdiction to increase their power. Federal judges would lean strongly in favor of the federal government. Federal judges would interpret the Constitution in all cases to enlarge their sphere of authority. Federal judges would always interpret the Constitution to extend the power of the federal courts (*Essay XI, 31 January 1788*).

Third, the federal courts would extend the federal government's legislative power. This, in turn, would increase the powers of the federal courts (*Essay XI, 31 January 1788*). Federal courts would authorize Congress to do anything that the courts judged would provide for the general welfare. The effect of these decisions would be to grant Congress a general and unlimited power to legislate (*Essay XII, Part I, 7 February 1788*).

Fourth, federal courts would steadily subvert the legislative, executive, and judicial power of the states, severely diminishing the power of state governments to make and execute laws. Federal courts would always limit the powers of the states. Federal courts would take from the state governments every power of either making or executing laws. Lastly, federal judges would construe the Constitution so that states would lose their rights "until they become so trifling and unimportant, as not to be worth having" (*Essay XI, 31 January 1788*).

Each of Judge Robert Yates's predictions has come true. The U.S. Supreme Court quickly fulfilled Judge Yates's first two predictions, that the Court would ignore the Constitution's text and increase its power by increasing its own jurisdiction. It fulfilled these predictions by granting itself the power of judicial review.

Article III, § 2 of the Constitution establishes the powers of the federal courts. Article III, § 2 does *not* grant the Supreme Court the power of judicial review over any other branches of federal or state governments. *See Eakin v. Raub,* 2 Sergeant and Rawle 330 (Pa. 1825) (Gibson, J., dissenting). Nevertheless, in 1803, the Supreme Court ignored Article III, § 2 and granted itself the power of judicial review over the executive and legislative branches of the *federal* government. *Marbury v. Madison,* 5 U.S. 137 (1803).

In 1810, the Supreme Court ignored both Article III, § 2 and the 10th Amendment to grant itself judicial review over the executive and legislative branches of *state* governments. *Fletcher v. Peck*, 10 U.S. 87 (1810). In 1816, the Supreme Court again ignored Article III, § 2 and the 10th Amendment to grant itself judicial review over the judicial branches of *state* governments. *Martin v. Hunter's Lessee*, 14 U.S. 304 (1816).

By these three decisions, the Supreme Court increased its power to become the final arbiter of all disputes in the United States. *Marbury v. Madison* (1803) violates the separation of powers by giving the judicial branch supremacy over the executive and legislative branches of the federal government. *Fletcher v. Peck* (1810) and *Martin v. Hunter's Lessee* (1816) violate federalism by giving the federal judicial branch supremacy over state governments.

Judge Yates's third prediction was that federal courts would extend the federal government's legislative power. The Supreme Court fulfilled this prediction by expanding Congress's powers under the Commerce Clause. Article I, § 8 gives Congress the power "to regulate Commerce with foreign Nations, and among the several States."

The Supreme Court expanded this power to include *any* activity that *impacts* interstate commerce, however slightly. The commerce power covers all such activities, even if the activity does *not* involve commerce, and even if the activity is *not* interstate. *Wickard v. Filburn*, 317 U.S. 111 (1942). This decision gives Congress an almost unlimited legislative power, just as Judge Yates predicted.

Judge Yates's fourth prediction was that federal courts would subvert the legislative, executive, and judicial power of the states. The U.S. Constitution establishes a federal system, splitting powers between state and federal governments. The 10th Amendment guarantees the legislative, executive, and judicial power of the states by providing "The powers not delegated to the United States by the Constitution, nor prohibited by it to the States, are reserved to the States respectively, or to the people."

Nevertheless, despite the 10th Amendment, the Supreme Court subverted the states' legislative, executive, and judicial powers in four steps. The Supreme Court's first step in subverting state powers was ruling that neither citizens nor states could sue the federal government to enforce the 10th Amendment. *Frothingham v. Mellon,* consolidated with *Massachusetts v. Mellon,* 262 U.S. 447 (1923).

The Supreme Court's second step in subverting state powers was nullifying the 10th Amendment. It held the 10th Amendment is only a meaningless "truism." The 10th Amendment does not limit the authority or powers of the federal government. *U.S. v. Darby Lumber,* 312 U.S. 100 (1941).

The Supreme Court's third step in subverting state powers was creating the legal fiction of the 14th Amendment, "incorporation." The Bill of Rights only applies to the federal government. *Barron v. Baltimore,* 32 U.S. 243 (1833). Nevertheless, the Supreme Court fictitiously "incorporates" the Bill of Rights into the 14th Amendment to make the Bill of Rights applicable to the states. The Supreme Court then uses provisions in the Bill of Rights to subvert the legislative, executive, and judicial powers of the states. *Mapp v. Ohio,* 367 U.S. 643 (1961) (forcing states to use the exclusionary rule in state criminal proceedings); *Baker v. Carr,* 369 U.S. 186 (1962) (forcing states to revise their congressional districts).

The Supreme Court's fourth step in subverting the powers of the states was legislating "implied" and "fundamental" rights not listed in the Bill of Rights. The Supreme Court then utilizes these newly created rights to subvert the legislative, executive, and judicial powers of the states. This technique supplants the rule of law with the rule of men. Any confederation of five Supreme Court justices now exercises an unlimited power to amend or ignore the Constitution.

The Supreme Court used an "implied" right of privacy to strike down state laws governing contraception, *Griswold v. Connecticut*, 381 U.S. 479 (1965); to strike down state laws governing abortion, *Roe v. Wade*, 410 U.S. 113 (1973); and to strike down state laws governing sodomy, *Lawrence v. Texas*, 539 U.S. 558 (2003).

The Supreme Court recently created a new, "fundamental" right to gay marriage. It then "incorporated" this right into the 14th Amendment to strike down state laws governing gay marriage. *Obergefell v. Hodges*, 576 U.S. __ (2015). By using these four legal steps, the U.S. Supreme Court has fully subverted the legislative, executive, and judicial power of the states, just as Judge Yates predicted in 1788.

Conclusion: Restoring the Rule of Law

The rule of law is preferable to the rule of men, and the laws must be just and sovereign. American jurisprudence established a system of just laws by adopting Blackstone's natural law jurisprudence. Natural law requires us "to live honestly, to injure no one, and to give every man his due." Laws that violate these precepts are unjust, invalid, and unenforceable.

The U.S. Constitution establishes a government of sovereign laws. Sovereign laws have three characteristics. First, they wield supremacy over magistrates. Second, they bind magistrates as fully as they bind other citizens. Third, magistrates must enforce sovereign laws. Rulers may not suspend enforcement of laws they dislike. Blackstone's "declaratory theory" of law enforces the rule of sovereign laws. Judges must decide cases, not by their own private judgement, but according to the known laws and customs of the land.

The judicial philosophy of legal positivism is the enemy of just laws. Legal positivism separates law from morality and knowingly enforces unjust laws containing "morally iniquitous provisions … which have no moral justification or force whatever." Stalin's Soviet Union and Hitler's Germany illustrate the folly of enforcing unjust laws.

The judicial philosophy of legal positivism is the enemy of sovereign laws as well. Legal positivism abandons Blackstone's "declaratory theory" of law and encourages activist judges to make new law in every case. Legal positivism destroys the rule of law by unifying the powers to make and enforce law in a single magistrate. The U.S. Supreme Court has effectively replaced the rule of law with the rule of men. Any confederation of five justices now exercises an unlimited power to amend or ignore the Constitution.

Representative republics cannot maintain themselves without just and sovereign laws. We must reawaken the rule of law in the United States and reject the rule of men. We must elect representatives who pass just laws, and we must appoint judges who respect the sovereignty of our laws and our Constitution.

Our first step should be to utilize Article III, § 2 of the Constitution. This section provides that, except for cases involving ambassadors and states as parties, "the Supreme Court shall have appellate jurisdiction, both as to law and fact, *with such exceptions, and under such regulations as the Congress shall make.*" [Emphasis added.]

Congress should invoke its powers Article III, § 2 and restrict the Supreme Court's appellate jurisdiction as follows. To restore the separation of powers, Congress should forbid judicial review of the legislative and executive branches of the federal government.

To restore federalism, Congress should forbid judicial review of the executive, legislative, and judicial branches of state governments. Congress should forbid the Supreme Court jurisdiction to invent new rights not contained in the text of the Constitution. Congress should also forbid the Supreme Court jurisdiction to incorporate these fabricated rights under the 14th Amendment. To restore federalism and the 10th Amendment, Congress should grant standing to states and citizens to sue and enforce the 10th Amendment against the federal government.

We must stop judicial activism. Our primary criterion for selecting judges must be their obedience to our Constitution and our established laws. We must remember that the Constitution creates the Supreme Court. The Supreme Court does not create the Constitution.

Lastly, we must remedy the Constitution's inadequate checks and balances on the federal judiciary. We must render activist judges accountable for their decisions like every other public official. We should enact a constitutional Amendment replacing life appointments to the federal bench with terms of years. Nothing less can free us from the rule of men and restore the rule of law.

RECOMMENDED READING

Aristotle, *The Politics of Aristotle*,
trans. Ernest Barker (Oxford University Press, 1946)

Sir William Blackstone, *Commentaries on the Laws of England*,
ed. Wilfrid Prest, vol. 1 (Oxford University Press, 2016)

Cicero, *De Re Publica (On the Republic) and*
De Legibus (On the Laws), trans. C.W. Keyes, ed. Jeffrey Henderson
(St. Edmundsbury, 2000)

Sir Edward Coke, *Institutes on the Lawes of England*,
in *The Selected Writings of Sir Edward Coke*,
ed. Steve Sheppard, vol. 2 (Liberty Fund, 2003)

John Locke, *Two Treatises of Government*, ed. Peter Laslett
(Cambridge University Press, 1963)

Charles de Montesquieu, *The Spirit of the Laws*, ed. Ann Cohler
(Cambridge University Press, 1989)

Plato, *Statesman*, in *The Collected Dialogues of Plato,*
including the Letters, trans. Lane Cooper, ed. Edith Hamilton and
Huntington Cairns (Princeton University Press, 1961)

EQUALITY

By Scott Robinson, PhD

PROFESSOR OF POLITICAL SCIENCE

T he concept of equality is at the heart of American political philosophy, and it shows up regularly in the political conflicts of American
history. It has animated almost all of the important policy fights regarding our social fabric. Much like the concept of liberty, this idea has deep
roots in Western political thought, which inspired the views of equality
on both the political right and the political left. Despite the intensity with
which policy issues are fought in our country, the concept of equality is
one in which all Americans believe. However, we often disagree over the
type and style of equality.

Classical Views on Equality

Equality was an important concept in the oldest influences on American
political thought and is preeminent in the work of both Plato and
Aristotle. Plato developed the idea that all members of a community must
share what the Greeks called *homonia*, or like-mindedness. He understood that for a society to function well, its members must understand
that they are united by a shared belief in the unity of their community.

It's important that community members feel that they are members of the same team. Plato conveys this idea through the well-known "myth of the metals" in his *Republic*. He suggests that a society have some unifying myth, for example, that everyone's ancestors were born from the same hole in the earth. Everyone shares an origin though some were marked by gold, others by silver, and still others by bronze. Plato was also an early proponent of something we all know today, that women are equal to men in their ability to perform most jobs.

Plato also developed a view of justice that would be influential in the subsequent evolution of the concept of equality. Though members of a society were members of a team, in a just society individuals would "mind their own business." This meant, for Plato, that individuals should perform the work in a society that is most fitting for their character; some should rule, others should be soldiers, and another group is most fit for labor. Though the concept of *homonia* suggested an underlying sense of equality amongst society members rooted in a common myth, it did not convey our more familiar concept of equality, which holds that we are thoroughly equal and that therefore no one is particularly determined to be a laborer or ruler by nature alone.

Plato's thoughts were not plucked from thin air. He had witnessed his home city of Athens suffer under a variety of political forms. The rule of the Thirty Tyrants was like it sounds; it was replaced with a democratic regime which, as Plato depicts in *The Apology* and *Crito*, condemned to death his philosophical mentor and dear friend Socrates, merely for thinking things of the gods that the majority of citizens did not believe. Plato's solution to the consistent problems that emanated from class differences—or inequalities—in his own day was to propose (perhaps ironically) that philosophers should rule in his most famous work, *The Republic*. The proposition would have seemed as fanciful then as it does today, and reader is left wondering whether such a regime could ever really come to be. It is fair to say that Plato grappled with, but failed to solve, the very tangible problems posed by the inequality of his own friends in his own society.

Aristotle articulated a view of equality that also acknowledged that individuals are different from one another and that a society needs these differences to function properly. He saw certain differences in humans as instilled by nature and essentially unavoidable. We should therefore expect to encounter all types of people in a society—those who are successful at amassing wealth, and those who do not amass much wealth. He referred to the wealthy class as oligarchs, and to the laboring class as democratic. Throughout his writings on politics, one of his key arguments is that, because humans tend to behave in a self-interested nature, the best way to achieve the *homonia* sought by his mentor Plato is to balance the interests of the oligarchs with the interests of the democrats. Creditors, for instance, should be balanced against debtors in the society's legislature, so that neither group may oppress the other through onerous laws.

Aristotle saw these divisions as "natural." They were, in other words, an indelible feature of human societies. Although we are equal in some basic sense, we are unequal in our specific abilities. Aristotle goes so far as to label those who cannot accomplish basic tasks without direction as "slaves by nature." Although this is a controversial claim today, it does reveal that the most important classical element of equality was its insistence that we are equal members of a community, or equally human, even if not equal in every capacity.

Aristotle further notes that a wise legislator is needed to create a successful city that balances the interests of the aristocrats and the interests of the democrats. There is no recipe for correct legislation, which is contingent on a host of variables. A wise legislator is capable of understanding precisely what is needed at the current moment to maintain the balance in his society—to keep the democrats from rebelling against the aristocrats, or vice versa. Such a legislator possesses "right reason," because he is able to understand the subtleties of the various possible contingencies. The city should have a natural balance between democrats and aristocrats. They are not equally endowed by God to do the same things, but they are equal members of a community, and that community's welfare is contingent on the happiness of all parties, not just some.

Cicero further developed the concept of equality through his use of "natural law" during the Roman Republic. He argues in *On the Laws* that the true origin of justice is not human laws, but rather "nature's leadership." In other words, nature created human beings with a unique and special place in the animal kingdom: "For although she made all other animate creatures face the earth for grazing, she made the human alone upright and roused him to look on the sky." Humans, possessing the unique ability to discern what is good and what is harmful for our race, are therefore uniquely situated to endeavor for their own welfare: "We have been made by nature to receive the knowledge of justice from one another and share it among all people." **A fundamental equality belongs to all humans insofar as we are each created by God for the purpose of organizing our own affairs for our own welfare.** We are not to be owned by one another in the same way in which humans own cattle, for we are equally created as free creatures.

Christian philosophers, most notably St. Thomas Aquinas, further developed the idea of equality in natural law. He weaves Cicero's notion of natural law into Christian terminology, arguing that all viable human laws (positive law) must be consistent with natural law, and that natural law can be discerned because natural law is that law that is consistent with divine law, which is created by God. Law may be viewed as hierarchically structured: God makes laws that dictate nature, nature makes laws as created by God that limit humanity, and humans discern divine and natural law, and establish positive laws meant to embody only that which is mandated first by God and nature.

In spite of Aquinas's ideas, political philosophies from the fall of the Roman Republic to the birth of the American Republic tended to be marked by kingships and hierarchies rather than a sense of equality. The English society, however, from about the time of the Magna Carta through the English Civil War (discussed below), developed a meaningful use of the concept of equality fundamentally in-line with the classical and Christian notions discussed above.

The Magna Carta made a major contribution to the development of equality, even though it merely granted some suffrage rights to some English nobles. When subsequent religious and political changes in England would aim for greater equality of common men, the Magna Carta served as a precedent to justify those changes, even if they would go much farther than the Magna Carta had in fomenting equality.

Richard Hooker's 16th-century work, *Of the Lawes of Ecclesiasticall Politie*, provided an important augmentation to the Anglican religious tradition. Hooker's work defended, in the tradition of Aquinas and the scholastics, the notion that revelation and reason worked concomitantly to reveal Truth to humans. His ideas were important in forming the Anglican Church in response to the Catholics and Puritans, both of whom favored a more rigid dependence on revelation. As this formula became influential in 16th-century England, it became an important tool, much as had the Magna Carta, in moderating the behaviors of English monarchs in accordance with the requests of English nobility. In essence, Anglo-Saxon norms—both legal and religious—from the Magna Carta through the Stuart Dynasty enforced the idea that revelation must also be reasonable. This tradition would help the English to effectively combat tyranny in the 17th century, as it provided a basic theoretical gateway to the development of the modern view of equality.

Modern Views on Equality

During the early Modern era, a new political philosophy called "the divine right of kings" emerged to combat the limitations that sometimes hampered medieval kings. Its proponents, such as the Stuart kings of England, said that kings were endowed by God with the right to rule their kingdoms authoritatively. The subjects of kings were bound by this divine dispensation to whatever policies the king might decide upon. As you can see, the ancient idea that all citizens of a city possessed an essential and natural equality to one another had vanished; the appeals for reason by the Scholastics and by Hooker were downplayed; the king was endowed by God to do whatever he pleased, regardless of what would be naturally best for his society.

Many of the arguments for equality that most impacted America were developed in England as a response to the "Divine Right of Kings." England had been embroiled in a Civil War from 1643 to 1649, which concluded with the execution of King Charles I and the temporary institution of a republic in England, which would last for about 10 years before the monarchy was re-instituted. During this time Thomas Hobbes wrote his famous work, *Leviathan*.

Hobbes developed an influential argument for government based upon consent. Hobbes begins by describing a "state of nature"; he argues that in a state without government we would be both "free" and "equal." In many ways our contemporary preoccupation with political equality begins in this work. Many modern thinkers following Hobbes also began from this template that man is primordially free and equal. In Hobbes's state of nature, however, freedom means that individuals would be free to kill one another. Equality means that individuals had relatively equal capacities to do so. Hobbes's well-known dictum, therefore, is that life in such a state would have been "solitary, nasty, poor, brutish, and short."

Hobbes develops this argument further by suggesting that individuals in such a state would eagerly find ways to improve their condition, and one way to do so would be to form agreements among themselves for protection. Individuals might agree to transfer some of their natural rights (he echoes Cicero with this lingo), such as the right to protect themselves if attacked to someone who could determine fault, to punish aggressors, and to deter future crime. In short, they could agree to form a government to protect themselves.

Hobbes is amongst the first modern thinkers to argue for the concept of popular sovereignty, which has been discussed throughout this volume. The government exists because the people will it. His work is especially helpful in clarifying that popular sovereignty is the linchpin in the relationship between individual autonomy and governmental authority. Though people had to relinquish the freedoms and equalities they had in the state of nature, the new government is justified because it is freely chosen by a body of equals.

In the end, Hobbes makes a compelling argument for a government based on equality. Without government, equality would only serve to harm us as individuals. The symbolic title, Leviathan, the biblical "king of the children of pride," is a way for Hobbes to note that the pride associated with human nature would lead to perpetual conflict without government to define justice and to legislate accordingly. However, Hobbes presented a limited view of equality in his work—it applied to the state of nature and to the moment when government was created. Once government was created through consent, the tone of Hobbes's argument changed. He suggested that an instituted governmental authority should be nearly absolute. Today's civil liberties like freedom of speech are completely absent from Hobbes. In fact, he isn't particularly clear about whether he favors a democracy or a kingship, and scholars continue to debate which side in the English Civil War he had intended to support with this work. His contemporaries believed him to be supporting the monarchy, and he suffered a very poor reputation in England for several generations.

Although Hobbes did not necessarily argue for any one form of government in *Leviathan*, Locke built on his idea of equality and thereby cultivated the modern era's insistence on political equality by his insistence that no one may be above the law.

Locke wrote about two generations after Hobbes. He penned his famous *Second Treatise* in the early 1680s during the Glorious Revolution, which finally removed the Stuart dynasty. We know that the primary goal of the *Second Treatise* was to cultivate antagonism against the Stuarts. Because England had granted so much political power to the nobility through the Magna Carta centuries prior, the English king could be attacked politically by affecting the outcomes of elections in the English Parliament. It was in these machinations during the 1680s that early political parties developed. The court supported the king, and the country opposed him. Locke's work was among a series of writings designed to foment support amongst everyday Englishmen for the country candidates for Parliamentary seats in the 1680s. Voter turnout in many boroughs had been traditionally very low and had been effectively coordinated by whatever noble possessed local power. The country plan relied upon increasing turnout among the rabble and separating them from their local nobility who supported the king. The electoral scheme worked, and by 1688 the Stuarts were forced to abdicate the throne. William of Orange succeeded them but with new constitutional restraints.

The idea of equality played a critical role in riling these common voters, especially by playing upon the notion that inequality in political representation was tantamount to tyranny. Locke borrowed from Hobbes to develop many of his basic arguments but took them much further than Hobbes had. For instance, Locke too touts the notion that in a primordial state of nature men would be "free" and "equal," but he argues that such a state would not be full of conflict and that life therein would not be as despicable as Hobbes had posited. Because most men are equal, they will realize that attempting to fight with one another would be dangerous. Instead, most of them will abide by the "law of nature," which consisted of refraining from harming others. Only in rare cases would some believe themselves to be superior to others and attempt to assert power over them. In such instances, Locke insists, the reasonability of the state of nature would compel everyone else to join together and defend themselves from this rare nefarious person.

Just as Hobbes had argued, government would evolve as a protective measure against harmful individuals. However, Locke argues that even after a society has been created by consent, the individuals composing it can never renounce the law of nature and are bound by it to overthrow tyrannical rulers if they infringe on "life, liberty, and property." Hence, Locke uses the idea of equality to suggest that all individuals, even kings, must abide by the law of nature, which is more authoritative than any mere king. By forming his argument in this way, Locke was able to effectively and logically attack the "divine right of kingship." Governments are created because of equality but may be overthrown if they violate the basic principle of equality under the law.

Equality in America

The American Founding Fathers relied on Locke's articulation of the essential equality of individuals. During the 1760s and 1770s, American colonists did not tend to view themselves as "Americans." Rather, they still understood themselves to be Englishmen. One of the main ways that they protested the Great Squeeze (the cumbersome series of tax laws passed from 1764 through 1773) was to argue that they were themselves Englishmen and that, as such, they were being denied their due representation in Parliament. Some writers and preachers took to referring to Americans as "the subjects of subjects"—a way of pointing out the fundamental inequality that characterized their relationship to other Englishmen. Though there were many supporters of the king in America during the 1760s and early 1770s, the argument made by supporters of independence that the colonies were being subjected to laws to which they had not consented increasingly gained traction as laws became more burdensome.

The language used to declare independence from England was profoundly inspired by the arguments of Hobbes and Locke, and the influence of their arguments regarding equality and consent are rather obvious in the Declaration's famous first two paragraphs:

> When in the course of human events it becomes necessary for one people to dissolve the political bonds which have connected them to another, and to assume among the powers of earth the separate and equal station to which the laws of nature and of nature's God entitle them, a decent respect to the opinions of mankind require that they state the causes which impel them to separation.

> We hold these truths to be self-evident, that all men are created equal; that they are endowed by their creator with certain inalienable rights; that among these are life, liberty, and the pursuit of happiness; that governments are instituted among men to secure these rights; that when a government fails to do so, it is the right, it is the duty, of the people to alter or to abolish it.

The Founders' interest in equality has been emphasized throughout American history. The triumph of the Democratic-Republican Party in 1800 ushered in a period in which a spirit of equality was prominent in American culture. In the early 1800s, Jefferson removed all taxes that directly affected individuals, and Jackson's famous "bank war" was undertaken in the name of protecting the common man. Both policies exemplify the way in which ideas about limited government were enacted in a spirit of equality during the early-19th century. Alexis de Tocqueville's famous *Democracy in America* was penned during this era, which we generally refer to as the "Era of Good Feelings." Tocqueville observed that "The common man in the United States has understood the influence that general prosperity exercises over his own happiness.... So, in public fortune, he sees his own, and he works for the good of the state." Tocqueville believed this civic attitude animated our ideal of popular sovereignty: "If there is a single country in the world where the true value of the dogma of the sovereignty of the people can be appreciated ... that country is assuredly America."

Behind the equality exhibited through civic participation in the "Era of Good Feelings" loomed the specter of slavery. The incongruence of slavery with the principles articulated in the Declaration came to a head in 1860. Abraham Lincoln's incipient Republican Party was founded on the idea of re-energizing the principle of equality and pointed specifically to the importance of the Declaration when arguing against slavery. He described the Declaration as "pictures of gold" around which the Constitution provided a "frame of silver." The fundamental laws provided by the Constitution existed to glorify the principles of the Declaration. We can see how, in Lincoln's view, the fundamental equality of "all men" animated our fundamental laws, and thereby justified the presidential decisions he made to preserve the Union. He re-emphasized this idea in the Gettysburg address, by declaring that "our nation was *conceived in liberty* but *dedicated to the proposition that all men are created equal.*"

The vision of equality as articulated by Lincoln made a profound impact on subsequent American history. Although both of today's predominant ideological views, conservatism and liberalism, tout versions of the equality of Jefferson and of Lincoln, conservatives and liberals today disagree about the practical implementation of those ideas. These differences can be traced easily to at least the rise of the Progressive Movement of the early-20th century. The Progressives arose in response to the political machines of the late 1800s, a political system dominated by pay-for-play elites and other forms of corruption. Progressives called for Lincoln-style equality as a way of correcting these problems, and have implemented measures to further equality in America from the early-20th century straight through to today. Indeed, progressivism was an important contributing force to the development of modern liberalism today. This influence is evident in a number of salient political issues throughout the 20th and 21st centuries.

Throughout the 20th century more people achieved political equality as they gained access to the political process. The Jim Crow-era obstacles meant to keep blacks from voting were dismantled. Women gained the right to vote in 1920, and eventually eighteen-year-olds would gain voting rights. The change in the method of election for United States Senators in 1917—from state legislature elections to popular elections —was also a progressive idea designed to promote democratic equality. The desegregation movement gained momentum during the Progressive movement and was finally fulfilled in the *Brown* rulings and in the Civil Rights policies of the 1960s. The Civil Rights movement sought specifically to reinvigorate the view of equality that Lincoln had emphasized by citing the Declaration's invocation of equality. Martin Luther King's "I Have a Dream" speech, like Lincoln's Gettysburg Address, also quoted the Declaration's invocation that "all men are created equal."

A number of policy areas throughout the late-20th century were conceived from this progressive heritage. The "Great Society" programs touted by the Johnson administration were implemented with a sociological understanding of crime and urban blight. The fundamental inequality of living conditions and of opportunities to advance out of such conditions buttressed many political initiatives, such as the creation of a cabinet-level agency, Housing and Urban Development, under Johnson. The Civil Rights laws of the late 1960s, moreover, prohibited discrimination by race or sex in a number of important areas of social life, such as employment and housing. More recently, discussions of universal Medicare and other government-directed proposals have evolved from this heritage.

The legacy of Lincoln's emphasis on the Declaration's principle of equality can still be seen in a number of increasingly controversial areas today. The gay rights movement of the 2000s is perhaps the best example of such policies today. Contemporary political theoreticians are also finding ways to apply the idea of equality to areas such as animal rights and trans-humanism (the notion of recognizing human attributes in artificial intelligence) as well. Cultural arguments about diversity, open-borders, and anti-bullying initiatives in schools are all manifestations of a deep American desire to facilitate equality.

It was, however, precisely this view of thorough and unfettered equality that had been rejected by classical and Christian thinkers. **Many scholars further contend that the emphasis seen in the Declaration on equality is more in-line with the classical view of limited equality than with the thorough equality that has emerged in the 20th century.** Indeed, it referenced the equality of men under law, and not the equal distribution of rights and property throughout every demographic within society.

Conservative arguments in this area, therefore, often invoke the language of equality as well, and posit that equality does not truly mean all that it has come to represent to modern liberals today. It is indeed noteworthy, if not confusing, that American conservatives also reference equality and Lincoln's philosophy in presenting the conservative view of equality. The "Equal Protection" clause of the 14th Amendment was designed to assure that formerly enslaved blacks were granted protection under the laws, a legal protection that is entirely consistent with today's conservative interpretation of the Declaration's view of equality. It is on this more basic view of equality as meaning that individuals should be treated equally under the law, as articulated by both the classic and modern influences discussed above, that conservatives and liberals today can agree on.

But the application of this legal doctrine to new and controversial claims of attributes of individual identity that should facilitate legal protections, such as homosexuality, creates conflicts with the long-standing First Amendment religious protections of Christians and others. This conflict between views of what attributes of one's identity should be viewed as the linchpin for equality in our country is a frequent and usually salient political issue. These fights frequently occur in our state legislatures, sometimes in Congress, and sometimes even in the Supreme Court of the United States. Indeed, a bevy of Supreme Court rulings have concerned the application of the equal protection clause, and the expansive nature of these cases speaks to just how important and controversial the concept of equality is in American society. One prominent and recent Supreme Court ruling, *Masterpiece Cakeshop v. Colorado Civil Rights Commission*, concerned a case in which a Christian baker in Colorado was sued by a gay couple when he refused for religious reasons their request for a wedding cake. The baker in this case argued that coercing him to violate his own religious beliefs was prioritizing gay rights ahead of his First Amendment free exercise of religion. In this case, both the baker and couple viewed their religious and sexual identities respectively as that attribute of their identities that should qualify their actions for legal protection on the basis of equal treatment. This conflict is difficult to disentangle as it involves contradicting claims to equal treatment, both of which are supported by different areas of law—the First Amendment and a Colorado state law, respectively; indeed, the Court tailored a very narrow ruling in this case, thereby refusing to pen a ruling that would deal broadly with such conflicts. We might expect quite a few more legal fights before this particular issue is settled. Such conflicts and outcomes should be expected in our often polarized contemporary society.

The thorough equality of liberals and the limited equality under the law of conservatives accentuate different elements of individuality and of society—they ask us to conceive of *homonoia* in different ways. And because equality is so important to all Americans, we are not quick to let go of our beliefs when we believe that equality has been wrongly defined or inappropriately applied in our society. In America, I am wont to conceive of anything throughout our history that has been of greater perennial concern to us than figuring out how to fulfill the Declaration's proclamation that "all men are created equal."

Changes in laws and the courts' interpretations of them through time provide different perspectives of equality that benefit various groups in our system at various points in time. When an attempt to benefit one group stretches too far, as we may be seeing in the current cases discussed above, our system provides various opportunities for our policies to balance themselves in the interest of equality and fairness. In America, equality is not merely an ideological catch-word used to justify our political prerogatives. In America, equality is evident in the fact that it is "we the people" who regularly voice our consent or opposition to the functioning of government and to the ideological notions represented therein. We are most equal in our ability to contemplate, discuss, vote, and share in the fate that we create for ourselves.

So, given that there has been an evident ebbing and flowing between the conservative and liberal emphases in equality in recent years, can we make any solid determinations about the general direction of equality in America over time? One basic observation seems appropriate. The general thrust of the American disposition toward equality was adequately described by Lincoln as one of dedication. There is not a major ideological current in America that does not endorse equality as one of its most fundamental tenets. This does not mean that there is unanimous agreement about exactly what equality means. Although there has traditionally been and there is presently much partisan wrangling to specifically define equality for our society, this fighting is often a contest over the same goal. By the time the political process has settled issues pertinent to equality, it is in the long run on the side of more and not less equality. English Tyranny was undone by the Declaration and by the Constitution, which enshrined its proclamation of natural equality; slavery was undone by an Amendment to that Constitution; Jim Crow and *Plessey*—do note the "separate *but equal*" language in that decision—gave way eventually to Civil Rights and *Brown*. When equality is viewed as beyond the partisan fighting about it, we may see quite clearly how meaningfully it has animated American history for the better.

RECOMMENDED READING

Plato, *The Republic*

Aristotle, *The Politics*

Cicero, *On the Republic* and *On the Laws*

Thomas Hobbes, *Leviathan*

John Locke, *The Second Treatise of Government*

Alexis de Tocqueville, *Democracy in America*

THE
DECLARATION
OF
INDEPENDENCE

By Anthony M. Joseph, PhD

PROFESSOR OF EARLY AMERICAN HISTORY

Like a celebrity known and admired by millions, the Declaration of Independence would seem to need no introduction. Most Americans understand what the Declaration of Independence accomplished on that portentous July day in 1776: Thirteen British colonies in North America confirmed in writing their separation from the British government and their new status as an independent nation on the world stage. But what more, if anything, did the Declaration mean?

The Declaration of Independence operated on at least two levels and understanding them will help raise your regard for the Declaration above a mere celebrity crush. The Declaration, first, provided a public record of a debate between the Americans and the British government over the meaning of the British Constitution. That debate was rooted in the politics of the British Empire and had been going on full-steam for more than a decade by the time the Declaration was drafted. Second, the

Declaration of Independence offered a political theory it held to be applicable to all times and places. That theory, known as the "social contract," made the consent of the people and the protection of their rights essential to the relationship between a government and its people. It defended a people's right to revolution in the event that a government failed to protect those rights.

The Declaration of Independence was thus a document centrally placed in the political maelstrom of the year 1776 and a statement of timeless political values. These two distinct dimensions in the document can sometimes give it a two-toned appearance. Some, preferring one tone over the other, have reduced the Declaration to a lifeless (albeit well-preserved) artifact of the past. Others, with an opposite preference, have converted it into an all-purpose instrument for radical change with little connection to its own history. In reality, the words of the Declaration of Independence remain today just what they were in 1776. Those words both justified American independence in a particular historical moment and carried a claim of universal truth that shaped the American constitutional order for the next two centuries and beyond.

The Coming of War—and Independence

The particular historical moment was the constitutional debate between the colonies and the British government. We cannot describe here the full history of that debate, but some sense of its basic shape is necessary to understand the structure and argument of the Declaration of Independence. An effective place to start is the Boston Tea Party of 1773. This bold colonial challenge to British authority worsened relations between the two sides and put them both on a course of war.

In late November 1773, the first of three tea ships of the British East India Company arrived at Boston. Under the Tea Act passed by Parliament earlier that year, the ship had 20 days to pay the tax on its cargo of tea or face seizure by customs officials. Even if the ship returned to England without unloading the tea, the law required payment of the tax before departure. Boston radicals, however, were determined to prevent payment of the tea tax under any circumstances. On December 16, just before the 20 days was to expire, about 50 men disguised as Indians boarded the three tea ships (the other two having arrived as well) and methodically threw all of their 342 tea chests overboard. With hundreds of Bostonians looking on, British troops and the Royal Navy decided not to intervene.

The Boston Tea Party incensed British political opinion. The British government did not let the misdeed pass. Initially, the government tried to prosecute the offenders, and even took some testimony. But the evidence proved insufficient to even bring the case to trial—Bostonians were unwilling to identify the culprits. Parliament, outraged by colonial lawlessness, enacted in early 1774 a series of four "Coercive Acts" intended to pull up the resistance root and branch. Two of the measures applied directly to Massachusetts. The Boston Port Act provided for the closure of the city's port unless and until the dumped tea was paid for (it was worth some £16,000). Bostonians refused to pay for the tea, and the port was promptly closed in June 1774. Parliament also passed the Massachusetts Government Act. This law converted the Massachusetts council from an elected to an appointed body and limited the colony's cherished town meetings to one per year unless the governor explicitly allowed more. The measure applied only to Massachusetts but threatened the rights of all the colonies: if Parliament could alter the government of Massachusetts, it could alter the government of any colony—even to the point of abolishing its elected assembly. To the colonists, Parliament seemed determined to deprive them of their constitutional "rights of Englishmen." To Parliament, by contrast, the Coercive Acts simply laid down the law: the colonies must submit to Parliament's rightful authority.

The Boston Tea Party also worked an important change upon the heart and mind of King George III. The king was a man of real cultivation and breadth of outlook. He knew French, German, and even some Italian. He had active interests in science, art, and music. Widely read, George III was an inveterate book collector. His personal library ultimately grew to the 65,000 volumes that became the founding collection of the British Library. This cultured young king was all of 22 years old when he ascended the throne in 1760, and he wisely left the details of American governance to his ministers. When he did express a view, though, it was often sympathetic to American grievances against Parliament. He said that the Stamp Act of 1765 was "abundant in absurdities" for first hampering the colonists' trade and then taxing it. He discouraged Parliament from altering colonial charters, noting that doing so "is at all times an odious measure." He even proposed an exemption on the tea tax for any colony that faithfully paid the remaining taxes levied by Parliament.

But the Boston Tea Party soured George III on the Americans and he never turned sweet again. Like Parliament itself, the king had no tolerance for Boston's law-breaking. George III came to believe that the British government had been too lenient with the colonies and now needed to take a firm, hard line toward them. In the aftermath of the Tea Party, the king strongly supported passage of the Coercive Acts and affirmed Parliament's claim of supremacy over the colonies. He believed the submission of the colonies was absolutely necessary to secure not only the authority of the Parliament but also the authority of the monarchy and the British Constitution itself. By 1775, George III had actually raced ahead of more cautious ministers and members of Parliament who still sought reconciliation with the Americans. Once on the gentler side of royal power, he had become a determined advocate of the use of force instead.

The turning of the king against the American cause was ultimately an essential step toward American independence. Because Americans viewed the king as their sovereign, they would have to declare independence from *him*, not from Parliament. And as long as Americans believed that the king was, at the very least, a neutral arbiter of their dispute against Parliament, independence was impolitic—a solution that did not fit the problem. In 1774, in fact, the colonists had not yet reached the conclusion that the king was willfully engaged in forcing their submission. When that realization did come, however, the colonists discovered the sovereign from whom they could declare themselves independent. He had been waiting for them since the early months of 1774.

One of the first actions George III took after enactment of the Coercive Acts was to appoint General Thomas Gage, who had once commanded the British Army in America, as governor of Massachusetts. The gloves were now off. Gage tried to make the new government under the Massachusetts Government Act work, but the king's appointed councilors refused to serve, and the members of the legislature refused to come when Gage called them into session. In the colony's courts, jurors refused to take the oath of allegiance to the new government. Meanwhile, in Philadelphia, representatives from each colony met for the first time as the Continental Congress. Their purpose was not to plan a war or revolution, but to complain. The Congress declared its opposition to all Parliamentary legislation concerning the "internal affairs" of the colonies, from the Stamp Act of 1765 to the Massachusetts Government Act of 1774.

The British government was no more intent on war than the Congress was. But given the objectives of both sides, violence was almost inevitable, and it came in April 1775. Preparing to defend themselves against British troops, colonists had built up a supply of arms at Concord, about 20 miles northwest of Boston. General Gage ordered some of his troops to seize the supplies. But the colonials were soon informed of the order, probably by Gage's own wife, the New Jersey native Margaret Kemble Gage. At dawn on April 19, some 700 British troops encountered 70 colonial militiamen at Lexington, about halfway between Boston and Concord. The militiamen were ordered to disperse, and they began to comply. But then a shot rang out—it was never clear from whom—and the British opened fire. At Lexington, 17 colonists became the first casualties of the Revolutionary War.

The British moved on to Concord, where they found most of the supplies gone. They burned what was left before encountering militiamen at Concord Bridge. Three British soldiers were killed there and, as the regulars headed back to Boston, they got hit by sniper fire all along the way. When it was all over, the British had lost some 275 men—almost three times as many as the colonists had.

Things did not get any better for the British when they reached Boston. On June 17, 1775, they launched an attack on colonial resisters at Breed's Hill, across Boston Harbor. The British succeeded in taking the hill, but only at the cost of more than 1,000 casualties, more than twice the losses suffered by the resisters. The battle was named after the largest hill of the area, Bunker Hill. It was such a costly victory for the British that it amounted almost to a colonial victory instead. The British had wanted to teach the untrained colonials a lesson, but instead those colonials had bloodied one of the finest armies in the world.

This was a war, definitely—but not yet a War of Independence. Both sides, in fact, hoped for some sort of reconciliation. Parliament had already approved the Conciliatory Proposal (February 27, 1775). Under this offer, Parliament agreed not to tax any colony that paid its share of the cost of defense and of salaries for royal officials such as governors and judges. The proposal seemed reasonable on its face. But the Continental Congress quickly rejected it. The proposal did not state the amounts each colony was expected to pay. Nor did it guarantee that Parliament would never tax the colonies. The plan fell far short of a Parliamentary acknowledgement that it had no constitutional right to tax or legislate for the colonies. And that is what the colonies insisted on.

The Continental Congress responded with its own effort at reconciliation, the Olive Branch Petition (July 8, 1775). The petition was addressed to King George III and asked that he mediate the dispute between Parliament and the colonies and stop all military action against the colonists. The petition reflected at least the public position of the American resistance: that King George III was the constitutionally neutral, common superior to both Parliament and the colonies and a potential ally in their grievances.

Whatever Americans may have believed privately about King George, the image of him as neutral arbiter was shattered by his response to the Olive Branch Petition. George III refused to even hear the Olive Branch Petition read out to him. With news of the Battle of Bunker Hill still ringing in his ears, the king instead issued a Proclamation of Rebellion (August 23, 1775), which formally declared the colonies in rebellion and commanded "all our Officers, civil and military" and even "all our subjects" to actively "suppress such rebellion, and to bring the traitors to justice." Rather than call off the dogs, George III affirmed the British military effort and ordered more of the same.

The Proclamation of Rebellion, certainly contrary to the king's intention, was another crucial leap forward on the road to American independence. It gave colonists who began to favor independence a huge new argument for the persuading of skittish American fence-sitters. The argument was straightforward: The king has broken away from us; we are now free to break away from him. That argument was founded on a widely accepted principle of English common law: *allegiance and protection are reciprocal duties.* Subjects owed the king their allegiance, while the king owed his subjects protection. The greatest luminaries of the common law tradition affirmed this dual obligation. Sir Edward Coke, in the famous *Calvin's Case* (1608), had explained that "as the subject oweth to the King his true and faithful ligeance and obedience, so the Sovereign is to govern and protect his subjects." More than a century later, William Blackstone, whose *Commentaries on the Laws of England* (1765–1769) became standard reading for budding lawyers on both sides of the Atlantic, noted that "Allegiance is the tie, or *ligamen,* which binds the subject to the king, in return for that protection which the king affords the subject."

This principle of reciprocal obligation could not alone justify American independence. For the relationship between king and subject could be understood as natural and therefore unalterable. Indeed, Blackstone, an ardent supporter of Parliamentary supremacy, asserted that the allegiance of a subject was perpetual and could not be abandoned except with the consent of a national legislature.

By the time of the American Revolution, however, an important addition to the principle had become widely accepted: a *right of withdrawal.* This right was grounded in the theory of the "social contract," an Enlightenment view that gained favor across Europe in the 18th century. In the English-speaking world, the theory was most closely associated with the English philosopher John Locke. **According to the social contract, government ruled by the consent of the governed in a kind of voluntary contract between the two parties. And, as with contracts generally, the violation of the terms by either party justified withdrawal from the contract by the party wronged.** Hence if a monarch withdrew his protection, his subjects could legitimately withdraw their allegiance. Subjects did not have the right to withdraw for trivial reasons, but a general loss of protection from the king would be sufficient cause.

We can see, then, how Americans welded together the ideas of allegiance, protection, and contract to create their case for independence. In declaring the colonies in rebellion, King George III had withdrawn his protection. The colonists, by the social contract, were now morally free to withdraw their allegiance and declare themselves independent. The king had laid the moral grounds for American independence in his Proclamation of Rebellion of August 1775.

Two months later, George III built on that foundation by telling Parliament that the Americans intended to establish "an independent Empire." Their "strong protestations of loyalty to me," he lamented, were "meant only to amuse." Soon Parliament took a similar line, enacting the Prohibitory Act in December 1775. This law ordered a blockade of American ports and the seizure of American ships and goods as if the colonies were "open Enemies" of the king. William Drayton, a South Carolina judge, concluded that the law had effectively "released America from Great-Britain" by declaring the colonies "out of the Protection" of the king and "actually dissolving" the contract between the king and the American people. Such sentiments became widespread in America over the course of 1775 and early 1776.

The loss of royal protection was, indeed, only one piece of the picture that Americans saw. Americans also believed that the British government, far from being toppled by rebellious Americans, was bringing about its own dissolution in the colonies. John Locke had explained that a government is dissolved when officials of the government act in violation of the Constitution and laws of the nation. The government in such a case is dissolved not from below (by the people) but from above (by the government itself). This understanding helps explain what the Declaration of Independence actually declared when it finally came in July 1776. The Americans considered British government in the colonies *already* dissolved by the British government itself. The Declaration formalized a dissolution of government wrongfully initiated and completed by the king and Parliament.

It was this work of dissolution that was in fact the real rebellion. For Locke had also argued that the true rebels in any conflict were the ones who had violated the constitution, not those who resisted the violation. When Americans applied a Lockean lens to the events of 1775–1776, they saw the rebellion of Parliament and king set against their own rightful resistance. "They are rebels who arm against the constitution," the *New York Constitutional Gazette* asserted in 1775, "not they who defend it by arms." Such language, of course, did not make its way into the text of the Declaration of Independence. The Declaration charged the king with attempting tyranny, not rebellion. But the moral force of the idea of dissolution and rebellion from above can be felt in much of the text. **British officials had rebelled against the very constitution they were supposed to uphold and had brought their own government down. The Declaration of Independence simply acknowledged these sad facts and cleared the way for a new government to take its place.**

At the time of the Proclamation of Rebellion, of course, the Declaration of Independence was nearly a year away. American opinion on independence continued to be divided, and it was impossible to fight a war for independence when so many colonists did not favor it. In most of the Thirteen Colonies, royal government broke down over the course of 1775–1776 and American resisters built new institutions of government to replace the collapsing edifices of British power. In five colonies, however—all of them in the mid-Atlantic region—assemblies continued to meet under British authority. Political leaders in these colonies formed the main block of resistance to independence. Some cautioned against moving too quickly. James Wilson of Pennsylvania, a future U.S. Supreme Court justice, worried that formally ending royal authority would cause "an immediate dissolution of every kind of authority.... Before we are prepared to build the new house, why should we pull down the old one, and expose ourselves to all the inclemencies of the season?" Others actively sought a way out of the impasse with Parliament. Joseph Galloway, also of Pennsylvania, proposed a colonial national legislature to govern American affairs jointly with Parliament. His proposal was never approved and Galloway himself became a Loyalist. New York's Peter Van Schaak, meanwhile, did not think that Parliament had undertaken a "preconcerted plan of enslaving us" and he therefore could not "think the government *dissolved.*" He also became a Loyalist.

American Loyalists, in fact, slowed the course of independence just as independence-minded patriots impeded efforts to reconcile the colonies to British rule. In the minds of Loyalists, *they* were the true patriots. They loved their country—Britain—and their king. They also believed resistance to the king and Parliament was morally wrong. Most Loyalists opposed Parliament's taxes and other measures, but they did not believe the colonists had a right to resist. The Loyalists' bottom line was that the king and Parliament had to be obeyed, even if they were wrong. War, in the Loyalists' view, would only produce new evils. They envisioned a long Civil War among the colonies if the effort to throw off British rule succeeded.

Estimates vary, but at least one in five Americans remained loyal. Loyalists were a diverse group. Many were government officials who believed their oaths of office compelled them to remain loyal. Many also were religious minorities of one sort or another—people who thought they had something to fear from an increase in the political power of their fellow colonists. Thus, Anglicans in New England, which was dominated by Puritans, tended to be Loyalists, while Anglicans in Virginia, where Anglicanism was the established Church, did not. Many Loyalists were pacifists who were morally opposed to war. Quakers in Pennsylvania were of this sort, though some broke off and supported the war, taking on the name "Free Quakers." African-Americans formed a sizable block of American loyalism. The British offered freedom in exchange for military service and at least 5,000 black Americans took advantage of the offer. Thousands more escaped their American masters and were ultimately evacuated from America by the British at war's end. Loyalists' social and geographic diversity made them an awkward body of colonials for the British to make effective use of. Nonetheless, some 19,000 Loyalists fought for the king in the Revolutionary War, and for much of the conflict, more Loyalists were enlisted in the king's army than patriots in Washington's. But still more Loyalists fled the colonies: some 80,000 departed for other parts of the British Empire, particularly Canada. Thus, the conflict between Loyalists and patriots made the Revolutionary War a civil war and the Declaration of Independence a contested document.

With such extensive opposition to independence—from fence-sitters as well as Loyalists—how did the Continental Congress come to declare independence in July 1776? Americans turned toward independence for an ever-growing list of reasons. First, patriots by mid-1776 had positioned themselves for independence. During the first year of fighting, they had succeeded in wresting military control from the British in each of the Thirteen Colonies. Political control, as we have seen, was harder to come by, but patriots had firm civil authority in eight colonies and powerful influence in those five mid-Atlantic colonies where British rule persisted. Also, the actual fighting hardened colonial opinion against the British. The British Army took on German mercenaries to fight the American resisters—a deep insult to Americans still sensible of their identity as Englishmen. And the British Navy had no qualms about bombarding colonial towns to bring about American submission. The British offer of freedom to slaves, meanwhile, was a profound threat to slaveholders as fear of slave revolts coursed through the southern colonies. With British rule dissolving, slaveholders reasoned, a formal declaration of independence could clear the way for a new government sufficiently strong to discourage slave resistance.

Military and economic concerns also contributed to the move toward independence. Patriot forces were desperate for supplies, and the colonial economy was shaken from the loss of British trade. George Washington was said to believe that "nothing else [but independence] will save us." While the colonies remained formally part of the British Empire, France was unwilling to fully assist them; if they became independent, that aid would be forthcoming. Independence would also free America to enter into trade agreements with other European powers. Independence thus became the necessary means of supplying the patriot army and making up for the loss of British trade. Fittingly, when Richard Henry Lee proposed independence to the Continental Congress on June 7, 1776, he also proposed that the Congress seek foreign alliances. The Declaration of Independence would ultimately reflect these twin concerns. Its conclusion announces independence using Lee's exact language of June 7 (replacing Jefferson's) and then asserts America's right to "contract Alliances."

These reasons for independence did not exhaust the list, however. A declaration of independence would respond affirmatively to the calls for independence coming from the American people. In the spring of 1776, some 90 American communities requested the Continental Congress to declare independence—citing, among other concerns, the king's withdrawal of protection and the political vacuum under which Americans lived until public authority was decisively re-established. The town of Leicester, Massachusetts, lamented the absence of legitimate government in Biblical language: "We are without form, and void, and darkness seems to cover the face of the land." Thomas Paine's *Common Sense*, published in January 1776, exhorted America to take the final step of separation. Paine depicted the British Constitution as a corrupt instrument by which "a Continent" had been "perpetually governed by an island." He urged the Americans to become independent and install on American soil a republic in place of the British monarchy. *Common Sense* became an instant bestseller and its radical perspective quickly worked its way into the American consciousness.

Finally, principles of English law and social contract theory imbued all of these reasons for independence with moral weight, with *gravitas*. Americans believed British actions had compromised the rule of law. The British government had violated its own Constitution. The king had withdrawn his protection and levied war on a people that, despite their grievances, still professed allegiance to him. Put simply, and in Locke's terms, British authority was dissolved from above by British rebels against the British Constitution. Under the social contract, the American people were not bound perpetually to live with that dissolution and rebellion. The contract between government and people was built on consent and mutual obligation: the consent could be withdrawn if the obligation went unfulfilled. Americans therefore had the moral right to separate from the dissolved government and replace it with a new one.

The Making and Meaning
of the Declaration of Independence

This logic of independence unfolded on the political scene in the spring and summer of 1776. On May 15, 1776, the Continental Congress voted to recommend the suppression of royal authority wherever it still existed —a measure aimed at supporting the patriot seizure of power in the mid-Atlantic. On June 7, Richard Henry Lee proposed a resolution that the colonies "are, and of right out to be, free and independent states, that they are absolved from all allegiance to the British Crown, and that all political connection between them and the State of Great Britain is, and ought to be, totally dissolved." The resolution was debated on June 8 and 10. Congress then postponed the matter for another three weeks. On June 11, however, Congress appointed a Committee of Five to draft a declaration of independence in the event that the Congress ultimately approved Lee's resolution. Years later, in 1805, John Adams recalled that the Committee of Five then appointed both he and Jefferson as a sub-committee to produce a text, and that Jefferson had then assumed the task after Adams declined. In Jefferson's account, by contrast, the Committee of Five appointed Jefferson alone to pen the draft. On balance, Jefferson's recollection is likely the more correct. But Adams's reasons for deferring to Jefferson—that Jefferson was an amiable Virginian who ruffled fewer feathers and wrote "ten times better" than Adams—may well have been similar to the full committee's reasons for appointing Jefferson. In any case, Thomas Jefferson was certainly the primary author of the original draft.

For the next two weeks, and amidst other pressing duties in Congress, Jefferson wrote a first draft of the declaration, received edits from both John Adams and Benjamin Franklin, incorporated further edits from the Committee of Five, and finally submitted on June 28 a revised draft to the full Congress for its consideration. The actual writing of the text may have taken him, as Adams later reported, "a day or two." Given Jefferson's productivity on other fronts, it certainly seems unlikely that he remained tied to his desk, quill in hand, for days on end refining the document. On July 2 the Continental Congress unanimously approved independence and then began considering Jefferson's draft. The delegates proved to be aggressive editors. By the time they were done one-fourth of the text had been stricken. Inelegant expressions were improved, needlessly harsh language softened, and untenable assertions corrected.

Congress's most significant change to Jefferson's draft was the complete elimination of his knife-sharp, 169-word attack on the British slave trade. Jefferson had charged the king with cruelly capturing a "distant people" who had "never offended him"; preserving a market for their sale and purchase; and using the royal veto to prevent legislation that would end or at least restrain "this execrable commerce." To complete the "assemblage of horrors," the king was now exciting the slaves to murder the colonists— "paying off" his crimes against the "*liberties* of one people" with crimes against the "*lives* of another." The Continental Congress, however, had no wish to see the history of British American slavery laid out thus, and instead inserted elsewhere in the text the less problematic charge that the king had "excited domestic insurrections among us," which referenced British efforts to arm both the slave and Loyalist populations in the colonies. The removal of Jefferson's passage against slavery would have portentous consequences for the American constitutional order. The excision deprived the Declaration of Independence of its most pointed argument for the liberty of all people within the borders of the United States. For generations, the Declaration's affirmation that "all men are created equal" was often read, in the absence of any declamation against slavery, as a mere platitude.

Two remaining passages of some length were also stricken by the full Congress. Both chastised the British people. In the first, Jefferson acknowledged that the Americans and their "British brethren" had both "adopted one common king" but he also insisted that "submission to their parliament was no part of our constitution." In the second, Jefferson blamed the British people for re-electing the "disturbers of our harmony" and allowing the British government to send Britons as well as foreign mercenaries to "invade and destroy us." Congress shortened and softened Jefferson's words—saying that the British people had proved "deaf" to America's claims and that the Americans were forced to "acquiesce in the necessity" of separation. Jefferson complained, of course, but the cuts were not only judicious but politic: Congress did not want to alienate any remaining supporters of the American cause in England.

On July 4, only two days after taking up Jefferson's draft, Congress approved the final text of the Declaration of Independence. News of the approval spread quickly, and public readings and celebrations followed as the document itself came into distribution. Jefferson himself was disgruntled at the changes made to his work and circulated copies of his own original draft as a final lament against his editors. His behavior was in permissibly bad taste, for he remained the Declaration's primary author, despite Congress's editorship. But what had Jefferson—and Congress—wrought?

The Declaration of Independence is not a simple stream of inspirational phrases about freedom. Its three main parts include philosophical maxims, constitutional claims, and political reflections that cohere into a single powerful rhetorical whole. The *preamble* asserts and explains the political theory on which American independence is based. The *charge and facts against the king* accuse George III of attempting an "absolute tyranny" and offer a list of constitutional misdeeds as evidence. The *conclusion* describes Americans' failed attempts to persuade Britain of the rightness of their cause before declaring that "all political connection" with Britain "is and ought to be totally dissolved."

The most famous part of the Declaration of Independence is the preamble. The preamble begins by stating the need to declare the causes that "impel" the colonies to separate from Britain. It then packs the powerful punch of a series of "self-evident" truths. Jefferson had originally described these truths as "sacred and undeniable" but one of his editors, possibly Benjamin Franklin, substituted "self-evident" instead. In the understanding of the time, self-evident truths were truths knowable by reason. Hence the Declaration immediately claimed a rational foundation for the truths that would follow. And since all human beings were held to possess the power of reason, the

Declaration was also asserting the universality of its truths—applicable to all peoples and nations, not just America and Britain.

The first truth, that "all men are created equal," was a commonplace of Christian reflection and Enlightenment political theory. God had instituted a natural equality among human beings. How Jefferson reconciled slaveholding with this equality is a puzzle that no amount of historical explanation can entirely solve. We can hardly propose that Jefferson was simply "a man of his time." For an English court in 1772 had declared that no argument from "natural" principles could provide legal sanction to slavery. And Massachusetts's Supreme Court would soon determine that the state's bill of rights, in declaring that all men were born "free and equal," prohibited slavery. And yet the centuries-old assertion of natural equality had frequently been considered consistent with various forms of inequality rooted in particular human cultures and institutions. In this respect, the acceptance of slavery by defenders of human equality was nothing new. Jefferson's assertion of human equality was in fact primarily a nod to contract theory: natural equality is what human beings have before they create government: each is equal in liberty, with none subject to the will of another. The Declaration attributes this individual liberty to the American people as a whole. It envisions a return to a state of equality between the American people and the rest of the world. America would no longer be a subordinate member of the British Empire but rather, in the Declaration's language, a "separate and equal" nation.

Equality also meant the equal possession of "unalienable Rights," including (but not limited to) "Life, Liberty, and the pursuit of Happiness." Here again Jefferson appealed to a substantial Western tradition. Unalienable rights were more than rights that could not be taken away: they were rights that could not be *given* away—not even with the consent of their possessor. For our rights were granted by God so that we might fulfill our

God-ordained duties to sustain our life and to seek our own well-being, our "happiness." To willfully forego our rights would be to incapacitate ourselves to do our duty. Hence our rights could not be given up any more than our duties could be. Both rights and duties were non-transferrable. In 1776, this understanding of rights had been most recently articulated by the Swiss natural law theorist Jean-Jacques Burlamaqui. Jefferson some years before had purchased a French edition of Burlamaqui's *Natural and Politic Law* and in any case was familiar with Burlamaqui's thought from James Wilson's *Considerations on the Nature and Extent of Legislative Authority of the British Parliament* (1774), which relied on Burlamaqui and which Jefferson had read.

Inalienable rights could not be fundamentally secured, however, simply by not giving them up. Men instituted government to protect them. But when a government became "destructive" of those rights, the people had the right "to alter or to abolish it, and to institute new government." Such a right should not be exercised lightly, the Declaration cautions, but when "a long train of abuses and usurpations" shows an intent to create an "absolute despotism," the people have not only the right but also the duty "to throw off such Government, and to provide new Guards for their future security."

Taken as a whole, the preamble so faithfully illustrates social contract theory that Jefferson has been accused of copying John Locke. Indeed, the phrase "long train of abuses and usurpations" is found in Locke's *Second Treatise of Government*. However, Jefferson himself never confirmed a unique connection between his Declaration and John Locke. The Declaration, he said, was founded on the "harmonizing sentiments of the day," available in conversation as well as written works, though he "turned neither to book nor pamphlet" in composing his draft. Given the time constraints Jefferson faced in June 1776, we have no reason to doubt him. Jefferson did make substantial use of George Mason's draft of the Virginia

Declaration of Rights. Jefferson's preamble contains similar ideas and similar language to the Virginia Declaration.

At a deeper level, however, both declarations drew from a fountain of Western thought that included authors whose ideas were appropriated and reused across the centuries until it became unclear to whom those ideas should be most closely attached. By 1776, the Lockean social contract had become clay in the hands of innumerable theorists, at least some of whom Jefferson was certainly familiar with, such as Burlamaqui and the Italian penal reformer Cesare Beccaria. The "happiness" of Jefferson's preamble, too, finds a place not only in Locke but in the Scottish philosopher Francis Hutcheson and European theorists who understood the promotion of happiness as an obligation of government. In short, a great many political writers of the revolutionary era could and did reference the ideas found in Jefferson's preamble. These ideas were on the tips of many pens.

Whatever Jefferson's sources for the preamble, the theory of government found therein is foundational to the American constitutional order. The preamble defines equality as a fact of our creation by God—an undeniable, unchangeable, "self-evident" fact. As we have seen, the preamble did not guarantee social or economic equality but did hold out the promise of a civic equality grounded on a natural equality to which, in the event of a failure of government, we could return. Further, the preamble defined life, liberty, and the pursuit of happiness as unalienable rights, and intimated that additional unnamed rights were also unalienable. And the government was obliged to protect all of these rights. If it failed to do so, the people had the right to alter or even abolish it. The preamble's articulation of rights ultimately found its way into the U.S. Constitution, both as originally ratified and as subsequently amended by the Bill of Rights. The right to abolish a government is the only preamble right that finds no home in the U.S. Constitution, for no constitution provides for its own destruction.

Even so, the Constitution does provide for its own amendment—making it possible to channel dissent against government into peaceful rather than violent change.

The preamble is the most cited portion of the Declaration of Independence today. In 1776, however, what followed the preamble drew the most attention—from Jefferson, from the Continental Congress, from everyone then living through the revolutionary drama. Having established the people's right to abolish a government that fails to secure their rights, the Declaration proceeds to charge the British government with that very failure. The focus was on the failure of the king, who is charged with attempting to establish an "absolute tyranny" over America.

That basic charge is then backed up with "facts," a long laundry list of 19 wrongs committed by the king or his agents—including his governors, his Parliament, and his military officers. To create this list, Jefferson made use of his own draft of the Virginia Constitution, which included a similar though somewhat shorter set of facts. Some of the facts charged in the Declaration seemed then and now to be vague, overly broad, or local to the point of obscurity. The very first fact, for example, charged that the king had "refused his assent to laws the most wholesome and necessary for the public good." Jefferson may have been comfortable with such an unspecified charge on the example of the English Declaration of Right (1689), which made a similarly broad charge against King James II. But what particular laws had George III refused? Thomas Hutchinson, a Loyalist and former governor of Massachusetts, speculated that Jefferson may have had in mind the British restrictions on the issuing of paper money in the colonies, but Hutchinson, close as he was to the American political scene, could not be sure. The charge was an apt beginning, Hutchinson declared, to the Declaration's "list of imaginary grievances." Other facts referenced events in particular colonies. The fourth fact, that the king had called legislatures to meet "at places unusual, uncomfortable, & distant" from their public records, was probably a reference to the moving of the Massachusetts assembly to Cambridge in 1768 on account of political discord in Boston.

After the philosophical heights of the preamble, the Declaration here seemed to be descending into the weeds of politics, all of which, as the saying goes, is local. But we must keep in mind that, however minute or unclear these facts may appear now, they were valuable to the Declaration's overall objective. Jefferson was in effect a lawyer laying out a case of "breach of contract" against the king (in English common law, the "declaration" was the first pleading submitted by the plaintiff). Jefferson thus had no interest in omitting any violation. He faced no risk in charging innumerable facts against the king so long as the facts were credible and at least some of them *stuck*.

Perhaps the most important fact charged was the 13th: that the king had "combined with others to subject us to a jurisdiction foreign to our constitution and unacknowledged by our laws; giving his assent to their acts of pretended legislation." Here the Declaration references the statutes enacted by Parliament. But why does the text not identify Parliament by name? The historian Carl Becker suggested long ago that the omission was deliberate. The Americans, Becker explained, so ardently rejected Parliament's claim of authority that they ignored "the very name" of the offending institution. And by abstractly referring to a "foreign jurisdiction," they showed that their case for independence was built on universal natural rights rather than the British Constitution. Becker surely overstated his point, as the passage makes explicit reference to "our constitution." Even so, the omission of the name of Parliament was consistent with Jefferson's effort to ground American independence *partly* on universal principles. No people could legitimately be made to submit to a "jurisdiction foreign" to them.

But what about that reference to "our constitution"? As with the preceding facts, the 13th fact charges violations of the British Constitution. What follows the 13th fact is a series of nine examples of Parliament's unconstitutional legislation, including its imposition of taxes without consent and its tampering with colonial charters. Strangely, the list of objectionable measures is not arranged in chronological order. Historian Pauline Maier has suggested that Jefferson arranged them instead in order of increasing gravity so as to maximize their rhetorical impact. Certainly, the scope of the measures cited expands: the first concerns the quartering of troops (Quartering Acts of 1765 and 1774) while the last cites Parliament's claim of the right to legislate for the colonies "in all cases whatsoever" (Declaratory Act, 1766). Whether the arrangement was intended for rhetorical effect or not, the 13th fact, with its nine subsidiary facts, is the heart of the Declaration's constitutional argument. No reader of the Declaration who did not accept the 13th fact could be much moved by what came before or after. The prior facts charging royal misconduct could be dismissed as temporary, remediable wrongs. The subsequent facts charging British warmaking on the colonies could be turned on their head and taken to describe the rightful suppression of a rebellion. The 13th fact contained the central constitutional quarrel regarding Parliament's authority over the colonies.

The 19 facts charged against the king constitute the largest section of the Declaration of Independence—the great ox's back of the document. They reflect the concern of Jefferson and the Continental Congress with the British Constitution and its violation by king and Parliament. However, we should view the Declaration as a single whole composed of the preamble, the charge and supporting facts, and the conclusion: independence. It is impossible to make sense of the Declaration of Independence without keeping this unity firmly in view. The Declaration is not merely an appeal to natural rights and Lockean contract theory. Nor is it merely an argument that king and Parliament violated the British Constitution. It is both of these things. It makes a Lockean argument by means of a constitutional one. King and Parliament broke the contract between the British government and the American people. That contract was the British Constitution. The resolution was to declare the contract dissolved and the Americans independent.

In 1776, the Declaration of Independence simultaneously rendered the colonies independent of the British king and established the United States of America. It also converted the Revolutionary War from a fight for constitutional rights under British rule to a fight for independence. The Declaration did not secure American independence but rather defined what the Americans were fighting for. That fight would go on for another five years. Real political independence would only come in 1783 when a defeated Britain formally recognized the United States in the Treaty of Paris.

The Declaration of Independence is the founding document of our nation. It not only defined the United States in 1776 but made possible the creation of the U.S. Constitution in 1787. It inspired not only the rights then and later incorporated into the Constitution but also, through its emphasis on the "consent of the governed," set the stage for the principle of popular sovereignty that undergirds the Constitution. Ultimately, the American people are in charge of our government.

Since 1776, the Declaration of Independence has undergone numerous changes in its place in American civic life. Independence began to be celebrated annually in 1777, and even on July 4, but initially the Declaration as a document was not central to those celebrations. Republicans began to acclaim the text itself in the 1790s not only for its anti-British posture but for the fundamental political values expressed in its preamble. They also celebrated the leader of their party, Thomas Jefferson himself, as its author. Jefferson for his part wondered "whether my country is the better for my having lived at all?" Initially, he answered, "I do not know that it is." By 1826, however, he counted his authorship of the Declaration as one of three achievements to be inscribed on his tombstone. By that time, too, the Republican Party he founded had become dominant and the esteem the Republicans had generated for the Declaration of Independence was firmly entrenched in American political life.

Henceforth the Declaration became an authoritative source for American political values rather than a mere addendum to Fourth of July celebrations. The dispute over slavery in particular brought the Declaration center stage. Abolitionists invoked the Declaration's appeal to human equality and charged Americans with hypocrisy. Slaveholders, meanwhile, clung to the Declaration's Lockean context and understood its principle of equality to be, in John C. Calhoun's words, a "hypothetical truism."

Because the Declaration of Independence ended a government rather than created one, it could not be directly enforced as law, on slavery or any other matter. But Abraham Lincoln laid out the final role of the Declaration of Independence in America's constitutional order. In his 1858 debates against Stephen Douglas, Lincoln insisted that human equality applied to all men—not just to the patriots of 1776. It applied to subsequent immigrants to the United States and to blacks already living in America. Indeed, the Declaration "contemplated the progressive improvement in the condition of all men everywhere." If it had done no more than justify independence in 1776, Lincoln insisted, then the Declaration of Independence was "of no practical use now—mere rubbish." Lincoln made the Declaration a text for all times and places, and especially for all *American* times and places. And, in reality, the Declaration of Independence has continued to inspire reflection, debate, and conflict on the meaning and reach of the American constitutional order, and likely always will, as long as that order endures.

* *

RECOMMENDED READING

Carl Becker, *The Declaration of Independence: A Study on the History of Political Ideas* (Harcourt, Brace & Company, 1922)

Pauline Maier, *American Scripture: Making the Declaration of Independence* (Knopf, 1997)

Morton White, *The Philosophy of the American Revolution* (Oxford, 1978)

Garry Wills, *Inventing America: Jefferson's Declaration of Independence* (1978)

RELIGIOUS
INFLUENCES

THE
ENGLISH
REFORMATION
AND THE
AMERICAN FOUNDING

By John O. Tyler, Jr. JD, PhD

PROFESSOR OF LAW & JURISPRUDENCE

ive principles define the American founding. First, all men are created morally and legally equal. Second, God endows men with
inalienable rights. Third, men establish civil governments through their
own actions. God does not establish kings by divine right. Fourth, the
powers of government depend on the consent of the governed. Fifth,
men may alter or abolish their government if it becomes destructive.

These principles are the product of the English Reformation, a religious
and political struggle that began with John Wycliffe's *On the Lordship
of God* in 1373 and ended with John Locke's *Second Treatise on Civil
Government* and *Letter Regarding Toleration* in 1689. The Reformers' goal
throughout the struggle was the liberty to believe and worship without
coercion from Church or state. This chapter explains how the struggle for

religious liberty in England produced our founding principles by surveying the works of five individuals. Augustine of Hippo (A.D. 354–430) provided the religious and political foundation for the English Reformation. John Wycliffe (1330–1384) and William Tyndale (1494–1536) freed men from the tyranny of popes, and John Milton (1608–1674) and John Locke (1632–1704) freed men from the tyranny of kings.

Augustine

Augustine of Hippo (A.D. 354–430) establishes the theological foundation for the English Reformation with his doctrines of scripture and predestination. Augustine establishes the political foundation for the English Reformation by separating the earthly and spiritual realms in *The City of God* (A.D. 413–427). Augustine's doctrine of scripture holds that scripture is the highest spiritual authority. Scripture is true, *Confessions*, 13.29 (A.D. 397–400), and scripture provides the standard for evaluating other teachings and writings. *Letter 82 to Jerome*, 1.3 (A.D. 405); *Letter 93 to Vincentius*, 10.35–10.45 (A.D. 408). Scripture, and scripture alone, is inerrant. *Letter 82 to Jerome*, 1.3 (A.D. 405). If scripture was not inerrant, the consequences would be disastrous. Every sentence of scripture becomes suspect. *Letter 28 to Jerome*, 3.3 (A.D. 394 or 395).

Augustine describes the predestination of the Elect in four works, *On Grace and Free Will* (A.D. 426), *On Rebuke and Grace* (A.D. 426), *On the Predestination of the Saints* (A.D. 428), and *On the Gift of Perseverance* (A.D. 428). God knew from eternity past that Adam and Adam's descendents would sin. God's foreknowledge, however, did not cause any man to sin. God permitted man to act from free will. Man's sin, inherited from Adam and committed during life, condemns every man to spiritual and physical death.

God is just, and every man's condemnation by sin is just. God has nevertheless resolved to reveal his grace and save some from damnation. God's election of these men is a function of God's grace, not human merit. Human merit is inadequate for salvation. God saves the elect by exercising His grace. All other men are condemned through their own fault.

Augustine separates the earthly and spiritual realms in *The City of God* (A.D. 413–427). The Visigoths under Alaric sacked Rome in 410 B.C. Many claimed the sack of Rome was Rome's punishment for abandoning its traditional religion for Christianity. *The City of God* argues that Christianity was not responsible for the sack of Rome. Human history is a conflict between the earthly City of Man and the spiritual City of God. The City of God will ultimately triumph because Christianity is the true faith.

Augustine contrasts the City of God and the City of Man by describing each city's citizens, dominant love, and virtue. Every person is a citizen of the City of God or the City of Man, but no person is a citizen of both. The City of Man's citizens are fallen men who reject God's love. The effects of sin dominate their lives, and Adam's sin condemns them. The City of God's citizens, however, are regenerated Christians who accept God's love. God's grace overcomes sin's effects. These people are out of place in the world because God is not immediately available for their enjoyment.

The love of self dominates the City of Man. The City of Man builds itself on self-indulgence, lust for material goods, and lust to dominate others. The love of God, however, dominates the City of God. The City of God builds itself on love for one's neighbor. Virtue is absent from the City of Man. Social customs and state coercion are required to enforce good behavior. Virtue is present, however, in the City of God. Good behavior results from God's grace overcoming the effects of sin.

Human government is necessary in the City of Man, but self-love dominates its actions, seeking power and self-aggrandizement. Government in the City of Man is organized oppression, using violence and threats to maintain its power. The City of God, however, has no human political institutions. Although the earthly City of Man and the spiritual City of God exist in wholly separate realms, both Cities share a common interest in promoting good behavior. They should therefore cooperate with each other to produce virtuous citizens.

Augustine's separation of the earthly and spiritual realms in the *The City of God* is metaphorical. John Wycliffe and the Reformers, however, will adapt Augustine's separation of the earthly and spiritual realms to argue for a *literal* separation of secular government from religious institutions.

John Wycliffe

John Wycliffe (1330–1384) was a priest, an Oxford professor, and the most prominent philosopher of his time. The popes in Wycliffe's time claimed to be Christ's representatives on earth, but they behaved like earthly kings. Pope Gregory VII's *Dictatus papae* (Dictates of the Pope) (1075) contains 27 declarations of power establishing a papal monarchy. These include declarations that "All princes shall kiss the feet of the pope alone." No one can judge the pope. The pope alone can depose emperors. The pope alone can make new laws. The Roman Church has never erred and never will err until the end of time.

The *Dictatus papae* claims "the Roman Church was founded solely by God," but Gregory's papal monarchy sacrificed its apostolic voice for earthly wealth and power. By Wycliffe's time the papacy was a spectacularly disgraced institution, utilizing the threat of eternal damnation to exact unquestioning conformity and external compliance. It claimed a monopoly on salvation, and when John XXII became pope in 1316, he developed a widespread system of indulgences that put salvation up for sale.

The Great Schism erupted in 1378, producing two rival popes who devoted their entire energy to destroying their rival. Pope Urban VI proclaimed a crusade against Clement VII and led an army of mercenaries across Italy until his death in 1389. In 1409, an assembly of churchmen at Pisa elected a third pope, Alexander V. Each pope excommunicated the other two.

Wycliffe's works combine a political revolt against the papal monarchy with the restoration of primitive Christian doctrines and practices. Four themes dominate Wycliffe's religious and political thought. Wycliffe's first theme is the authority of scripture. Scripture is absolutely true, divine in origin, and provides the sole authority for Christians and the Church. Wycliffe's second theme is lordship. Lordship is the right to exercise authority and, indirectly, to own property. Lordship depends on God's grace, and man can forfeit lordship by sin. Wycliffe's third theme is the doctrine of the Church. Wycliffe distinguishes the true Church of the elect from the visible, earthly Church. Wycliffe's fourth theme denies the doctrine of transubstantiation. Priests have no divine power to transform bread and wine into the physical body and blood of Christ.

Wycliffe presents his first theme, the authority of scripture, in *De Veritate Sacrae Scripturae* (On the Truthfulness of Holy Scripture) (1378). Wycliffe replaces the authority of the Catholic Church with the authority of scripture. *De Veritate Sacrae Scripturae* makes three significant claims. First, scripture is inerrant. Second, scripture is the measure and norm of all truth and knowledge, and scripture contains all that is necessary to man for salvation. Third, all Christians have a right to read scripture for themselves in their own language. Every believer is a priest, and every believer is capable of understanding the Bible through study, prayer, and faith. The literal sense of the text should always be the starting point of interpretation, and the layman can grasp the right meaning of scripture through the instruction of the Holy Spirit.

Wycliffe's second theme is his doctrine of lordship. *De Dominio Divino* (On the Lordship of God) (1373) provides Wycliffe's prescription for reviving the Church by reforming the clerical hierarchy. *De Civili Dominio* (On Civil Lordship) (1377) provides Wycliffe's prescription for reordering society. Wycliffe builds his theory of lordship on three pillars.

The first pillar of lordship is that all lordship depends on God's grace. No one in mortal sin, including kings and popes, has any right to any power or property from God. Every man who stands in grace, however, receives the right of lordship and possesses every gift of God. God's divine lordship is permanent, but man's civil lordship is transitory and conditioned on service. Kings must serve God, and popes must serve God and their fellow man. Any king, pope, or layman who falls into mortal sin forfeits his lordship and any claim to power or property. Kings who use the land and the Church for their own gain are tyrants. Subjects may resist tyrannical kings with force, particularly if the king endangers his subjects' souls by fostering ecclesiastical decay.

The second pillar of lordship is that a righteous man has lordship of the entire physical world. Even if a righteous man is afflicted in life, he still has true possession of the whole universe. If God gives, he gives abundantly. If a man possesses anything, he possesses everything. All things work together for good to the righteous man. Since there are many righteous men, they own the whole universe in common. This common ownership provides the starting point for John Locke's famous theory of private property. (Locke, *Second Treatise*, §§ 25–32).

The third pillar of lordship is the separation of secular government from religious institutions. Augustine's *City of God* (A.D. 413–426) describes a *metaphorical* separation of the secular and spiritual realms. Wycliffe's doctrine of lordship describes a *literal* separation. The Church suffers in its spiritual worth when it ventures into secular affairs and pursues secular interests. Secular government is supreme over the Church in secular affairs. The Church's powers are limited to its spiritual office. If the Church exercises financial or territorial functions belonging to the state, then the state should intervene and reclaim the misused revenues and territories.

Wycliffe's third theme is the doctrine of the Church. The true Church, the community of the elect, is distinct from the visible Church. Wycliffe limits the power of the visible Church on earth in *De Civili Dominio* (1377) and *De Ecclesia* (On the Church) (1378). The lordship of the visible Church is subject to God's law as manifested in scripture. Since we cannot know the elect, there is no reason to recognize the authority of the visible Church and no reason to obey it. No man has any duty to obey any cleric, including the pope, unless the cleric is true to scriptural precepts. Wycliffe limits the powers of the pope and priests in *De Ecclesia* (On the Church) (1378) and *De Potestate Papae* (On the Power of the Pope) (c. 1379). Ordination in itself offers no certainty of divine approval or authority. Believers have the right to question the legitimacy of the clergy and its actions by comparing them to scripture.

Wycliffe gives the king power over the Church. *De Civili Dominio* (1377); *De Ecclesia* (On the Church) (1378); and *De Officio Regis* (The Office of the King) (1379). The pope represents the humanity of Jesus, but the king represents the divinity of Jesus. Secular powers also have authority to deprive unworthy priests of their benefices.

Wycliffe argues further that the visible Church, the "prelates and priests, monks and canons and friars," cannot justify its own existence. Wycliffe's *De Ecclesia* (On the Church) (1378) adopts Augustine's doctrine of predestination. God fixes salvation from eternity past by predestination. The visible Church cannot help any man to gain salvation or perform any of its attributed functions.

Wycliffe's fourth theme is the denial of transubstantiation. Wycliffe denies that Catholic priests have a divine power to transform bread and wine into the physical body and blood of Christ. Christ is *figuratively* present in the elements, but not *physically* present. Wycliffe attacks the doctrine of transubstantiation on historical, scriptural, and philosophical grounds in *De Eucharistia* (On the Eucharist) (1379) and *De Apostasia* (On Apostacy) (1379). Wycliffe's historical attack relies on the fact that transubstantiation did not become Catholic dogma until the Fourth Lateran Council in 1215. Wycliffe rejects the claimed power of priests "to make the Body of Christ." No creature has the power to make his own Maker.

Wycliffe's scriptural attack argues that neither scripture nor the Church Fathers give clear support to transubstantiation. Since Christ did not give his living body and blood to the disciples at the Last Supper, the doctrine of transubstantiation contradicts the clear sense of the Gospels. The doctrine promotes idolatry by encouraging the worship of the bread and the wine, and it subjects Christ's body to accidental indignities.

Wycliffe's philosophical attack involves the "problem of universals," the great philosophical controversy of the medieval period. "Realists" believed that universal ideas, such as "redness," have their own existence apart from red objects such as apples. Nominalists, however, believed that universal ideas are merely names with no separate existence. Supporters of transubstantiation were Nominalists who argued that transubstantiation annihilates the "essence" or substance of the bread, but leaves the "accidents" or appearance of the bread unchanged. Wycliffe was a Realist who argued it was impossible to separate the appearance of the bread from its substance. Bread, if truly annihilated, cannot appear intact.

The Church prosecuted Wycliffe for heresy three times without success. Armed men under John of Gaunt rescued Wycliffe from his first trial in 1377 at St. Paul's in London. An order of the queen rescued Wycliffe from his second trial in 1378 at Lambeth Palace, London. The third trial attempted to try Wycliffe *in absentia* at the Blackfriars Priory, London in 1382. The Dover Straits earthquake ended that trial just as the Archbishop of Canterbury William Courtenay finished reading the charges against Wycliffe.

Wycliffe was the driving force behind the first complete English Bible, a translation of the Vulgate that first appeared between 1380 and 1382. Approximately 170 Wycliffe Bibles survive today. Wycliffe also trained a band of "Poor Preachers," Oxford scholars who preached the Gospel across England and criticized the power and corruption of the Catholic Church. The Poor Preachers inspired the Lollard movement, described below.

Wycliffe died in 1384. The Council of Constance condemned Wycliffe on 260 counts in 1415, ordering Wycliffe's bones exhumed and cast out of consecrated ground. In 1428, to prevent Wycliffe's bodily resurrection, Pope Martin V ordered Wycliffe's remains dug up, burned, and the ashes scattered. Bishop Richard Fleming of Lincoln carried out the pope's orders. Forty-four years after his death, Wycliffe's ashes were scattered in the Speed, a brook that flows into the Avon River. Wycliffe's ashes became the emblem of his beliefs, and a local rhyme foretold Wycliffe's impact on the future: "The Avon to the Severn runs. The Severn to the sea. And Wycliffe's dust shall spread abroad, wide as the waters be."

The Lollards

Wycliffe's opponents called his followers "Lollards," a derisive term taken from the Dutch word *lollen* meaning to mumble. The historian Henry Kneighton (d. 1396) wrote that Lollards "everywhere filled the kingdom. A man could scarcely meet two people on the road but one of them was a disciple of Wycliffe." The Lollards applied the standard of scripture to Church teaching and practice, and they became politically powerful as many nobles embraced Wycliffe's teaching.

In February, 1395, Lollards presented a manifesto to Parliament entitled the "Twelve Conclusions" and nailed copies to the doors of St. Paul's Cathedral and Westminster Abbey. The Twelve Conclusions complained that the Church was too involved in temporal affairs. Priests and bishops were not scriptural. Vows of celibacy induced sodomy among the priests. Transubstantiation led innocent people into idolatry. Men who held high office in the Church should not hold high secular office. Offering prayers for the dead in exchange for money was simony. The worship of crosses and the veneration of relics were idolatrous. The claims that confession to priests was necessary for salvation and that priests had the power to grant forgiveness of sins were blasphemous. Only God could forgive sins and save man. Crusades and holy wars violated Christ's commands to love and forgive our enemies. The Church wasted time and money on beautiful but unnecessary works of art in violation of scripture.

The political climate that once favored Wycliffe and the Lollards now turned. Archbishop of Canterbury William Courtenay sent a copy of the Twelve Conclusions to the pope, and the pope complained to King Richard II. The king compelled Lollard knights and nobles to disavow their views. When Archbishop Courtenay died in 1396, the new Archbishop Thomas Arundel petitioned the king and Parliament for the power to burn Lollards at the stake.

Wycliffe's powerful patron and protector John of Gaunt died in 1399. Richard II had previously exiled Gaunt's son Henry Bolingbroke and Archbishop Arundel. Richard now confiscated Bolingbroke's inheritance. Bolingbroke returned to England and deposed Richard II. Bolingbroke restored Arundel as Archbishop, and Archbishop Arundel crowned Bolingbroke King Henry IV.

Henry IV was king but his throne was insecure. Henry agreed to exterminate Lollardy in exchange for Church support of his crown. In 1401 Parliament passed the infamous statute *De Haeretico Comburendo* ("Concerning the Burning of Heretics") giving English bishops the power to "utterly destroy" the Lollards. Any person who preached, taught, believed, or wrote anything "contrary to the catholic faith or determination of the Holy Church" would "be burnt, that such punishment may strike fear into the minds of others." In 1408 Archbishop Arundel issued the Constitutions of Oxford, declaring it heresy to translate any part of the scripture into English, to read scripture without a bishop's prior permission, or to discuss any of Wycliffe's writings. In 1412 Arundel ordered the burning of all of Wycliffe's works. When sheriffs refused to burn Lollards convicted under the 1401 statute *De Haeretico Comburendo*, Parliament passed an act in 1413 requiring all sheriffs in England to take an oath that they would burn any heretic within 10 days. Parliament also passed *An Act Suppressing Lollardy* in 1414, providing that anyone reading the scriptures in English forfeited their life, their property, and all their family's property.

The persecution of the Lollards eroded their support among the nobility and drove the movement underground among the common people. The Lollards continued to criticize the Church, distribute copies of the Wycliffe Bible, and attack the doctrine of transubstantiation, but they were too low in society to achieve institutional reforms. Ironically, the Lollards' low social status preserved Lollardy from obliteration. In 1523, Cuthbert Tunstall, Bishop of London, wrote to Erasmus of "the great band of Wycliffite heretics" that remained in England. Later that year Erasmus wrote to the new Pope Adrian VI that religious persecution was "remarkably useless." The persecution of the Lollards by the English kings had "overcome" the Lollards, but it could not "extinguish" them.

The doctrines of the Lutheran Reformation differed little from Lollardy, but they appealed more effectively to politicians and learned men. The lower classes of England who read Wycliffe's Bible faithfully every night awoke to find Europe convulsed by their ideas. Wycliffe planted the seeds of the Reformation in England, and the Lollards carefully tended the fields. William Tyndale would now begin the harvest.

William Tyndale

William Tyndale was born in 1494 and received his Master of Arts from Oxford in 1515. He was in Cambridge in 1516, where he possibly met Erasmus, and he returned to his native Gloucestershire in 1520 as chaplain to Sir John Walsh. One evening a priest taunted Tyndale's love of scripture by stating "we are better to be without God's laws than the Pope's laws." Tyndale replied, "I defy the Pope and all his laws. If God spare my life ere many years, I will cause the boy that drives the plow to know more of scriptures than you." Tyndale's New Testament (1526) gave God an English voice and brought scripture to every Englishman.

Tyndale's 1526 New Testament exceeded Wycliffe's 1382 translation in quality and impact. Wycliffe translated Jerome's Latin Vulgate. Scribes required more than a year to make one copy. Two developments prepared the way for Tyndale's improved translation. First, Gutenberg perfected his printing press in 1439, enabling Gutenberg to produce about 60 Bibles per year. Tyndale published more than 3,000 copies of his New Testament in Germany in 1526.

The second development was the revived study of Greek, the original language of the New Testament and the "Septuagint," the widely accepted translation of the Old Testament by Jewish scholars in the third century B.C. Knowledge of Greek was largely lost in the West until Constantinople fell to the Turks in 1453. Scholars fled to Italy with their Greek manuscripts, and knowledge of Greek spread as exiled scholars began to teach in European universities. Erasmus of Rotterdam created a sensation by publishing a Greek New Testament in 1512, with corrected editions in 1519 and 1522. Both Luther and Tyndale used Erasmus's Greek New Testament for their translations.

Tyndale was ordained a Catholic priest in 1522. In 1523 he requested permission from Bishop of London Cuthbert Tunstall to translate the Bible into English. When Tunstall refused, Tyndale lodged with a London merchant and continued translating. German merchants encouraged Tyndale to complete the work in Germany and offered to smuggle the Bibles into England. Tyndale went to Germany in 1524 and completed his New Testament. Tyndale began printing his New Testament in Cologne in 1525. Bishop Tunstall sent agents to arrest Tyndale, but he fled to Worms and continued printing the New Testament. The printer completed the first copies in February, 1526. They arrived in England the next month, smuggled in bolts of cloth.

In October, 1526, Bishop Tunstall directed his agents to acquire every Tyndale New Testament they could. Tyndale's agents intentionally sold copies to Tunstall's agents at exorbitant prices. Tunstall burned the New Testaments at St. Paul's Cathedral on October 27, 1526. Tyndale used Tunstall's money to finance his efforts, and eventually smuggled more than 18,000 copies into England.

Unable to stop the flow of Tyndale's works into England, Tunstall recruited Sir Thomas More to discredit Tyndale's scholarship. More's *Dialogue concerning Heresies* (1529–1530) claimed Tyndale intentionally mistranslated six Greek words in his New Testament. The six words were *Ekklesia* (which Tyndale translated as *congregation* rather than *Church*); *Agape* (which Tyndale translated as *love* rather than *charity*); *Presbuteros* (which Tyndale translated as *elder* rather than *priest*); *Paraptoma* (which Tyndale translated as *faults* rather than *sins*); *Exomologeo* (which Tyndale translated as *acknowledge* rather than *confess*) and *Metanoeho* (which Tyndale translated as *repent* rather than *do penance*). For the reformers, Tyndale's translations of these six words discredited the powers claimed by the Church for popes and priests, discredited the claim that human works are necessary for salvation, and discredited the sacraments as conditions of salvation.

Tyndale published an influential political work, *The Obedience of a Christian Man*, in 1528. After reading it, Henry VIII sent Stephen Vaughn to Europe to find Tyndale and persuade him to return to England. Tyndale refused to return unless Henry permitted the publication of the English Bible. On May 21, 1535, after 10 years of pursuit, Tyndale's pursuers finally apprehended him. Henry Phillips, an agent of the Bishop of London John Stokesley, pretended to befriend Tyndale and then betrayed him. The Bishop's agents imprisoned Tyndale in Vilvorde Castle, six miles from Brussels, and charged Tyndale with heresy.

A commission of 17 members, including three theologians, three canons, and a representative of the Inquisition, tried Tyndale for heresy. The commission prolonged the trial for months in hopes of getting Tyndale to renounce his beliefs. Tyndale spent 500 days in prison, without heat, without warm clothing, without books, and without light. The commission finally abandoned its efforts and burned Tyndale on October 6, 1536. The executioner, as a sign of respect, strangled Tyndale before burning his body. Tyndale's last words were "Lord! Open the king of England's eyes."

Tyndale wrote *The Obedience of a Christian Man* (1528), subtitled *"and how Christian rulers ought to govern,"* to disprove Catholic claims that reformers were preaching sedition and inciting political violence. Tyndale's preface argues that every man has the right to read scripture for himself in his own language. Tyndale's prologue argues that scripture does not support disobedience to civil authority. Disobedience comes instead from "the Bloody doctrine of the Pope which causeth disobedience, rebellion, and insurrection." Tyndale concludes the prologue by instructing the readers to compare all his arguments against scripture.

The main body of *Obedience* has three sections. The first section explains God's law of obedience, which applies to all people, particularly kings, governors, and rulers who enact God's justice. No one is exempt from God's law of obedience, including monks, friars, bishops, and popes. Tyndale's doctrine of nonresistance holds that the law of obedience requires submission to civil authority, even if civil authorities are tyrants. The king, even if a tyrant, is a minister of God for our welfare.

The second section of *Obedience* describes how kings, judges, and officers should rule. Following Augustine and Wycliffe, Tyndale argues for the separation of secular government from religious institutions. "To preach God's word is too much for half a man. And to minister a temporal kingdom is too much for half a man also." Men holding high Church office should forsake the world and preach the Word of God as a full-time occupation.

Secular rulers are God's representatives on earth, and God gives kings supremacy over the Church. Resisting secular authority is resisting God's authority. Bishops have wrongfully resisted the authority of secular rulers, and secular rulers must reestablish their authority over the bishops. The pope, for example, currently controls the English king. This divides England into two nations in which the king and the pope fight for supremacy. The king should assert his supremacy over the Church and unify his nation.

The third section of *Obedience* addresses the proper interpretation of scripture. For more than a thousand years the Church had applied four methods of interpretation to every word of scripture. The *literal* interpretation of scripture, long discounted by the Church, teaches actual deeds and events. This method interprets "the city of Jerusalem" as a literal city. The *allegorical* interpretation of scripture teaches what we should believe. This method interprets "the city of Jerusalem" as the Church. The *tropological* or moral interpretation of scripture teaches us what we should do. This method interprets "the city of Jerusalem" as the believing soul. The *anagogical,* or "leading up" interpretation of scripture, teaches us where we should set our aim. This method interprets "the city of Jerusalem" as the heavenly city of God.

Tyndale argues that the literal sense of scripture is the only *true* sense of scriptural interpretation. The Church uses the other three methods to interpret scripture however it pleases and to deny scripture to the laity, arguing that only learned men can interpret scripture. The Church denies access to scripture to hide its false teachings. Jesus commanded the people to read scripture for themselves so they would know when false prophets tried to deceive them. The English people should follow Christ's command and read scripture for themselves so they will know when the Church tries to deceive them.

Tyndale closes *Obedience* by exhorting Henry VIII to take political and financial actions against the Catholic Church. Politically, the king should impose his political supremacy over the Church "to rid his realm from the wily tyranny of the hypocrites and to bring the hypocrites under his laws." Financially, the king should calculate how much money he spent helping Pope Julius II in the Holy League to force the invading French king out of Italy. Tyndale estimates Henry spent more than $686 million. Henry should make the pope refund it all.

Tyndale's *Obedience* influenced every level of English society including the king. John Foxe reports that Anne Boleyn obtained a copy, gave it to Henry VIII, and asked him to read it. "The King did so, and delighted in the book. For, saith he, this is a book for me and all kings to read." In 1529, one year after publication of *The Obedience of a Christian Man,* Henry began replacing clerics holding high positions in his government with laymen. He replaced his Chancellor Cardinal Wolsey with Sir Thomas More, the first layman to hold that position. Henry eventually formalized his break with Rome with the Act of Supremacy (1534), which made Henry the head of the English Church. The Treason Act (1534) made disavowing the Act of Supremacy a capital offense.

Henry did not obtain the papal reimbursement of Holy League expenditures urged by Tyndale, but he more than recouped his expenses. The Act of First Fruits and Tenths (1534) diverted the traditional taxes paid to the pope into Henry's treasury. The First Suppression Act (1536) and the Second Suppression Act (1539) dissolved the approximately 900 monasteries, priories, convents, and friaries in England, Wales, and Ireland. Henry seized their property, appropriated their income, and disposed of their assets.

Henry also embraced Tyndale's English Bible. In July 1536, a convocation called by Henry issued the 10 Articles, a new statement of doctrine for the Church of England. The first Article provided that the Holy Scriptures and the three Creeds are the basis and summary of the true Christian faith. In September 1538, Henry's Chancellor Thomas Cromwell ordered every parish in England to purchase a copy of an English Bible and place it in "some convenient place" for all to see and read. To meet this demand, Cromwell commissioned Tyndale's close associate Miles Coverdale to prepare the "Great Bible," so called because of its size, utilizing Tyndale's translation. Printers produced more than 9,000 copies. God granted Tyndale's last request to open the King of England's eyes.

The title page of the Great Bible illustrates the ideal kingdom described in Tyndale's *Obedience* and Wycliffe's writings. It shows Henry VIII on the throne. God gives the *Verbum Dei*, the word of God, directly to Henry. Henry hands a copy of the Bible in English to the Archbishop Cranmer on his right and another to Chancellor Cromwell on his left. The Archbishop distributes the Bible from the king to the parish priests, and the chancellor distributes the Bible from the king to the nobility. There is one nation, joined together at Henry's feet and proclaiming "God save the king." The message is clear to every person who sees it. There is one England. There is no pope. The king answers to God, the king is supreme over the Church and his subjects, and every person can read scripture for himself in his own language.

Englishmen after Wycliffe and Tyndale could read the Bible in their own language, but they still did not enjoy religious liberty. England at this point had only exchanged the tyranny of the pope for the tyranny of the king, and Tyndale's doctrine of nonresistance permitted no human remedy for tyrannical kings. Religious persecution under Mary I and Charles I will lead the Puritans to abandon Tyndale's doctrine of nonresistance.

John Milton

The Puritan John Milton (1608–1674), author of *Paradise Lost* (1667), is England's greatest advocate of liberty after John Locke. Milton's works reflect the religious and political thought of John Calvin (1509–1564). Milton validates all five principles of the American founding, and he champions most of the liberties contained in the Bill of Rights. Milton rejects Tyndale's theory of nonresistance and justifies a right to armed rebellion and regicide.

Milton builds all his arguments on scripture. Like Wycliffe and Tyndale, Milton's *On Christian Doctrine* presents scripture as divinely inspired, inerrant, and containing all that is necessary for salvation. Scripture provides the only source of Christian doctrine, and every believer should read and interpret it for himself.

Calvinism took root in England through the "Marian Exiles," described below. Henry VIII died in 1547. Henry's Protestant son Edward became king but died in 1553. Henry's Catholic daughter Mary succeeded Edward and took bold action to reverse the English Reformation. In 1554 Mary revived the Heresy Act (1382), the statute *De Comburendo Haeretico* (On the Burning of Heretics) (1401), and the Act Suppressing Lollardy (1414). Mary executed 283 Protestants for heresy, most by burning, and many for following Wycliffe in denying transubstantiation.

Approximately 800 Protestants fled Mary's persecution during the "Marian Exile." Most gravitated to Calvinist enclaves in Holland and Switzerland, returning to England as confirmed Calvinists when Mary died in 1558 and Elizabeth I came to the throne. Elizabeth quickly imposed a Religious Settlement restoring Henry VIII's Reformation through two statutes. The Act of Supremacy (1558) restored the Crown as the head of the Church in England and abolished the authority of the pope. The Act of Uniformity (1559) regulated worship. Elizabeth's Religious Settlement followed a "*via media*," a middle path that was neither Protestant nor Catholic. It sought instead to conform to the teachings of the early Church fathers.

Charles I abandoned the *via media* when he became king in 1625. His persecution of Calvinist Puritans drove many to Holland and America. Twenty thousand left England in 1632. Archbishop William Laud purged Calvinists from English pulpits. Charles and Laud strengthened the power of the bishops and ecclesiastical courts, and they pilloried, whipped, and imprisoned dissenters who criticized their policies. They punished the Puritan lawyer William Prynne by cutting off his ears and branding his face.

Charles was a political tyrant as well. He attempted to rule without Parliament during his "Personal Rule" from 1629 to 1640, imposing crushing taxes without the required consent of Parliament. Charles attempted to impose his religious policies on Calvinist Scotland, triggering the Bishops Wars of 1639–1640. The Scots occupied northern England and held it for ransom, forcing Charles to call a Parliament to raise the ransom funds.

The "Long Parliament" convened in 1640 and immediately began reversing Charles's policies. Parliament abolished the Star Chamber and the

High Commission, reduced the power of the bishops, removed all clergy from the House of Lords, outlawed taxation without Parliament's consent, and passed an act requiring the king to call a Parliament at least once every three years. Parliament convicted the Earl of Stafford, Charles's primary advisor, and Archbishop Laud for treason. Parliament executed Stafford and imprisoned Laud.

Charles entered the House of Commons with 400 armed men on January 3, 1642, to arrest five members for treason. The result was civil war. Parliament's forces took Charles prisoner in 1647. A High Court of Justice convicted Charles of treason and beheaded him on January 30, 1649. Charles's beheading provoked a firestorm of protest in England and Europe. John Milton responded to these protests in three works, *The Tenure of Kings and Magistrates* (1649); *A Defense of the People of England* (1651); and *A Second Defense of the People of England* (1654).

The Tenure of Kings and Magistrates (1649) validates all five principles of the American founding. First, all men are created morally and legally equal. God created man in his own image, creating every man to command and not to obey. Second, God endows men with inalienable rights. God gives all men the right to defend and preserve themselves, as well as the right to choose and change their government.

Third, men establish civil governments through their own actions. God does not establish kings by divine right. Civil government originated after Adam's fall as conflicts led to violence. To prevent their mutual destruction, men formed a league for their joint defense. Commonwealths resulted from this agreement.

Fourth, the powers of government depend on the consent of the governed. Every man has an inalienable right to defend and preserve himself, but men favor themselves in exercising this right. To solve this problem, men delegate their individual rights to defense and self-preservation, in trust, to a central authority. All powers of government flow from this delegation.

Fifth, men may alter or abolish their government if it becomes destructive. God grants political supremacy to the people, who delegate their power to kings on condition that kings exercise it for the people's good. Kings who rule otherwise are tyrants, and the people may depose and kill tyrants. Milton gives three justifications for regicide. First, the Gospels do not shield tyrants from justice. Second, historical precedent supports killing tyrants. The Greeks and Romans considered tyrannicide "lawful, glorious, and heroic." Third, legal precedent supports killing tyrants. The peers and barons of England have an ancient legal right to judge the king.

The French scholar Salmasius responded to Milton's *Tenure of Kings and Magistrates* in *A Defense of the Reign of Charles I* (1649). Salmasius defended the divine right of kings and called on the kings of Europe to restore Charles I's son as king of England. Milton responded to Salmasius in *A Defense of the People of England* (1651). Milton rejects the divine right of kings as an old superstition. None of the best writers among the Jews, the Greeks, or the Romans provide any precedent for such a right. Furthermore, kingship is irreconcilable with Christianity. Christ only commanded men to render their coins unto Caesar, not their freedom. The coin's face bore an image of Caesar. Men's faces bear the image of God. We are God's property. Surrendering ourselves to tyrants dishonors our Creator.

Pierre Du Moulin (1568–1658), a French Huguenot minister, responded to Milton's *Defense of the People of England* (1651) with *The Cry of the Royal Blood to Heaven* (1652). Du Moulin presents Charles I as a type of Christ and his execution as a greater crime than Christ's crucifixion. The Jews were blind to Christ's glory, but the English knew what they were doing. England's Puritans pose a mortal danger to all Protestant monarchies.

Milton responds to Du Moulin in his *Second Defense of the English People* (1654), observing that "there are three species of liberty which are essential to the happiness of social life: religious, domestic and civil." The following recounts Milton's writings on these three types of liberty and how the U.S. Constitution and Bill of Rights adopt Milton's views.

Milton addresses *religious liberty*, the liberty of conscience and freedom of worship, in five tracts against the clergy in 1641 and 1642. Milton's *Treatise on Civil Power in Ecclesiastical Causes* (1659) argues for liberty of conscience, freedom of worship, open toleration for all peaceable biblical religions, separation of church and state, and the disestablishment of religion. The Establishment and Free Exercise Clauses of the First Amendment preserve these liberties.

Milton's writings on *domestic or private liberty* argue that education is "the only genuine source of political and individual liberty," and "the only true safeguard of states." Parents are entitled to nurture and educate their children in their own faith and values, with due regard for each child's nature and gifts. American Constitutional law protects this liberty as a "fundamental right." Milton argues that homes and private papers should be free from unreasonable searches and seizures. The Fourth Amendment and the exclusionary rule preserve this liberty.

Lastly, Milton presents a sophisticated theory of *civil or political liberty*. The most important political liberty is the right to elect public officials. Article I preserves the right to elect Congress and Article II preserves the right to elect the president. Milton argues that the people should have the right to petition these officials, a right preserved in the First Amendment. The people should not be taxed or sent to war without their consent, rights preserved in Article I. Milton advocates the separation of powers, established in Articles I, II, and III. The people should have the right to remove officials who no longer serve or please them, a right preserved in the Impeachment

Clauses of Articles I and II. The people should have the right to criminal and civil jury trial, rights preserved in the Sixth and Seventh Amendments. Milton advocates broad freedom of association, religion, speech, and press, all rights preserved in the First Amendment.

Milton's *Areopagitica* (1644) defends freedom of the press from Parliament's June 14, 1643, Licensing Order requiring government licensing of all materials before printing. Parliament empowered censors "to break open Doors and Locks" to search, seize, and destroy any offensive materials. The censors could also imprison writers, printers, and publishers indefinitely.

Milton presents four arguments in support of his request that Parliament withdraw its Licensing Order. First, licensing is the invention of the Roman Catholic Church. Second, reading is necessary to acquire knowledge of good and evil in our fallen world. Licensing books is no more effective in suppressing seditious and libelous books than shutting fence gates to imprison crows. Third, the Licensing Order denies our God-given reason and freedom to choose. Removing books with bad content denies our opportunities for acquiring, generating, and practicing virtue. "How much we thus expel of sin, so much we expel our virtue." Fourth, the Licensing Order discourages learning and the pursuit of truth. If we fear each book before we even know its contents, we create a "second tyranny over learning."

Milton closes *Areopagitica* by appealing to national pride. England is the new chosen nation, an earthly example of Augustine's City of God, and the English people are potentially a "nation of prophets, sages, and worthies." The Licensing Order, however, will lessen the learning of the English people and their willingness to write and speak. Let Truth and Falsehood grapple in the open. Truth will win.

Milton's last political work is *The Readie and Easie Way to Establish a Free Commonwealth* (1660). Milton foresees the Restoration and warns that restoring the monarchy in England will diminish liberty and virtue. The whole freedom of man, Milton explains, consists of two components. The first is spiritual liberty, the liberty of conscience. This is the most precious liberty, and England's history shows that only a commonwealth, not a monarchy, will protect it. The second component of freedom is civil liberty. Monarchies centralize political power, and monarchs will not diminish their own powers to protect the civil liberties and rights of their subjects.

The U.S. Constitution incorporates many of Milton's recommendations in *The Readie and Easie Way*. Milton argues the best governmental structure for protecting civil liberty is a federal republic. Each county retains control of its elections, makes its laws, administers its system of justice, and establishes its system of education. The 10th Amendment establishes a federal system, with states retaining control of local affairs. Milton's central government resolves disputes between counties, a principle established in Article III, § 2. Milton calls for abolishing all distinctions between lords and commoners, a policy adopted in the Titles of Nobility Clause of Article I, § 9. The people should elect representatives for the central government, and the people should change a third of the representatives every two or three years. Article II adopts a similar rotation in the U.S. House and Senate.

John Locke

The English physician and philosopher John Locke (1632–1704), like Milton, wrote during a period of religious tyranny and revolution. The Restoration placed Charles II on the throne in 1660, and his Catholic brother became James II in 1685. James employed five strategies to force England back into Catholicism.

First, he corrupted the courts to establish a "dispensing" power. James used this power to suspend England's religious laws and place Catholics in control of the army, the Privy Council, the courts, the universities, and the

Church of England. Second, James usurped Parliament's power by rigging Parliamentary elections to "pack" Parliament, prosecuting opponents in Parliament, and finally dissolving Parliament altogether. Third, James used the threat of force to control his Protestant subjects by raising an illegal standing army, placing the army under Catholic command, and disarming Protestants. Fourth, James weaponized the courts by illegally denying Protestants due process. Fifth, James established an illegal Ecclesiastical Commission to persecute ministers and university officials who resisted Catholicization.

James suspended England's religious laws on April 4, 1688. Seven Anglican bishops presented a lawful petition to James claiming he had no authority to suspend the laws. James responded by prosecuting them for sedition and libel. The jury acquitted the seven bishops on June 30, 1688. The Glorious Revolution soon followed. James II fled England for France on December 10, 1688. William and Mary consented to the English Bill of Rights on February 13, 1689, prior to taking the throne. Forty-one provisions of the U.S. Constitution and Bill of Rights adopt principles from the English Bill of Rights. The chapter on "The English Bill of Rights" details these provisions.

John Locke's works capture the political thought supporting the Glorious Revolution and the American founding, and Locke's ideas are firmly rooted in the English Reformation. Locke's works accept the truth, authority, and inerrancy of scripture expounded by Augustine, Wycliffe, Tyndale, and Milton. Locke's *Essay Concerning Human Understanding* (1689) holds that God reveals the precepts of natural law in scripture (Locke, *Essay*, 2.28.8), and his *Second Treatise of Government* (1689) holds that scripture establishes the validity standard for human laws. (Locke, *Second Treatise*, § 136). Locke's influential work on religious liberty, *A Letter Concerning Toleration* (1689), adopts the separation of secular government from religious institutions advanced by Augustine, Wycliffe, and Tyndale. It also adopts Milton's arguments for religious liberty.

Locke's *Second Treatise* adopts two important aspects of Wycliffe's theory of lordship. Locke's theory of private property adopts Wycliffe's view that all men own the world in common. (Locke, *Second Treatise*, §§ 25–32). Second, Locke follows Wycliffe's idea that civil lords forfeit their right to lordship through wrongful conduct. Locke holds that tyrants forfeit their right to rule. (Locke, *Second Treatise*, § 232).

Locke's *First and Second Treatises of Government* (1689) owe much to Milton. Locke devotes his entire *First Treatise* to arguing against the divine right of kings. Locke's *Second Treatise* follows Milton's *Tenure of Kings and Magistrates* in advocating the five principles that define the American founding. First, all men are created morally and legally equal. Men, by nature, are "all free, equal, and independent." (Locke, *Second Treatise*, § 95). The state of nature is a state "of equality, wherein all the power and jurisdiction is reciprocal, no one having more than another." (Locke, *Second Treatise*, § 4). There is no subordination among men in the state of nature, and no man may destroy or use any other men. (Locke, *Second Treatise*, § 6).

Second, God endows men with inalienable rights. Every man has the right to preserve himself, and no man may "harm another in his life, health, liberty, or possessions." (Locke, *Second Treatise*, § 6). The right to liberty includes freedom from government without one's consent. (Locke, *Second Treatise*, § 22).

Third, men establish civil governments through their own actions. God does not establish kings by divine right. Locke's *First Treatise* (1689) argues that God does not establish kings by divine right. Locke's *Second Treatise* (1689) explains the origin of civil society. Man initially lives in a state of nature. The state of nature is generally peaceable, but three defects make it difficult to protect private property. There is no consent to a common law, there is no impartial judge of disputes, and individuals do not have power to execute just sentences. (Locke, *Second Treatise*, §§ 124–126). Men form a social contract to correct these defects. (Locke, *Second Treatise*, § 21). Man in the state of nature has the right to exact retribution for crimes committed against him. Each man gives up this right under the social contract in exchange for impartial justice backed by overwhelming force. (Locke, *Second Treatise*, §§ 128–131).

Fourth, the powers of government depend on the consent of the governed. The people always remain sovereign. Every man has the right to be free from any government without his consent. (Locke, *Second Treatise*, § 22). No one can be compelled to enter a society without his consent. (Locke, *Second Treatise*, § 95). After one consents to form a government, however, he consents to government by majority rule. The consent of the governed justifies majority rule and makes it binding. (Locke, *Second Treatise*, § 99).

Fifth, men may alter or abolish their government if it becomes destructive. The governed have the right and duty to resist tyrannical government. Government acts tyrannically when it fails to govern according to known and established laws. "Wherever law ends, tyranny begins." Government exists by the consent of the people to protect the rights of the people and to promote the public good. The people should resist and replace any government that fails in these duties. (Locke, *Second Treatise*, § 202).

Government use of force without right violates the rights of subjects and seeks to enslave them. Such acts forfeit the powers entrusted to the government by the people, void the social contract, place the government in the state of nature, and create a state of war against its subjects. Reversion to the state of nature cancels all ties between government and the governed, and every person has the right to defend himself and resist the aggressor. (Locke, *Second Treatise*, § 232).

Lastly, Locke's *Letter Concerning Toleration* (1688) argues that government has no right to coerce men in religious matters. Neither God nor men commit the care of their souls to the state. Neither scripture nor Christ support coercion as a means to salvation. Furthermore, coercion cannot compel belief. Man believes what he thinks is true, not what government compels him to do.

Conclusion

Five principles define the American founding. First, all men are created morally and legally equal. Second, God endows men with inalienable rights. Third, men establish civil governments through their own actions. God does not establish kings by divine right. Fourth, the powers of government depend on the consent of the governed. Fifth, men may alter or abolish their government if it becomes destructive.

These principles are the product of the English Reformation, the religious and political struggle that began with John Wycliffe's *On the Lordship of God* in 1373 and ended with John Locke's *Second Treatise on Civil Government* and *Letter Regarding Toleration* in 1689. Augustine's doctrines of scriptural authority and predestination provided the theological foundation for the English Reformation. Augustine's separation of the earthly and spiritual realms in *The City of God* provided the political foundation.

The English Reformation had two phases. Wycliffe and Tyndale freed men from the tyranny of popes during the first phase of the English Reformation. The political climax of the first phase was Henry VIII's break with the Roman Catholic Church in 1534. The religious climax of the first phase was the publication of the Great Bible in 1538. Englishmen after Wycliffe and Tyndale could read the Bible in their own language, but they still did not enjoy religious liberty. England at this point had only exchanged the tyranny of the pope for the tyranny of the king, and

Tyndale's doctrine of nonresistance permitted no human remedy for tyrannical kings.

Milton and Locke freed men from the tyranny of kings during the second phase of the English Reformation. This phase of the English Reformation produced the five principles that define the American founding. The political climax of the second phase was the Glorious Revolution in 1688, codified in the English Bill of Rights in 1689. The religious climax of the second phase was the Toleration Act of 1689. Most Protestants obtained religious liberty under the Toleration Act, but the Act still excluded Roman Catholics from its protection. The First Amendment finally realized the ideal of religious liberty in 1791: "Congress shall make no law respecting an establishment of religion, or prohibiting the free exercise thereof." As demonstrated above, the struggle for religious liberty in England created or enhanced every right preserved in the U.S. Constitution and Bill of Rights.

Religious liberty and political liberty are inseparable. They rise and fall together, and history proves that destroying religious liberty inevitably destroys political liberty as well. John Milton warned that liberty is always threatened, and religious liberty now faces its greatest threat in American history. Since the Supreme Court decision in *Employment Division v. Smith*, 494 U.S. 872 (1990), religious liberty is the *only* right in the Bill of Rights that does not receive strict scrutiny protection. The great task before our nation is preserving religious liberty. Political liberty cannot and will not flourish in its absence.

RECOMMENDED READING

Benson Bobrick, *Wide as the Waters:*
The Story of the English Bible and the Revolution It Inspired
(Penguin, 2001)

K. B. McFarlane, *The Origins of Religious Dissent in England*
(Collier, 1952)

Reginald Lane Poole, *Wycliffe and the Movements for Reform*
(Longmans, 1889)

David Teems, *Tyndale: The Man Who Gave God an English Voice*
(Nelson, 2012)

John Witte, Jr., *The Reformation of Rights*
(Cambridge University Press, 2007)

AMERICAN CHURCHES

AND THE

FIRST AMENDMENT

By Anthony M. Joseph, PhD

PROFESSOR OF EARLY AMERICAN HISTORY

The First Amendment to the U.S. Constitution, ratified in 1791, prohibits Congress from making any law "respecting an establishment of religion, or prohibiting the free exercise thereof." Thomas Jefferson famously stated that these religion clauses of the First Amendment created a "wall of separation between Church & State." At the time of the Amendment's passage, however, the phrase "wall of separation" had no legal meaning in the United States. And the more expansive modern interpretation of Jefferson's phrase—that government must remain untouched by Churches and the law untouched by religious values—provides us no reliable understanding of the First Amendment or the historical situation that led to it.

Instead, we must look to America's complex religious diversity at the time the First Amendment was ratified. Some Americans then lived in states where a particular Christian denomination was the "established Church," receiving the exclusive support of the government. Establishment did not necessarily imply full persecution of other denominations and faiths, but it did mean that public funds could be channeled to the favored Church and that non-members could be made to pay taxes for that purpose. Other Americans lived in states that had no established Church and accorded religious liberty to a great extent. Virtually all Americans, wherever they lived, had direct experience with religious pluralism. This diversity had proved difficult to manage politically in the individual states; that difficulty would have been dizzyingly multiplied if Congress had had to craft a single national policy on religion. Not surprisingly, Congress and the states declined to shoehorn the American people into a single national religion. The new federal government would not grant to any religious body its exclusive support. There would be no national established Church. On its face, the First Amendment did not prohibit a state from maintaining an established church or restricting religious liberty. However, both before and after the Amendment's passage, the states swung—some quickly and some gradually—toward application of the same twin principles that the First Amendment expressed: no to establishment, yes to religious liberty.

Established Christianity, North and South

That portentous transition was the climax of a story long in the telling. For most of the 17th century, American religion was dominated by established churches—Anglicanism in the southern colonies and Congregationalism in New England. Then, toward the end of the 1600s, new colonies founded in the Mid-Atlantic dispensed with establishment, allowing Christian sects (non-established churches) to grow and ultimately rival the established churches in popularity. By the eve of the Revolution, American religious life was a complex weave of diverse confessions and church-state regimes.

The southern United States began in the Chesapeake Bay region with the founding of Jamestown, Virginia, in 1607. The settlers of Virginia made Anglicanism—the Church of England—their established Church. Public funds drawn from local taxes paid for the ministers' salaries, the construction and repair of churches, and other expenses of Church life. The funds were not particularly abundant, however. Many of Virginia's 35 Anglican parishes existed only on paper. More than half had no minister, and many lacked a Church building. The Virginia population was heavily unchurched as a result. Most white infants (and all black ones) went unbaptized and marital unions were often made without the sanction of a Church ceremony.

A similar pattern of relatively low religious zeal appeared in other southern colonies founded in the 1600s. Maryland, begun in 1634, initially bore the stamp of its Catholic founder, Cecilius Calvert, Lord Baltimore, who intended the colony as a haven of toleration for his fellow Catholics. Maryland attracted more Catholics than the other English colonies, but it became majority Protestant nonetheless. Lord Baltimore advised the Catholic minority to worship "as privately as may be" and to refrain from public discussions of religion. Any indication that Catholics came to Maryland to convert Protestants would jeopardize the status of the colony with the English government. The quieting of Catholicism in Maryland did not, however, necessarily translate into an active Protestantism in the colony. Only a handful of Protestant congregations existed in Maryland. Probably to an even greater degree than Virginians, Marylanders were unchurched. The colony of Carolina, founded in 1663, followed a similar course. French Huguenots established an early presence in Carolina, but the earliest record of a Church for English-speaking Christians dates only to the year 1698.

By then, however, Anglicanism in the British colonies had begun to expand. The Anglican Church was formally established in Maryland in 1692. South

Carolina (1706) and North Carolina (1715) followed. In each case, the colony was divided into parishes and taxes for their support were introduced. Within two years of the establishment of Anglicanism in Maryland, some 22 churches had been built. In the Carolinas, public funds enabled the construction of churches similar to those that dotted the landscape of rural England. No Anglican bishop was ever appointed to the Anglican Church in America. In that respect, the Anglican project in America remained unfinished business at the time of the Revolution. Yet Anglicanism by the mid-1700s was unquestionably a more vital American presence than it had been a century before.

Little more than a decade after the founding of Jamestown, Puritans began to build their own form of established Christianity in America. Influenced by the teachings of Protestant theologian John Calvin (1509–1564), Puritans were worried that the Anglican Church was becoming more like the Catholic Church in matters of doctrine and ritual. The Puritans got their name from their desire to "purify" the Anglican Church of such tendencies.

In the early 1600s, some Puritans were so unhappy that they separated from the Church of England and left England altogether. These became known as "Separatist" Puritans. In 1607, just as Jamestown was being founded, they began to move to Holland, where a variety of religious denominations were tolerated. For a time, this was satisfactory, but the Separatists did not like to see their children growing up Dutch and they themselves were not allowed the same economic opportunities as native-born Dutch. With England beginning to colonize America, the Separatists thought they saw a chance for a new life in America. Some of them decided to migrate once more, this time to American shores. These Separatist migrants to America became the "Pilgrims." They sailed on the Mayflower in 1620 and founded Plymouth Colony. King James I gave them an informal assurance that they would be allowed to practice their religion freely in the New World.

Plymouth Colony was eventually absorbed into a much larger Puritan colony—Massachusetts Bay. To a greater degree even than Plymouth, Massachusetts Bay was founded for religious reasons. It was the fruits of the religious vision of Puritans, who in the 1620s became vexed by changes in the Church of England, that were even more dismaying than those that prompted the Separatists to head to Holland two decades before. Anglicanism seemed to be moving even more in the direction of Catholicism. The power of Anglican bishops was enhanced. Puritan lay preachers were stripped of their licenses to preach. Anglican Churches were beautified in ways that reminded Puritans of Catholicism. Most Puritans reacted by staying in England and playing a significant role in the devastating civil war that broke out there in the 1640s. But some Puritans took a different approach. Instead of trying to reform England, they journeyed to the New World and attempted to build a true Christian society from the ground up. They formed the Massachusetts Bay Company. From around 1630 to 1640, Puritans led a migration of some 14,000 settlers to New England.

The Puritans of New England did not officially separate from the Church of England. Instead, they created a denomination called Congregationalism that for all practical purposes operated outside the authority of the Anglican Church. Indeed, Congregationalism quickly became the established Church of Massachusetts Bay. The colony's government paid the salaries of Congregationalist ministers and required attendance at Church services. Local town selectmen and parish vestries controlled the hiring and paying of ministers. Despite their public character, Congregationalist Churches were selective in membership. Only persons who had demonstrated by their personal testimony that they had been saved could become church members.

A high spiritual standard of admission kept many settlers off the membership list. And only full members had the right to vote in public elections. Open opposition to Puritan teaching was punishable by the government. **The Puritans had fled religious persecution in England not because they thought it wrong to have an established Church but because they thought Anglicanism was the wrong established Church to have.**

Established Congregationalism in Massachusetts, however, could no more eliminate religious variation than established Anglicanism had in England. And variation led to the creation of additional colonies in New England. Thomas Hooker and several other Puritan ministers considered the standard for Church membership in Massachusetts too strict. In 1636, they founded Hartford, the beginnings of the colony of Connecticut, with its own version of established Congregationalism. Roger Williams, also a Puritan minister, argued vehemently for the complete "disestablishment" of Congregationalism. "Forced worship stinks in God's nostrils," Williams said. He also criticized the Massachusetts government for distributing lands that belonged to Native Americans. Banished from Massachusetts in 1636, he founded the town of Providence on Narragansett Bay and lived out his long life as a critic of the Puritans and a friend to the local Indians. Anne Hutchinson, a Boston midwife, dared to conduct religious services in her home and accused the Puritans of trusting in their good works for their salvation. She, too, was expelled from Massachusetts. She headed for Narragansett Bay and helped found Newport and Portsmouth, which joined with Williams's Providence to form Rhode Island. Shaped by her and Williams's example, Rhode Island embraced religious toleration. It was the only New England colony that had no established Church.

Thus, the Anglican South and Congregationalist New England offered two forms of established Christianity. In the South, an underachieving Anglicanism began to expand in the late 1600s and early 1700s.

In New England, except for tolerant Rhode Island, an established Congregationalism showed great vitality. Taken together, the Anglican South and Congregationalist New England formed the heart of American Christianity in the 17th century. By 1700, some 90 percent of all Christian congregations in the colonies belonged to one or the other of these established Churches. Not all of these congregations were equally active. Government preference did not directly translate into evangelical zeal. Even so, insofar as 17th-century Americans practiced the Christian faith, they usually practiced it within the parameters of a government-supported Church. The people of these colonial regions became accustomed to a close intertwining of Church and state not unlike what they and their ancestors had experienced in Europe.

The Middle Colonies and the Rise of Sectarian Christianity

The Middle Colonies—Pennsylvania, New York, New Jersey, and Delaware—created a truly different model of church-state relations. Here, religious toleration and the absence of an established Church became the norm. This distinctive pattern was owing partly to the Dutch and their founding of the colony of New Netherland, from which the Middle Colonies sprang. The Dutch founded New Netherland primarily for trade. The Dutch Reformed Church was the colony's established Church, but the colonial government freely admitted a variety of European nationalities and allowed them to settle in spiritually— Lutherans, Puritans, Quakers, Mennonites, Catholics, and Jews. When the English under James, Duke of York, conquered New Netherland in 1664, they inherited a small but religiously diverse population that would have been impossible to corral into an established Anglican Church. The British quickly spun off New Netherland into the colonies of New York, New Jersey, Pennsylvania, and Delaware. Partly in imitation of the Dutch, they allowed religious diversity to flourish in the region.

That practice was accentuated by the important role the Quakers played in the settlement of the region. James granted New Jersey to two noblemen, one of whom subsequently sold his share to a group of Quakers. Among those Quakers was William Penn. Penn was a wealthy English gentleman who had become a Quaker at a time when few members of the English gentry had any attraction to the new, radical sect. Quakers were pacifists who not only opposed war but also any government coercion in matters of religion. Penn envisioned founding a new colony that would become a haven not only for Quakers but for all of Europe's troubled religious communities. He needed a grant of land, however, to make this happen. Ironically, the pacifist Penn's best playing card was his father's military service. Sir William Penn had been an admiral in the English wars against the Dutch. For supplies and services that he had provided, the English Crown owed the elder Penn some £16,000, a sum that passed to the younger Penn when his father died. In lieu of a cash payment of the debt, King Charles granted Penn some 45,000 square miles of land west of the Delaware River. Penn named it Pennsylvania in honor of his father. Quakers poured into Pennsylvania, but so did Germans and Scots—all of them attracted by inexpensive land and religious freedom. Pennsylvania filled up quickly with Quakers, Presbyterians, Lutherans, and German Reformed, among others. None of these denominations had the cultural or political wherewithal to attempt an established church on American soil. And in any case the Quakers would have opposed them if they had tried. Unlike the Puritans, the Quakers embraced religious freedom as a universal principle, not as a means of establishing the preeminence of their own faith.

The Middle Colonies became the most religiously diverse region of the future United States. While Boston was the capital of a Protestant sect that became an established church, Philadelphia became the capital of Protestant sects that remained sects—and flourished. And they proved themselves fully capable of self-government without the aid of public authority. Quakers established the Philadelphia Yearly Meeting shortly after the founding of Pennsylvania. The Meeting, led by "Public Friends" who were in effect ministers, exercised authority over local Quaker meetings across the region. Baptists began in the Middle Colonies as a handful of small congregations that formed the Philadelphia Baptist Association in 1707. The Association answered questions of theology and governance, established norms for admissions and appointments to the ministry, and addressed disputes in local congregations. By 1776 the Association had incorporated some 42 congregations and provided administrative infrastructure for the growth of the Baptists in the post-revolutionary era. Presbyterianism, too, charted an organizational course outside the light (or shadow?) of government support. In 1706 Presbyterian ministers founded the Presbytery of Philadelphia. The Presbytery established standards for the education of ministers and for their appointment by local congregations. Expanded and reorganized as the Synod of Philadelphia in 1716, the association enjoyed steady growth throughout the 18th century. By 1770, the Synod included more than 120 ministers representing congregations throughout the Middle Colonies and even northern Virginia.

The Middle Colonies contained one significant departure from this pattern. New York adopted a partial establishment. In New York City and its surrounding counties, elected parish vestrymen chose ministers without any requirement as to denominational affiliation. Anglican clergymen managed to win most of the available positions, but they had to politic for them. And the New York model of "multiple establishment," in which more than one religious body could conceivably secure government support, would become an enticing example for others to follow in the revolutionary era.

The Revolution in Church and State

On the eve of the American Revolution, eight of the Thirteen Colonies had established churches, either Congregationalist or Anglican. One—New York—had a unique partial-multiple establishment. The remaining four colonies had no established church at all. Taken together, perhaps two-thirds of Americans lived in jurisdictions with established churches. And yet in no colony did the established Church dominate to the exclusion of the sects. By 1776, the sectarian Baptists and Presbyterians had roughly the same number of church members as the established Congregationalists and Anglicans.

Awash in religious diversity, Americans during the revolutionary era debated church-state relations and altered their church-state regimes. The most important outcome initially was the movement toward multiple establishment along the lines of colonial New York. Maryland in 1776 provided for a tax to support the "Christian religion." A year later, while New York itself abandoned multiple establishment, Georgia embraced it, giving public support to "Protestant" denominations. South Carolina in 1778 also authorized a multiple establishment. Presbyterian minister William Tennent had challenged established Anglicanism as contrary to religious liberty, but he was satisfied with South Carolina's measure, which would give each denomination equal status and make "Christianity itself" South Carolina's established religion. In New England, meanwhile, Congregationalism also yielded to multiple establishment. Massachusetts, Connecticut, and New Hampshire all permitted some Christian dissenters to claim exemption from parish taxes. The web of multiple establishments within each of these revolutionary states was an attempt to preserve government support for the Christian religion without prejudicing the religious liberty of any Christian body of worshippers. Additional laws preserved government support for Christianity generally. One or more states outlawed blasphemy, excluded Jewish congregations from legal privileges, required profession of the Christian faith for holding public office, or made Church attendance compulsory.

The shift toward multiple establishment, however, ultimately proved to be merely a transitional stage. The church-state debate in Virginia, the most populous state in the young United States, helped make it so. Virginia was officially and assertively Anglican, but the state's Baptists and Methodists had become vigorous rivals and critics of the Anglican establishment. This religious conflict exploded into a full-blown political contest in the middle of the Revolutionary War. By 1779, two distinct church-state proposals were on the table in the Virginia Assembly. One proposal was to create a multiple establishment along the lines of South Carolina. The other measure, put forward by Thomas Jefferson, would prohibit taxation in support of "any religious worship, place, or ministry whatsoever." Neither measure passed. In 1784, Patrick Henry proposed another multiple establishment bill. More than 10,000 Virginians petitioned the Assembly against his measure. Virginia evangelicals argued that religion lay outside the jurisdiction of the state and that the Christian faith did not require the support of the government for its growth. James Madison joined the opposition, arguing that religious duties were an obligation of the individual, not the society or the state. Historically, Madison further argued, civil authority in the hands of religion had proved a springboard for "spiritual tyranny." Ultimately, Virginia's Anglicans, now severed from their parent Church across the Atlantic, could not sustain the case for even a multiple establishment in the state—the evangelicals were too strong. The Virginia Assembly in 1786 voted the bill down and passed instead Jefferson's "Act For Establishing Religious Freedom." The law abandoned the language protective of Christianity found in the multiple establishment measures of other states. Instead, it prohibited government compulsion in all matters of religion and held religious freedom to be a natural right.

It certainly seems a short step from Jefferson's law to the First Amendment: "Congress shall make no law respecting an establishment of religion, or prohibiting the free exercise thereof." However, the First Amendment did not forbid *any* laws respecting religion. **Indeed, many Americans understood the protection of religious liberty to be a fundamental purpose of government, along with the protection of property and civic liberty.** For a time, at least, James Madison seemed to diverge from this view. He wrote in the mid-1780s that religion was "not within the purview of Civil Authority" and, again, that "religion is wholly exempt" from the cognizance of government. Such expressions could be taken to mean that government ought to be entirely silent regarding religion—neither protective nor hostile. But Madison was content with the Amendment language that emerged from Congress in 1789.

Indeed, Congress's crafting of the establishment clause of the First Amendment seems to have been mainly an effort to forestall unintended interpretations of religious liberty rather than introduce complete secularism to American government. Some members of the House of Representatives were concerned that the proposed Amendment language, "no religion shall be established by law," might be misread to mean the abolition of religion altogether. Another suggested that the Amendment prohibit the establishment of "religious doctrine" rather than "religion." That change would prevent favoritism toward a particular denominational theology. Others feared that the Amendment might be taken to disestablish or prohibit established Churches in the states. It was even suggested that non-established, privately incorporated Churches might prove unable to enforce their own bylaws in federal courts, since support from such courts might be viewed as an establishment of religion. To address such threats to Churches in the states, James Madison proposed that the word *national* be inserted before *religion*. But that change could give the impression that the Constitution had created a national government—a notion with which many Americans disagreed. Madison withdrew his proposal and, as passed in the House, the Amendment simply stated Congress "shall make no law establishing religion." The Senate, meanwhile, preferred "articles of faith, or a mode of worship" instead of "religion." The final version used "establishment of religion." It also introduced the word "respecting" so as to place both the establishment of a national Church and the disestablishment of state Churches outside Congress's authority.

The religion clauses of the First Amendment reflected a nascent consensus in the United States on church-state relations. **The new federal government would neither establish nor disestablish any churches.** The states, meanwhile, would work out their own policies based on their own unique histories and religious configurations, with a strong trajectory toward full disestablishment and complete religious freedom. Indeed, states that had embraced multiple establishment during the Revolution abandoned even that—among them Georgia (1789), South Carolina (1790), and Maryland (1810). Established-Church Christianity did persist in parts of New England—lasting longer there than anywhere else in the young United States. Connecticut continued to administer its contentious system of tax exemptions for non-Congregationalists until 1818, when voters finally scrapped the system in approving a new state constitution. Massachusetts gave up a similar arrangement only in 1833.

At the heart of the First Amendment consensus, however, was not state disestablishment, whether accomplished rapidly or slowly. Nor was it the full-blown secularization of government and law preferred by many Americans today. Rather, Americans of the founding era agreed upon a kind of spiritual federalism: the states would be allowed supreme authority in matters of religion. The greatest "wall of separation" in 1791 was the wall separating the federal government from the religious diversity that flourished in and among the states.

RECOMMENDED READING

Jon Butler, *Awash in A Sea of Faith:*
Christianizing the American People
(Harvard University Press, 1990)

Philip Hamburger, *Separation of Church and State*
(Harvard University Press, 2002)

Mark A. Noll, *A History of Christianity*
In the United States and Canada
(Eerdmans, 1992)

Bernard Schwartz, *The Bill of Rights:*
A Documentary History, 2 vols. (McGraw Hill, 1971)

LEGAL
INFLUENCES

THE
MAGNA CARTA

By David J. Davis, PhD, FRHistS

PROFESSOR OF BRITISH HISTORY

It is safe to say that Americans have long been fascinated by the Magna Carta. In fact, we probably love it much more than our English cousins, who still use it as part of their legal system. In 1957, the American Bar Association paid for the construction of a memorial to the Magna Carta in England, on the very ground where it was first agreed upon in 1215. Also, the Supreme Court along with several lower American courts cite the Magna Carta as part of the American legal tradition. And a depiction of the signing of the Magna Carta even appears on the bronze doors of the U.S. Supreme Court.

Much earlier in American history, the first permanent colonies in the 17th century were established in a period when the Magna Carta was being held up by key members of Parliament like John Selden and Edward Coke as a fundamental document of the English constitutional tradition. It influenced some of the earliest American documents, including the Virginia Charter (1606) and the Massachusetts Body of Liberties (1641).

Also, it was among some of the first texts to be printed in Philadelphia (by William Penn in 1687 [part of his volume titled *Excellent Privilege*]), and during the American War for Independence, the Massachusetts colonial seal was changed from a Native American to a colonial soldier holding a sword in his right hand and a copy of the Magna Carta in his left.

In both the liberties that the Magna Carta sets out and the manner in which it establishes them, the Magna Carta is an early chapter in the larger historical narrative of how the American colonies claimed their independence. Of course, like so many things in history, the reasons and events that both shaped the creation of the Magna Carta and subsequently its influence upon the English government have been glossed over too often. Because of this fact, it is easy to forget that, while the Magna Carta's importance is timeless, the original purpose of the Magna Carta was not. It was written within a particular historical moment and with a very specific purpose; and unlike the Constitution of the United States, the writers were not charting the course of a new form of government or establishing a new nation. The Magna Carta was created to resolve particular problems of a particular period. In order to understand what it achieved, we must pay attention to how it came to be and how its significance has changed over time. Between 1215 and 1600, what began as a document of established liberties transformed the English legal system as well as the cultural understanding of political and legal power in England.

Establishment of the Magna Carta

The original Magna Carta was set down in the summer of 1215 by King John of England, one of the most hated kings in English history. The document was intended to be a peace treaty of sorts between the king and several of his English barons from the north and east of England who had rebelled against the king. In June, John met his barons at a field called Runnymede, west of London along the Thames River. The barons had seized the city of London, along with a few other castles, and were insisting that John fulfill what they saw as the king's obligations and responsibilities to their traditional English liberties. However, this was not a revolution over civil liberties in the same way that the American War for Independence was. The barons' rebellion was the last straw, a violent necessity, precipitated by years of abusive policies enacted by John in the hopes that the king would be forced to come to terms.

When John became king of England in 1199, he also became the most powerful nobleman in France, controlling territories that stretched from the Pyrenees mountains, extending north along the western French coastline and east to the cities of Tours and Rouen. This "Angevin Empire," which included lands in Ireland and Wales, was a complicated mix of different governmental structures and economic systems that his brother Richard I and father Henry II had carved into a single territory through marriage and conquest. The most important marriage was Henry's union with Eleanor of Aquitaine, John and Richard's mother, giving Henry one of the most important fiefdoms in France (Aquitaine). Unfortunately for John, his succession to the throne lacked support from several nobles across the empire, and he faced a considerable threat from King Phillip II of France who plagued John's early reign with constant efforts to conquer the duchy of Normandy, another one of John's key territories in France.

Although John's reputation as a ruler and a man has suffered over the years, the reality is that his policies and kingship varied very little from that of his elder brother Richard and their father. For one thing, beyond basic feudal obligations to his nobles, there was no consistent model or philosophy for kingship in 12th-century England. Like those that preceded him, John ruled very pragmatically, sometimes ruthlessly, in order to secure his own power. If this pragmatism is the measure of kingship in the period, then John was quite adept at the position. As historian J. C. Holt comments,

> King John's character left deep marks on this period for the crisis called forth all his genius for political maneuver, through the whole range of moves from dictatorial bullying to bribery and shallow promises.... Financial need, suspicion of treachery, and the desirability of buying support combined to give John's policy towards his subjects a complex, almost contradictory, appearance ... hence, while he bullied and laid insupportable financial burdens on some, he wooed and conciliated others.

John's taxes, which are the stuff of legend, in some instances matched the total taxes raised by the previous three monarchs. He introduced new taxes on income and moveable goods. For those unwilling or unable to pay, particularly among the nobility, he threatened to seize lands and titles, take hostages, and even imprison the debtors until payment was made. When noble titles and lands came available through death or imprisonment, he sold the appointments at a premium.

Given John's position, the draconian measures seemed an unfortunate necessity. He was quickly losing territory in France, and constantly fighting battles he could not pay for. So, he took every opportunity to fill his pockets with tax money. For example, when Pope Innocent III placed England under interdict, because John refused to recognize Innocent's choice for archbishop, John made use of this punishment by seizing Church lands and requiring higher payments from the Church's lands. By 1213, John had lost large swathes of territory, despite several attempts to retake the land, and Phillip was preparing an invasion of England, intending to set up his son as king. Perhaps the last straw for his barons was John's devastating loss at the Battle of Bouvines (1214) in the Flemish countryside, which sent the king back to England defeated and bankrupt.

By early 1215, John began positioning himself against a growing faction of barons, who were dissatisfied with royal policies and failures. The king declared himself a vassal of the Pope and promised to go on crusade if the papacy would support him against his barons. Also, he began organizing a mercenary army with troops from the European continent, anticipating that it was only a matter of time before violence broke out. However, before John could strike, the barons captured the capital city without too much resistance, along with key cities like Exeter in the southwest and Lincoln in the north.

When the two sides met in June, the king was not prepared for a full-scale war, and the barons had no intention of removing the king from power. The matter of the Magna Carta was a matter of opposing sides of a feudal conflict, meeting on neutral ground to renegotiate their contractual obligations. The details of the Magna Carta echo the typical language of a medieval feudal agreement between a lord and a vassal. **The Magna Carta was a guarantee in the name of the king to grant liberties and freedoms to his vassals (the barons, bishops, and other nobles of England). This was not intended to be a constitution in any sense of the word.** It was a charter: a legal contract or grant, not the skeletal framework for any government.

The opening statement of the Magna Carta makes this point clear:

> JOHN, by the grace of God King of England, Lord of Ireland, Duke of Normandy and Aquitaine, and Count of Anjou, to his archbishops, bishops, abbots, earls, barons, justices, foresters, sheriffs, stewards, servants, and to all his officials and loyal subjects, Greeting.

> KNOW THAT BEFORE GOD, for the health of our soul and those of our ancestors and heirs, to the honour of God, the exaltation of the holy Church, and the better ordering of our kingdom,

at the advice of our reverend fathers Stephen, archbishop of Canterbury, primate of all England....

Unlike later documents like the Petition of Right (1628) or the Declaration of Independence, this was not written from the perspective of the people. King John, regardless of how much he may have despised the details of the Magna Carta, was the one speaking. It was in the king's name, and the liberties are granted with his sovereign authority. As the 18th-century Whig politician Edmund Burke explained, "Their idea of liberty was not ... perfectly free; and they did not claim to possess their privileges upon any natural privileges or independent bottom, but just as they held their lands from the king."

The details of the agreement were hashed out by both sides in the days and weeks leading up to the actual meeting. The barons based many of their liberties upon the Charter of Liberties issued by Henry I in 1100, which granted English nobles certain property and marriage rights, as well as guarantees about forest land and financial debts. And, in this regard, the Magna Carta was not innovative. It claimed liberties and privileges that had been customary for over a century. The bulk of the clauses in the Magna Carta dealt with matters of ecclesiastical privilege, taxation, land and inheritance rights, and economic matters like the king's forests and money-lending. Today, the clauses dealing with things like trial by jury and due process of law are seen as the most significant, and they certainly were important. However, the emphasis in the early-13th century was on the immediate abuses of the king, particularly in matters of taxation and ecclesiastical rule.

Nevertheless, the agreement of the Magna Carta did not settle matters between John and his barons. In fact, since neither side fulfilled the original terms of the agreement and the pope declared the document "illegal and unjust," rather than establishing an immediate peace, war quickly followed the meeting at Runnymede. Over the next two years, a civil war between the two sides morphed into an international conflict with an invasion from France, who hoped to capture the English throne. However, after John's death from dysentery in 1216, the purpose for the war died with him, and his son Henry III was named king.

Despite the fact that the Magna Carta was annulled by the pope, the custom of the king affirming certain documented privileges and liberties slowly became a customary part of the English government. The Magna Carta was renewed by Henry III in charters (also called the Magna Carta) in 1216, 1217, and 1225 and again by Henry's son Edward I in 1297, cementing a custom that was, in certain respects, unique in the medieval world. These charters did not fundamentally change how kingship operated in medieval England. They, however, did set down certain liberties and protections for the people, certain expectations about how a monarch should rule. Also, they laid a groundwork upon which the constitutional tradition that was codified in the 17th and 18th centuries could be established.

For the time being, the Magna Carta, as part of the English law code, was only significant insofar as it was enforced and affirmed by government officials and the courts. In the 14th century, the Magna Carta was widely enforced. Parliaments and kings reaffirmed the 1297 charter, and judges, particularly on the high courts known as the King's Bench, applied the statutes of the Magna Carta with regularity to private lawsuits over land sale and inheritance cited the charter. For example, in 1299 John, Earl of Warenne, filed suit cited the Magna Carta as a precedent against the King's Exchequer, who John claimed granted too large of a dowry to a widow whose husband had been a tenant on John's land. After the man's death, according to the law, John was expected to pay the dowry. However, in the suit, he claimed that the king's officials had not followed the appropriate protocol in assigning the value of the dowry. Then, in 1315, the King's Bench heard the case of another widow, named Isabel wife of Hugh Bardolf. Isabel filed a suit against her landlord, citing the Magna Carta, because the landlord had removed her family from their tenement property without "reasonable judgment," after Hugh's untimely death.

Similarly, in 1318, Margaret de Clare based her legal petition upon the Magna Carta to have her deceased husband's lands and titles passed to her second husband, Hugh d'Audley. Margaret had been married to Piers (Peter) Gaveston, Earl of Cornwall, a favorite courtier of Edward II, who was executed illegally by a group of his fellow nobles in 1312. Gaveston was from humble origins and had been given Cornwall by Edward. When Edward traveled to France for his own marriage in 1308, he made Gaveston his regent in England, and this favoritism made several nobles jealous of the king's attention and favors. While Hugh was not made Earl of Cornwall, a title that Edward would give to one of his sons, Hugh later was named the Earl of Gloucester.

What these examples demonstrate is that the Magna Carta was no longer simply an agreement made between nobles at the beginning of the 13th century. It was not only statute law but was also developing a certain *mythos* around it. By 1369, the Magna Carta, along with other royal decrees like the *De Tallagio Non Concedendo* (1299), which became the precedent for the American colonists to claim "no taxation without representation," were considered to be more essential to English government than other laws. Edward I's grandson, King Edward III, even declared that the Magna Carta overruled any other statute, investing it with an almost constitutional quality.

The Longevity of the Magna Carta

Despite its popularity in the 14th century and the fact that sessions of Parliament regularly affirmed (and even read) the Magna Carta, by the middle of the 15th century, the charter had slipped into something of legal obscurity.

It is unclear what created this obscurity. England was embroiled in the Hundred Years War until 1453, and then a series of dynastic wars known as the War of the Roses until 1487. These conflicts may have played a role in the Magna Carta's slip into increasing insignificance. Whatever the reason, from 1450 to 1600, the Magna Carta stood like a dusty monument in statute law that lawyers and officials knew was there but did not deploy terribly often. The 1297 charter was printed as part of the royal statutes issued by the royal printer Richard Pynson, and an English translation first appeared in 1534. Yet, it played little role in the lawsuits of the period, and its function in Parliament was little more than that of a mascot. It was taught in the curriculum of the Inns of Court (London's law school); however, the Magna Carta rarely served as much more than a marginal citation in obscure legal debates. The exception to this obscurity seems to have been the first clause, concerning ecclesiastical liberty. It reads:

> FIRST, THAT WE HAVE GRANTED TO GOD, and by this present charter have confirmed for us and our heirs in perpetuity, that the English Church shall be free, and shall have its rights undiminished, and its liberties unimpaired. That we wish this so to be observed, appears from the fact that of our own free will, before the outbreak of the present dispute between us and our barons, we granted and confirmed by charter the freedom of the Church's elections—a right reckoned to be of the greatest necessity and importance to it—and caused this to be confirmed by Pope Innocent III. This freedom we shall observe ourselves, and desire to be observed in good faith by our heirs in perpetuity.

The fundamental and unqualified phrase "shall be free" is speaking specifically about the election of bishops (a process known as *investiture*), which had been a point of conflict between the Church and state since the 11ᵗʰ century. However, there is nothing in the clause that would necessarily limit ecclesiastical liberty to this particular issue.

In two key moments during the 16ᵗʰ century, this clause would be put to the test, and the Magna Carta would emerge from its obscurity to help shape English religious history. First, in 1536, as a response to King Henry VIII's break with the Roman Catholic Church and the subsequent dissolution of monasteries throughout England and Wales, uprisings appeared in the north and west of England. Protestors from across the social spectrum condemned the violent changes that Henry had enacted against the traditional religion. The movement led by the lawyer Robert Aske and the nobleman Thomas Darcy came to be known as the Pilgrimage of Grace. Referring to the Magna Carta's defense of the Church's liberties against royal authority, the Pilgrimage accused the king of breaking statute law, because he failed to respect and defend the freedom of the Church of England. Even though the king had named himself the Supreme Head of the Church, Aske and his followers did not believe this act superseded the Magna Carta.

At its height, tens of thousands of commoners were in open rebellion against the monarchy, winning widespread support throughout the north, even occupying Lincoln Cathedral for a brief time. In the end, in spite of the initial successes, the Pilgrimage was poorly organized and lacked a specific purpose beyond voicing their dissent. It was summarily crushed in 1537 by the king's armed forces; its leaders and hundreds of participants were executed for treason.

In a second event, 40 years later, the Protestant Bishop of Worcester John Whitgift employed the Magna Carta's first clause in a completely different manner. Bishop Whitgift was known for being something of a High Church firebrand. During a successful career at Cambridge University, Whitgift made a name for himself in condemning the excesses of the puritan groups among English Protestants, which included having the puritan leader Thomas Cartwright stripped of his academic fellowship at the university. While he felt no compulsion to defend the liberties of puritans, Whitgift insisted upon the Church of England's liberties against any violations of its autonomy. In 1578, Queen Elizabeth's royal commissioners visited Worcester in order to survey potential ecclesiastical lands that the Crown may want to seize. Whitgift wasted little time reminding Her Majesty of her commitment to the Church's liberty. In a speech aimed at the Queen, he warned Elizabeth not to follow the example set out by her father Henry VIII, who broke his coronation oath "to which he had sworn in Magna Carta." Whitgift continued, "God did so far deny him his restraining grace, that as king Saul after he was forsaken of God, fell from one sin to another … till at last he fell into greater sins than I am willing to mention." Church lands in England, which had been dedicated to Christ, could not be so stripped away from ecclesiastical authority without inviting a divine judgment. It is somewhat surprising that not only did Elizabeth accede to Whitgift's warning, but she also established him as her archbishop five years later.

What these examples demonstrate is that the Magna Carta, while it had diminished in popularity from centuries past, remained a bulwark of individual and corporate liberty. It was a bulwark that even in obscurity still carried significant weight in the eyes of the English people.

The Establishment of Parliament

Perhaps the most important contribution that the Magna Carta makes to constitutional history is that it called for an assembly of nobles to adjudicate any abuses that the monarch may commit. Clause 61 of the 1215 Magna Carta even gave this body the right to seize the monarch's property until a redress of the abuses had been made:

We give and grant to the barons the following security:

Namely, that the barons choose any twenty-five barons of the kingdom they wish, who must with all their might observe and hold, and cause to be observed, the peace and liberties we have granted and confirmed to them by this our present Charter. Then, if we, our chief justiciar, our bailiffs or any of our officials, offend in any respect against any man, or break any of the Articles of the peace or of this security, and the offence is notified to four of the said twenty-five barons, the four shall come to us—or to our chief justiciar if we are absent from the kingdom—to declare the transgression and petition that we make amends without delay.

And if we, or in our absence abroad the chief justice, have not corrected the transgression within forty days, reckoned from the day on which the offence was declared to us ... the four barons mentioned before shall refer the matter to the rest of the twenty-five barons. Together with the community of the whole land, they shall then distrain and distress us in every way possible, namely by seizing castles, lands, possessions and in any other way they can (saving only our own person and those of the queen and our children), until redress has been obtained in their opinion. And when amends have been made, they shall obey us as before.

Although the notion of a noble assembly to redress grievances and advise on executive decisions had deep roots in the Anglo-Saxon history of England, clause 61 provided statutory permanence to this older custom. Of course, this is not exactly what we think of today when we reference Parliament. This assembly was not a legislative body by any means. Nor did it have any authority to remove a particular monarch for abuse of power. It was a contact point, an intermediary, between monarch and kingdom in order to restore the equilibrium between ruler and ruled.

Early on, parliaments were called only intermittently, when the monarch needed the support of his nobles, often for taxation purposes. It was only with the accession of Edward I in 1272 that parliaments slowly became a normal part of English government, and it was not until Edward III that a House of Commons appeared as something permanent and distinct from the House of Lords.

However slow and messy the evolution of the English Constitution was, the assembly would eventually assert its own precedence over and above that of the English monarchy. The assertion of this precedence eventually erupted in the English Civil War of the 17th century, but the beginnings were not nearly as antagonistic. First, during the reign of Edward III (1327–1377), several laws reinterpreted portions of the Magna Carta in broader terms than were intended originally. Clause 39 was a particular focal point of this reinterpretation:

> No free man shall be seized or imprisoned, or stripped of his rights or possessions, or outlawed or exiled, or deprived of his standing in any way, nor will we proceed with force against him, or send others to do so, except by the lawful judgment of his equals or by the law of the land.

First, the phrase "judgment of his equals (or peers)" was reinterpreted to mean trial by jury, a practice that was much rarer in the 13th century. Second, the phrase "law of the land" was understood by the phrase "due process of law," which involved either a legal writ or a jury. Then, the phrase "no free man" became in a 1354 statute, "no man of whatever estate or condition he may be." Although these were technically narrow reworkings of statutory law, they established an important precedence in the history of the English Parliament: that the assembly can, and should when they deem it necessary, reinterpret established law in order to better provide for the kingdom.

In the 16th century, a second step toward Parliament's expanded position in English government was taken when the Tudor monarchies began to rely upon the authority of Parliament as a legislative body. Parliament's importance in the 16th century can be seen in how often, and how long, they were in session, when compared to the previous century. Henry VII, who ruled for 24 years, called seven Parliamentary sessions, which met for a total of 25 weeks. His son, Henry VIII, ruled for 37 years, with Parliamentary sessions lasting a total of 183 weeks. This trend of longer sessions continued for the reigns of Henry's three children: Edward VI, Mary, and Elizabeth I.

The impetus for Parliament's growing importance seems to have been the Protestant Reformation, or at least Henry VIII's motivations for breaking away from the authority of the Pope. When Henry VIII's efforts to obtain a divorce from Queen Katherine of Aragon failed, Henry turned to his Parliament to assist him in separating the Church of England from the Roman Catholic Church. The king's Parliament at the time, often referred to as the Reformation Parliament, issued seven key pieces of legislation between 1529 and 1534 that deprived the Pope of any legal authority in Henry VIII's kingdoms, transferred all ecclesiastical revenues to the Crown, and established the king as the Supreme Head of the Church of England. Although the king seized new power for himself, he simultaneously was establishing certain expectations about the monarch's relationship to Parliament. Its role as a legislative body was becoming entrenched in the constitutional and cultural mind of England. Already by the middle of the 15th century, it was customary for members to insist upon their right not to be imprisoned during sessions, except in cases of treason or other high crimes. And by the 1520s, there were appeals to the monarch to permit free speech in Parliament, so that members could voice their opinions without fear of reprisal.

However, Parliament remained subordinate to the monarchy, and both institutions perceived their roles in government as established to maintain harmony, with the monarch as the head of the government. Parliament may debate intensely certain pieces of legislation. They may voice opposition to the ecclesiastical settlement established by Queen Elizabeth. They may demand that the Queen execute her imprisoned cousin, Mary Queen of Scots. And they did! For the time being at least, it was considered the monarch's prerogative to disregard Parliament's advice. While the Tudor monarchs did not consider themselves to be absolute monarchs, they also did not consider the whims and opinions of Parliament things that must be obeyed.

At the turn of the 17th century, Parliament's role in the English government remained secondary to the monarchy. However, there was already evidence that this monarchical prerogative would not last forever. When James I succeeded Elizabeth in 1603, he became king of England and Scotland, uniting the two independent kingdoms under one flag. And as one might expect, this Scottish king was not accustomed to English forms of policy and procedure. In the first few months of his reign, King James had upset key factions in England. In 1604, a committee formed by the House of Commons drafted a petition to the king that outlined some of their complaints against his actions. Although the petition, known as "A Form of Apology and Satisfaction," was read before the entire House, it was never voted upon and likely never seen by King James. Nevertheless, the text reveals some startling views about the relationship between king and Commons. Beginning in a conciliatory way, understanding how James might not be fully familiar with the English Constitution and may have been given misinformation from counselors, the House desired to clarify their position. They claim that "our privileges and liberties are our right and due inheritance," and that these liberties "ancient and undoubted" cannot be "withheld … denied, or impaired" without harming the entire kingdom. The petition goes on to explain that the House is "a Court of Record" with the "highest standing in the land," and that the king has no right to bar members access to the assembly, which James had done recently with the member Sir Francis Goodwin because of accusations against Goodwin for outlawry. The petition concludes with a return to the traditional role of Parliament, as an intermediary between the king and the kingdom. This time, however, Parliament claimed a level of authority that was unprecedented:

> We stand not in place to speak or do things pleasing; our care is and must be to confirm the love and tie the hearts of your subjects the commons most firmly to your Majesty.... There was never a prince entered with greater love, with greater joy and applause of all his people. This love, this joy, let it flourish in their hearts forever. Let no suspicion have access to their fearful thoughts that their privileges, which they think by your Majesty should be pro-tected, should now by sinister informations or counsel be violated or impaired, or that those which with dutiful respects to your Majesty speak freely for the right and good of their country shall be oppressed or disgraced. Let your Majesty be pleased to receive public information from your Commons in Parliament as to the civil estate and government, for private information pass often by practice: the voice of the people, in the things of their knowledge, is said to be as the voice of God.

While much has been made over the years about the divine right of kings in this period, here is an elected assembly asserting its own divine right. Less than 25 years later, Parliament would issue another document—the Petition of Right. The Petition demanded that James's son, King Charles I, recognize the same sorts of liberties that Parliament believed were enshrined in the tradition of the Magna Carta. Except this time, it was not the king granting the liberties to his nobles. The Petition was addressed "To the King's Most Excellent Majesty," reminding him that "the good laws and statutes of this realm," and not the monarch, guarantee the liberties of the realm.

RECOMMENDED READING

J. C. Holt, *Magna Carta,*
3rd edition (Cambridge University Press, 2015)

Faith Thompson, *Magna Carta:*
Its Role in the Making of the English Constitution, 1300–1629
(Sutton Press, 2007)

THE
ENGLISH
BILL OF RIGHTS

By John O. Tyler, Jr. JD, PhD

PROFESSOR OF LAW & JURISPRUDENCE

M any provisions of the U.S. Constitution reflect lessons learned from the history of England under the Stuart kings, particularly the reign of James II from 1685 to 1688. James II was a Roman Catholic who abused his powers to return Protestant England to Roman Catholicism. His abuses of power eventually provoked the Glorious Revolution in 1688, and Parliament adopted the English Bill of Rights into law on December 16, 1689.

James employed five strategies to Catholicize England. First, he corrupted the courts to establish a "dispensing" power. This power allowed the king to suspend laws without Parliament's consent. James used this power to suspend religious laws prohibiting Catholics from holding public office. He then placed Catholics in control of the army, the Privy Council, the courts, the universities, and the Church of England.

Second, James usurped Parliament's power. He illegally interfered with Parliamentary elections to "pack" Parliament and secure repeal of the religious laws. When Parliament refused to repeal the religious laws, James persecuted opposing members of Parliament and eventually dissolved Parliament altogether. Third, James sought to control his Protestant subjects through military force by illegally raising a standing army and disarming Protestants. Fourth, James weaponized the courts against Protestants by illegally denying them due process. Fifth, James established an illegal Ecclesiastical Commission, using its inquisitorial powers to persecute Anglican ministers and university officials who resisted Catholicization.

James suspended England's religious laws on April 4, 1688. Seven Anglican bishops presented a lawful petition to James claiming he had no authority to suspend the laws. James responded by prosecuting them for sedition and libel. The jury acquitted the seven bishops on June 30, 1688. The Glorious Revolution soon followed. James II fled England for France on December 10, 1688. William and Mary consented to the English Bill of Rights on February 13, 1689, prior to taking the throne.

Forty-one provisions of the U.S. Constitution and Bill of Rights adopt principles from the English Bill of Rights. The following discussion explains James II's abuses of power, the English Bill of Rights provisions addressing each abuse, and the clauses of the U.S. Constitution and Bill of Rights adopting these provisions.

James II's First Strategy: Impose the Dispensing Power

The Magna Carta (1215) and the Petition of Right (1628) forbid the dispensing power because it places the king above the law. James ignored these provisions to impose a dispensing power and suspend laws prohibiting Catholics from holding public office. James's predecessor Charles II attempted to suspend these laws, known as the Clarendon Code, by royal declarations in 1662 and 1672. Parliament forced Charles to withdraw both declarations, however, and the House of Commons passed a resolution in 1673 that the king could not suspend laws without Parliament's consent. Parliament then passed two new laws, the Test Acts of 1673 and 1678, forbidding Catholics from holding office.

James turned to the courts to impose his dispensing power. He corrupted the courts by firing 12 justices, including Chief Justice Thomas Jones of the Court of Common Pleas, who opposed the dispensing power. James then arranged a collusive suit, *Godden v. Hales* (1686), to uphold the king's dispensing power. Eleven of the 12 remaining common law justices upheld the king's dispensing power to suspend laws without Parliament's consent.

James used his dispensing power under *Godden v. Hales* (1686) to appoint Catholic army officers and replace Protestant judges and justices of the peace with Catholics. He replaced Protestants on the Privy Council with five Catholics, and he placed Catholics in positions of authority in the Church and the universities. James suspended the Test Acts in 1687 and prosecuted any official who enforced them.

Paragraphs 1 and 2 of the English Bill of Rights reestablish the sovereignty of English law over the king providing that he has no dispensing power. He cannot suspend any laws unless Parliament consents. Two provisions of the U.S. Constitution have similar provisions. Article I's Supremacy Clause establishes the Constitution, the laws, and U.S. treaties as the supreme law of the land. They bind all judges in every state. Article II's Take Care Clause requires the president to "take care that the laws be faithfully executed."

James II's Second Strategy: Usurp Parliament's Power

James used voter fraud and *Quo Warranto* lawsuits to "pack" Parliament illegally in 1685. The *Quo Warranto* suits revoked the charters of 66 English towns and cities. The Crown then controlled selection of the Members of Parliament for those 66 towns and cities. Only 55 of the 507 members of this "Loyal Parliament" were Whigs opposing the King. The Loyal Parliament's first Act was to grant James II revenues for life.

Paragraph 8 of the English Bill of Rights reestablishes free elections to Parliament. Two provisions of the U.S. Constitution guarantee free elections to the U.S. Congress. Article I's Elections Regulation Clause gives the states the power to determine the times, places, and manner of congressional elections, subject to alteration by Congress. Article I's Qualifications and Quorum Clause provides that each house of Congress is the judge of its members' elections.

When the Loyal Parliament persisted in refusing to repeal the religious laws, James persecuted his opponents in Parliament. The Parliamentary Privilege Act (1512) gives Members of Parliament total immunity for their official acts. James ignored this statute. One target was Sir William Williams, the Protestant Speaker of the House of Commons. James brought an action against Williams for slander and libel in May 1686. Williams's only offense was authorizing the publication of testimony given by Thomas Dangerfield to the House of Commons in 1680. Williams was fined £10,000 ($2,335,491) despite his immunity under the Parliamentary Privilege Act (1512). The House of Lords also published Dangerfield's testimony, but James took no action against them.

Paragraph 9 of the English Bill of Rights reestablishes Parliamentary privilege by providing that no person can impeach or question any speech, debate, or proceeding in Parliament in any court or place other than Parliament itself. The U.S. Constitution establishes the same privilege for Congress. Article I's Speech and Debate Clause provides that Senators and Representatives cannot be questioned outside Congress "for any speech or debate in either House." Article I's Privilege from Arrest Clause provides that no Representative or Senator can be arrested while attending a session of Congress, or while traveling to or from a session, except for treason, felony, and breach of the peace.

When Parliament persistently refused to repeal the religious laws, James simply decided to rule without it. Since the Loyal Parliament foolishly granted James revenues for life in 1685, James had no further need of Parliament. James ignored statutes passed in 1330 and 1362 requiring that Parliament meet at least once every year. He ignored the Triennial Act (1641) providing that no more than three years could pass without a Parliament. James also ignored the Act to Prevent Inconveniences (1641) providing that the king cannot dismiss Parliament without Parliament's consent. James prorogued Parliament six times beginning November 16, 1686, and he illegally dissolved Parliament without Parliament's consent on July 2, 1687. Parliament never met again during his reign.

Paragraph 13 of the English Bill of Rights reestablishes frequent Parliaments. Article I's Meetings of Congress Clause requires Congress to meet at least once in every year.

Lastly, James illegally collected import and export duties without Parliament's consent beginning on February 9, 1685. James ignored the many laws requiring Parliament's consent for these levies, including Clauses 12–15 and 30 of the Magna Carta (1215), the No Tallage or Aid without Consent of Parliament Act (1306), a 1485 statute of Henry VII, the Petition of Right (1628), the Tonnage and Poundage Act (1641), and the Ship Money Act (1641).

Paragraph 4 of the English Bill of Rights provides that the Crown may not levy any taxes without Parliament's consent. Two provisions of the U.S. Constitution reflect this requirement. Article I's Spending Clause provides that only Congress can levy and collect taxes, import duties, and export duties. Article I's Origination Clause requires all bills for raising revenue to originate in the House of Representatives.

James II's Third Strategy:
Control Subjects Through Military Force

James sought to control Protestant subjects who resisted Catholicization through military force. James raised an illegal standing army, placed it under illegal Catholic command, and posted a large contingent outside the center of Protestant resistance in London. James then illegally disarmed his Protestant subjects.

Cromwell taught England that standing armies in peacetime threaten freedom. Parliament passed the Disbanding Act of 1660 to disband Cromwell's standing army, and Parliament passed the Militia Acts of 1661, 1662, and 1663 to prevent standing armies in the future. The Militia Acts severely limited the king's military power. Local landowners funded the militia and the lords-lieutenants of each shire appointed the officers. Almost all militia officers came from the local gentry. The king could only call up the militia for 14 days per year unless a military emergency arose. Even in military emergencies, the burden of paying for the militia shifted to the king, and Parliament could control the army by refusing funding.

Charles II and James II supported disbanding Cromwell's army because its soldiers opposed the Stuart monarchy. Once Cromwell's army was disbanded, however, Charles and James schemed to emulate Cromwell and create their own standing army. The political justification they needed came in 1661 with "Venner's Insurrection."

Thomas Venner was a cooper and leader of the "Fifth Monarchy Men." These men believed that Charles I and Cromwell fulfilled prophesies in Daniel Chapter 7 and Revelation Chapter 20, making Christ's return imminent. On January 6, 1661, the Fifth Monarchy Men attempted to seize the government, usher Christ's return to earth, and inaugurate Christ's millennial kingdom. Most of Venner's men were killed or captured. Venner and 10 others were hanged, drawn, and quartered.

Charles and James used Venner's Insurrection to persuade the Privy Council that the king needed a loyal bodyguard. The Council permitted Charles three regiments, which Charles used as the nucleus of a new standing army. This force soon grew to 5000. Despite two resolutions passed by the House of Commons to disband Charles's standing army in 1674 and 1677, the standing army grew to 8700 before James II ascended the throne on February 6, 1685.

Charles II's illegitimate son, the Protestant Duke of Monmouth, led a rebellion against James in June and July 1685. James used the rebellion to justify growing his illegal standing army to 53,716 officers and men. James illegally placed Catholics in command. London was the center of Protestant belief, and James posted 13,000 soldiers in west London on Hounslow Heath "to overawe the capital." The English reviled James's standing army as a menace to their liberties and their religion.

Paragraph 6 of the English Bill of Rights provides that the king can neither raise nor maintain a standing army in peacetime without Parliament's consent. The U.S. Constitution grants Congress control of raising and maintaining military forces. Article II's Commander-In-Chief Clause provides that the president is commander-in-chief of the armed forces and the militia when they are called into service. Article I, § 8, however, grants all other powers over the armed forces and the militia exclusively to Congress.

The Declare War Clause gives Congress the power to declare war. The Army Clause gives Congress the power to raise and support armies. Remembering the Loyal Parliament's folly in giving James lifetime revenues at the beginning of his reign, the U.S. Constitution limits military appropriations to two years. The Navy Clause gives Congress the power to provide and maintain a Navy. The Military Regulations Clause gives Congress the power to make rules for the government and regulation of the army and navy.

The Militia Clause gives Congress the power to call forth the militia to execute federal laws, suppress insurrections, and repel invasions. The Organizing the Militia Clause gives Congress the power to organize, arm, and discipline the militia, and to govern such part of the militia as may be employed in the service of the United States. However, reflecting the English Militia Acts of 1661, 1662, and 1663, the appointment of all militia officers and the authority for training the militia are reserved to the states.

Charles and James next disarmed their Protestant subjects despite centuries of custom, statutes, and common law establishing the right to bear arms. Seven statutes between 1141 and 1541 imposed a duty to bear arms to keep the peace, serve in the militia, and pursue and capture lawbreakers. The common law also recognized an absolute and inalienable right to own, bear, and use arms to protect one's liberty, personal security, family, servants, and property.

Charles II obtained two statutes from Parliament limiting the right to bear arms. First, the Militia Act of 1662 permitted militia officers and their agents to search and disarm anyone they judged "dangerous to the Peace of the kingdom." Second, the Game Act of 1671, under the pretext of game conservation, prohibited the possession of firearms and bows for most Englishmen other than landed gentry and their gamekeepers.

Charles used these statutes to disarm his political enemies, and James used them to target Protestant subjects. On December 6, 1686, James utilized the Militia Act of 1662 and the Game Act of 1671 to enforce a general disarmament by seizing all firearms.

Paragraph 6 of the English Bill of Rights restores the rights of Protestant subjects to keep and bear arms. The Second Amendment extends the right to keep and bear arms to all Americans.

James II's Fourth Strategy: Weaponize the Courts

James weaponized the courts against Protestant subjects by denying due process of law. Due process protects the innocent by permitting proof of innocence through reasonable means. Due process has three requirements. Defendants must receive full and fair notice, prior to trial, of all charges and potential punishments. Defendants must receive a fair trial, and defendants must receive an impartial tribunal.

James's corrupted courts denied Protestants full and fair notice by imposing illegal punishments. They denied Protestants fair trials by imposing excessive bail and packing juries. They denied Protestants impartial tribunals by permitting "begging" of fines and forfeitures and by imposing excessive fines.

The right to full and fair notice of potential punishments was denied in two infamous cases. Titus Oates was convicted in 1685 for perjury in the 1679 treason trials of five Jesuit priests. Although whipping was not an authorized punishment for perjury, the infamous judge George Jeffreys ordered Oates whipped from Aldgate to Newgate, a distance of 1.07 miles. Oates was whipped again two days later from Newgate to Tyburn, a distance of 2.74 miles. Jeffreys, who regretted that he could not condemn Oates to death, ordered Oates whipped five times a year for life.

The Reverend Samuel Johnson was convicted of sedition and libel in 1686 for writing that Protestant soldiers should not serve under Catholic officers. Johnson argued this "unequally yoked" Christians to unbelievers in violation of II Corinthians 6:14. Although whipping was not an authorized punishment for seditious libel, the judge sentenced Johnson to be whipped from Newgate to Tyburn. Johnson received 317 lashes with a whip of nine knotted cords.

Paragraph 10 of the English Bill of Rights responds to the illegal whippings of Oates and Johnson by prohibiting the infliction of "cruel and unusual punishments." The Eighth Amendment does the same.

The right to fair trial prohibits punishment before conviction. The Magna Carta (1215), the Liberty of Subject Act (1354), and the Petition of Right (1628) forbid imprisonment without conviction. Nevertheless, Charles II illegally imprisoned Protestants without trial.

Charles jailed them outside England so they were not protected by the Habeas Corpus Act (1640). Parliament responded by passing the Habeas Corpus Act of 1679. The 1679 Act prohibited transporting prisoners to deny their right to habeas corpus, but the 1679 Act had a loophole. It left the amount of bail to the discretion of the judge.

Charles's corrupt judges used this loophole to impose excessive bail and keep Charles's political opponents in jail without trial. The diarist Samuel Pepys was arrested and charged with treason in the Popish Plot in 1679. His bail was set at £30,000 ($6.5 million). The London merchant George Speke was arrested and charged with slander in 1683 after Speke legally requested the mayor of London to petition the king to call a Parliament. Bail was set at £100,000 ($22.7 million). Since neither man could pay their bail, both remained in prison without trial.

Paragraph 10 of the English Bill of Rights prohibits excessive bail. The Eighth Amendment does the same.

The right to fair trial also requires trial procedures that enable defendants to prove their innocence through reasonable efforts. Charles II and James II denied Protestants fair trials by packing juries in treason prosecutions. The Magna Carta (1215) guarantees the right to trial by jury, and Parliament passed statutes in 1414 and 1451 to prevent packed juries in treason cases. These statutes required jurors in treason cases (a) to be freeholders, (b) to reside in the shire where the treason occurred, and (c) to have income of at least 40 shillings ($2527) per year. Treason defendants had the right to remove jurors who failed any of these requirements.

Sheriffs selected juries, and Charles and James obtained control of the London sheriffs in 1683 using the same Quo Warranto suits they used to "pack" Parliament. Charles and James used these sheriffs to pack juries and obtain death sentences in 1683 against two Protestant political opponents, Lord William Russell and Colonel Algernon Sidney. The infamous George Jeffreys prosecuted Lord Russell and presided as judge over Colonel Sidney's trial. Corrupt judges, aware of the packed juries, denied Lord Russell and Colonel Sidney their statutory right to remove unqualified jurors. Packed juries convicted both men on perjured testimony, and Lord Russell and Colonel Sidney were both beheaded.

Paragraph 11 of the English Bill of Rights responds to the Russell and Sidney cases by prohibiting jury packing and by requiring that all jurors in treason cases be freeholders. Three clauses of the Sixth Amendment protect the right to jury trial for criminal defendants. These clauses guarantee (a) a speedy trial, (b) a public trial, and (c) an impartial jury drawn from the state and district where the crime was allegedly committed.

The right to an impartial tribunal requires judges without bias for or against any party. James denied impartial tribunals to Protestant subjects by permitting the illegal practice of "begging" for fines or property. Convicted traitors forfeited their property to the king under the Treason Act (1351). Courtiers often "begged" to receive fines and forfeited property from pending cases *before* the defendants were tried. The chancellor, the treasurer, and other

Crown officials often granted these requests, placing judges in a conflict of interest. The Crown was responsible for administering justice, but the desire of Crown officials to please favored courtiers conflicted with this responsibility. Courtiers' desire for private lucre often resulted in unjust prosecutions and convictions and deprived defendants of an impartial tribunal.

"Begging" for fines and forfeitures prior to judgment violated chapter 29 of the Magna Carta (1215). Parliament outlawed "begging" prior to judgment in the Escheators' Act (1429). Nevertheless, begging became so widespread under Charles II that the Crown received only negligible revenue from forfeitures.

The most egregious example of "begging" occurred in the 1685 "Bloody Assizes" after the Monmouth Rebellion. James II appointed the infamous Judge George Jeffreys to try approximately 1,300 captured rebels. The property of all the prisoners was confiscated. Jeffreys executed 320 prisoners by hanging, drawing, and quartering. Jeffreys then posted the quartered corpses at every crossroads, in every marketplace, and on every village green in Devonshire.

Jeffreys transported 841 prisoners. Couriers "begged" for consignment of the prisoners before they were tried, in violation of the Magna Carta (1215) and the Escheators' Act (1429). Even the queen received a consignment of 100 prisoners. The courtiers and the queen sold them into slavery in the West Indies for a period of at least 10 years. Each prisoner brought a profit of about $3,100.

Paragraph 12 of the English Bill of Rights outlaws the practice of "begging" by pronouncing all grants of fines and forfeitures before conviction to be illegal and void. The Due Process Clauses of the Fifth and 14th Amendments provide that no person shall be deprived of life, liberty, or property without first receiving due process of law.

James's denial of impartial tribunals to Protestants was also manifest by excessive fines against Protestants. The problem of excessive fines first arose with the Normans, who replaced Alfred the Great's fixed system of fines with a system of discretionary fines known as *amercements*.

Paragraph 20 of the Magna Carta (1215) establishes three protections against excessive fines. First, fines must be proportional to the gravity of the offense. Second, a fine may not be so great that it prevents any man, free or villein, from making his living. Third, fines may only be imposed by one's peers. The First Statute of Westminster (1275) requires that all *amercements* be reasonable, be proportional to the offense, and without impairment to anyone's ability to make their living. In *Hodges v. Humkin* (1615), the Court of the King's Bench extended these proportionality requirements to imprisonment as well as fines.

Stuart monarchs ignored these laws, persistently utilizing excessive fines and imprisonment to disable and punish political adversaries. Charles II and James II routinely levied excessive fines against Protestant opponents. In 1680, a committee of the House of Commons reviewed the fines issued since 1677 by the Court of the King's Bench. The committee concluded that the Court of the King's Bench treated Catholics leniently while intentionally imposing excessive fines on Protestant subjects, and the House of Commons drafted a bill to end the abuse of Protestants. Nevertheless, the excessive fines continued, as illustrated by three cases recounted below.

In 1684, John Hampden, the Protestant grandson of the John Hampden involved in *Hampden's Case* (1637) regarding ship money, was fined £40,000 ($9,341,962) for a misdemeanor conviction. A single witness alleged, without corroboration, that Hampden was involved in the Rye House Plot to assassinate Charles II and James II.

In 1686, Sir William Williams, the Protestant Speaker of the House, was fined £10,000 ($2,335,491) for libel against the future James II. This was the highest libel fine in English history. Williams's only offense was authorizing the publication of *Dangerfield's Narrative* recounting the testimony of Thomas Dangerfield before the House of Commons regarding the "Popish Plot." Williams was fined despite his immunity under the Parliamentary Privilege Act (1512). The House of Lords printed the entirety of *Dangerfield's Narrative* in its own journal, but no legal action was taken against any of its members.

In 1687, the Court of the King's Bench fined the Protestant Earl of Devonshire £30,000 ($7,144,345). His only offense was striking a man with a walking stick. The earl desired satisfaction for an earlier affront the earl had suffered from Colonel Thomas Culpepper. The earl confronted colonel Culpepper in the king's palace at Whitehall and demanded that the colonel go downstairs with him. When the colonel refused to go, the earl struck him with his walking stick.

The three men described above, Sir William Williams, John Hampden, and the Earl of Devonshire, were all members of the 1689 Bill of Rights Committees in the House of Commons and the House of Lords. In response to the excessive fines described above, paragraph 10 of the English Bill of Rights prohibits the imposition of excessive fines. The Eighth Amendment does the same.

James II's Fifth Strategy:
Establish an Illegal Ecclesiastical Commission

James established an illegal Ecclesiastical Commission, using its inquisitorial powers to persecute Anglican ministers and university officials who resisted Catholicization. The Ecclesiastical Commission was the successor to the Court of High Commission established by Elizabeth I in 1559. The

High Commission originally supervised clerical discipline, but it quickly expanded its jurisdiction to include lay offences and became a tool of political oppression. The High Commission's secret proceedings ignored the due process and jury trial guarantees of the Magna Carta (1215), utilizing the *ex officio* oath and other procedures of the Inquisition.

The *ex officio* oath, forced on the defendant before giving him notice of any charges, required the defendant to swear to answer fully and truthfully any question posed by the High Commission. Defendants who submitted to the *ex officio* oath were compelled to choose between testifying against themselves or committing perjury. Those who refused the *ex officio* oath could be imprisoned indefinitely without trial. The High Commission routinely transferred refusing defendants to the infamous Court of Star Chamber, where they could be tortured and imprisoned indefinitely without trial.

The High Commission had broad powers, unlimited discretion, and there was no appeal from its decisions. James I and Charles I utilized both the Court of High Commission and the Court of Star Chamber as instruments of tyranny. The common law judges, led by Sir Edward Coke, opposed them at every opportunity, and the "Long" Parliament abolished them both in 1641. The Act Abolishing the Court of High Commission (1641) also abolished the *ex officio* oath and forbade the re-establishment of the Court of High Commission or *any similar court* at any time in the future.

Nevertheless, James II ignored the 1641 Act and reinstated the Court of High Commission in July 1686, renaming it the Ecclesiastical Commission. The Ecclesiastical Commission returned the Inquisition to England. James appointed the despised Judge George Jeffreys of the Bloody Assizes as its president.

James directed the Ecclesiastical Commission to persecute any cleric who criticized Catholicism. The Commission's first target was Henry Compton, the Bishop of London. In 1686, the Ecclesiastical Commission ordered Bishop Compton to suspend John Sharp, Dean of Norwich and Rector of St. Giles in the Fields, after Sharp gave a sermon criticizing Roman Catholicism. Bishop Compton delayed the suspension to conduct his own investigation, so the Ecclesiastical Commission suspended Bishop Compton.

James also used the Ecclesiastical Commission to Catholicize the Universities of Cambridge and Oxford. In February 1687, the king ordered Cambridge to grant a degree to a Benedictine monk, Alvin Francis, without the oaths of supremacy and allegiance required by English statutes. These oaths were adopted to prevent Catholics from receiving degrees. When the Vice-Chancellor of Cambridge refused to break the law and grant the degree, the Ecclesiastical Commission removed him from office.

On April 5, 1687, the king ordered the Fellows of Magdalen College at Oxford to elect Anthony Farmer, a Catholic sympathizer of bad character, as its president. The Fellows refused and elected one of the fellows as president. The Ecclesiastical Commission expelled them all from their fellowships and replaced them with Catholics. The new Catholic fellows elected the Catholic Bonaventura Gifford as their president.

Paragraph 3 of the English Bill of Rights declares the Ecclesiastical Commission "illegal and pernicious." The U.S. Bill of Rights adopts numerous guarantees against the inquisitorial procedures utilized in the High Commission, the Court of Star Chamber, and the Ecclesiastical Commission.

The Due Process Clauses of the Fifth and 14th Amendments forbid the government from depriving a person of their life, liberty, or property without due process of law. Due process requires full and fair notice, a fair trial, and an impartial tribunal. The inquisitorial procedures utilized in the High Commission, the Court of Star Chamber, and the Ecclesiastical Commission violated each of these elements.

The Establishment Clause of the First Amendment prohibits the government from establishing religious courts. The Free Exercise Clause of the First Amendment prohibits government regulation of religious belief, worship, and lifestyle. The Self Incrimination Clause of the Fifth Amendment prohibits the *ex officio* oath by providing that no person "shall be compelled in any criminal case to be a witness against himself." The Sixth Amendment guarantees criminal defendants the right to a public and speedy jury trial, as well as the right to assistance of counsel.

The final straw for the English people came on April 4, 1688, when James suspended England's religious laws in his Declaration of Indulgence. James issued a revised Second Declaration of Indulgence on April 27, 1688, and on May 4, 1688, the Privy Council ordered that Anglican clergy distribute and read the Second Declaration during worship services, from every pulpit, to every congregation in England. Any clergyman who refused to read the Declaration was subject to ejection from his benefice by the Ecclesiastical Commission.

On May 18, 1688, two days before the ordered reading of the Second Declaration, seven Anglican bishops filed a lawful petition with the king. The petition requested the king to rescind the order requiring Anglican priests to distribute and read the Second Declaration. The bishops claimed, contrary to the collusive decision in *Godden v. Hales* (1686), that the king did not possess the dispensing power, and that Parliament had often declared the dispensing power illegal. James angrily responded, "God has given me the dispensing power and I will retain it!"

English common law permitted this petition, as did the Act against Tumultuous Petitions (1661). James nevertheless arrested the seven bishops and prosecuted them for sedition and libel. The jury acquitted the seven bishops on June 30, 1688, to tumultuous celebrations across England. The Glorious Revolution followed soon after "without bloodshed, without proscriptions, and without any important breach of public order." James II fled England for France on December 10, 1688. William and Mary consented to the English Bill of Rights on February 13, 1689, prior to taking the throne, and Parliament enacted the Bill of Rights as law on December 16, 1689.

Paragraph 5 of the English Bill of Rights responds to the Trial of the Seven Bishops by establishing the right of every subject to petition the king. All commitments and prosecutions for doing so are illegal. The First Amendment similarly establishes "the right of the people ... to petition the government for redress of grievances."

Conclusion

The English Bill of Rights did more than respond to illegal abuses of power. It restored the sovereignty of English law; it restored England's mixed constitution; it restored the due process of law; and it restored the liberty of the English people. It also inspired key provisions of the U.S. Constitution and Bill of Rights.

The religious struggles between James II and the English people also inspired the United States' greatest political innovation, true freedom of religion. Three provisions of the Constitution and Bill of Rights guarantee this freedom. The No Religious Test Clause of Article VI forbids religious test laws like the Test Acts of 1673 and 1678. The First Amendment's Establishment Clause forbids state Churches like the Church of England. The First Amendment's Free Exercise Clause forbids government agencies like the Ecclesiastical Commission from interfering with religious worship, lifestyle, and belief.

Lastly, the English Bill of Rights reminds us that we must vigilantly protect our Constitution and Bill of Rights. The English Bill of Rights did not create any new liberties. It only restored well-established liberties that the English people failed to protect. Once lost, restoring these rights required a century of struggle, including three civil wars and the Glorious Revolution.

* *

RECOMMENDED READING

John Dykstra Eusden, *Puritans, Lawyers, and Politicians*
in Early Seventeenth-Century England
(Yale University Press, 1958)

Thomas B. Macaulay,
The History of England from the Accession of James II, vol. 1
(Harper, 1879)

Lois G. Schwoerer, *The Declaration of Rights 1689*
(Johns Hopkins University Press, 1981)

J.R. Tanner, *English Constitutional Conflicts of the Seventeenth Century,*
1603–1689 (Cambridge University Press, 1962)

G.M. Trevalyan, *England under the Stuarts*
(Folio Society, 1996)

COVENANTS, COMPACTS, AND CHARTERS:

THE EMERGENCE OF AN AMERICAN CONSTITUTIONAL TRADITION

By Chris Hammons, PhD
PROFESSOR OF POLITICAL SCIENCE

In the hallways of schools, government buildings, and civic organizations across America, our nation's founding documents are customarily displayed to memorialize the origins and history of our republic. These "Freedom Shrines," as they are sometimes called, typically include our Constitution, the Bill of Rights, and the Declaration of Independence. You're also likely to find other documents from American history, such as the Gettysburg Address and the Emancipation Proclamation. You might come across FDR's "Four Freedoms" or MLK's "I Have a Dream" speech. You can sometimes even find, though it seems increasingly rare, one of the earliest documents to contribute to our constitutional tradition. It's a very short document known as the Mayflower Compact.

Drafted in 1620, the Mayflower Compact is considered by many scholars as the first "constitutional" document created in North America. There are a handful of colonial charters that predate the Mayflower Compact, but these were brought from England. The Mayflower Compact was drafted completely in the New World. At only 195 words, it is an exceedingly short document. It's shorter even than Lincoln's Gettysburg Address, which is frequently noted for its brevity. Yet the Mayflower Compact remains one of the most remarkable documents in our constitutional story because it is the first in a long American tradition of writing down constitutional principles on paper. It is also unique because it predates many of the frequently cited historical and philosophical influences on American constitutionalism. In short, the Mayflower Compact might be considered "the seed of American constitutionalism"—a seed planted by the Pilgrims almost two centuries before our Founding Fathers met in Philadelphia.

The Mayflower Compact

The significance of this important document is tied to the story of the Pilgrims who came to the New World in a tiny ship for which the Compact was named. The Pilgrims were looking for a new home and a place they could worship as they pleased. Like many Englishmen, the Pilgrims felt that the Church of England had been corrupted by Catholic and High-Church influences. They objected to the pageantry, the ritual, and the affluent trappings of the Church. The Puritans wanted to purify the Church (hence their name) and return to a simpler focus on the Bible, without all the pomp and circumstance of fancy religious services.

Though they are often described as Puritans, it is more accurate to refer to the Pilgrims as *Separatists*. Like the Puritans, they too felt the Church of England was corrupt, but they believed it was so tainted that it was beyond saving. The Separatists felt that the only way to escape the corrupt influence of the Church of England was to leave it. The problem for these Pilgrim Separatists was that the Church of England was the official Church of the realm. Unlike in the United States today, you couldn't just start up a new church on a corner lot. To attempt such a thing was punishable by prison or death. Lacking religious freedom in England, these Pilgrim men and women, looking for a new home for their families, sold their belongings, loaded up their children, and left.

Their initial escape took them to Holland. Why Holland? Well, it's closer than North America for one. In addition, it was the most prosperous commercial nation on the planet, rife with opportunity for gainful employment. Most importantly for the Pilgrims, it was a very diverse and tolerant society. The Dutch wouldn't care about the religious practices, doctrines, or lifestyles of a small group of Pilgrims from England. It would be the perfect place to start over.

The Pilgrims moved to Holland and lived there for a dozen years. They prospered, though life was tough and the expense of living in a major commercial area made it difficult to get ahead financially. Their finances, however, were the least of their concerns. Having lived in Holland for over a decade, they had another problem. Their children were growing up eating Dutch food, singing Dutch songs, and playing Dutch games with Dutch children. Many of the youngest children had never know any different. These Pilgrim children were losing their English identity.

The Pilgrims figured they needed to go somewhere far away, where they could raise their kids free from all the distractions of windmills and tulips, and the wilderness of North America looked pretty good. It was isolated. Land was plentiful and cheap. And they would be free from any sort of religious restrictions imposed by England. They pooled the money they had saved over the past decade and purchased a ship to get them across the Atlantic to the New World. The ship was called the *Speedwell.*

The *Speedwell* was exactly the sort of ship you would expect Pilgrims—with scant funds and limited seafaring knowledge—to buy. In fact, the *Speedwell* was in such bad shape that the Pilgrims realized that it would be dangerous to travel the Atlantic without another ship in tow. They sailed the leaky *Speedwell* from Holland to South England, and begin planning their departure to the New World.

Using an idea they borrowed from the Dutch, the Pilgrims formed what is called a joint-stock company. They raised money from investors with the promise that raw materials found in the New World would be exported and sold at a profit. The investors would share in these profits, sort of like today's venture capitalists. The Pilgrims raised good money from these investors, and secured additional funds by selling passage on the voyage to young men looking for adventure and fortune. With the money raised they purchased some land in America, a second boat called the *Mayflower*, and set sail on September 6, 1620.

After 66 days at sea, the *Mayflower* pilgrims reached the shore of America in late November of 1620. The journey across the ocean was not easy. The *Mayflower* nearly sank during a terrible storm. It was saved due to the heroic response of the Pilgrim men, impressing both captain and crew of the tiny vessel. The other ship, the *Speedwell*, never made it far from England. The crew found that the ship leaked terribly, just as the Pilgrims had feared. The *Speedwell* turned back to port and left the *Mayflower* Pilgrims to cross the ocean alone.

After the harrowing voyage, the passengers and crew were exhausted and anxious. The deteriorating conditions onboard the tiny ship—packed with 102 passengers, 30 crew, and various livestock—were miserable. The travelers were desperate to set foot on land. Though eager to get to shore, the Pilgrims sat on the deck of the little ship and looked out at the misty virgin wilderness of North America ... and were scared to death.

The long journey and terrible storm had pushed them hundreds of miles from their planned landing. Their charter was valid only for settlement in "Northern parts of Virginia." The Pilgrims knew they were well outside the jurisdiction of their charter, but weren't sure where exactly they were (we know the area now as Massachusetts). They were effectively adrift in the New World.

The Pilgrim men stood on the deck of the tiny ship across from the other passengers they had picked up in England—young men seeking adventure, fortune, and all the things from which the Pilgrims were trying to escape. With growing trepidation, the Pilgrims realized they were at risk of exposing their families to chaos and lawlessness in a New World wilderness far from home. Already, the "Strangers," as the Pilgrims referred to these other passengers, were contemplating setting up camp for themselves and striking out on their own, contending that the group's charter had no authority in this uncharted land. If ever there was such a time as a "state of nature"—a world without order, or government, or law—this was it.

William Bradford, future governor of the colony, noted that it was the "discounted and mutinous speeches" by the Strangers, who threatened to "use their own liberty," that led the Pilgrims to act. In a pivotal moment in American history, all of the men on the tiny ship gathered in the hull. Fathers and bachelors, Pilgrims and Strangers, men of faith and men of fortune, gathered together and drafted a mutual agreement. It is this agreement, or compact, that bears the ship's name. These 41 men made a pledge ... that though they had no government, no laws, and no means to enforce them, they would pledge themselves to abide by the will of the majority, for the good of the colony. And all signed their names to this document, which became known as the Mayflower Compact.

The Mayflower Compact, 1620

In the name of God, Amen. We, whose names are underwritten, the Loyal Subjects of our dread Sovereign Lord King James, by the Grace of God, of Great Britain, France, and Ireland, King, defender of the Faith, etc.:

Having undertaken, for the Glory of God, and advancements of the Christian faith, and the honor of our King and Country, a voyage to plant the first colony in the Northern parts of Virginia; do by these presents, solemnly and mutually, in the presence of God, and one another; covenant and combine ourselves together into a civil body politic; for our better ordering, and preservation and furtherance of the ends aforesaid; and by virtue hereof to enact, constitute, and frame, such just and equal laws, ordinances, acts, constitutions, and offices, from time to time, as shall be thought most meet and convenient for the general good of the colony; unto which we promise all due submission and obedience.

In witness whereof we have hereunto subscribed our names at Cape Cod the 11th of November, in the year of the reign of our Sovereign Lord King James, of England, France, and Ireland, the eighteenth, and of Scotland the fifty-fourth, 1620.

The document contains the signatures of men from various social groups. Some of the men were wealthy, like merchant John Carver, while others were from more modest occupations as sailors, carpenters, or even servants. These men set aside their differences to establish a government for their mutual preservation. It was an agreement—that "social compact" that you read about earlier—formed for the common good. And most importantly, it was done freely, showing that governments could be established by "reflection and choice" rather than "accident and force."

The Compact didn't establish a system of government. It is not a consti-tution in the traditional sense of a document that "sets up a government." There are no institutions created, powers allocated, or even limitations placed on political authority. Rather, the document is an agreement that the colonists will "covenant and combine ... together into a civil body pol-itic; for our better ordering, and preservation"—meaning that they will come together to form some kind of governing body, though the form or scope of that body would be determined later. The men would then "enact, constitute, and frame, such just and equal laws, ordinances, acts, constitu-tions, and offices, from time to time, as shall be thought most meet and convenient...." In other words, when finally assembled, the men would pass laws that they deemed necessary for the "good of the colony."

These initial laws would be formulated and passed based on majority rule. Once the majority agreed on a law, all the men of the colony promised "all due submission and obedience" to uphold the law. This raises an interest-ing question as to the enforcement mechanism, or the executive power, in the Mayflower Compact. How do you enforce such an agreement, thou-sands of miles from the King's courts and soldiers? It would have been very easy for the Pilgrims or the Strangers to ignore the Mayflower Compact if they had so chosen, yet it worked surprisingly well. Why?

Lacking any means of enforcing the Compact, other than ink and honor, the Plymouth colonists relied largely on their tremendous faith to bind each other to the agreement. Here in the wilderness of North America, where the King of England could not reach, these men relied on mutual trust and faith in each other, and in a higher power. The opening line of the Compact, "In the name of God, Amen," is an invocation of a higher power to which men swore their obedience. In fact, the religious nature of the document is further evident in the use of the phrase "*covenant* and combine." The idea of a *covenant* is an intrinsically religious concept that implies the agreed-upon arrangement is not only amongst men but with God as well. In essence, it a Compact between Pilgrims, Strangers, *and* God. Ironically the term "Compact" nowhere appears in the document, and a better name for the document might be the Mayflower Covenant, reflecting the religious nature and ideals of the people who crafted it.

The Mayflower Compact exemplifies several principles of American constitutionalism almost 200 years before our national Constitution was drafted. Immediately evident in the Compact is the principle of "Popular Sovereignty," reflected in the creation of a "civil body politic" comprised of the people. In this aspect, the Mayflower Compact looks a lot like the social contract theories of Hobbes and Locke, even though these works don't arrive for another generation or two. John Quincy Adams got it right when he noted that the Mayflower Compact is the only actual instance in human history of the theoretical "social compact" written about by political philosophers.

The Compact also invokes a higher power to which men are beholden. This is an idea that runs through much of the political philosophy of the founding era—Locke, Montesquieu, and Blackstone among the most prominent. Though the phrase "natural law" or "laws of nature" is never used, the deistic element in the invocation and the idea of a binding covenant reflect the idea of a higher moral truth in political affairs beyond just the words on paper. Sadly, the opening invocation of the Compact is often excised from reprints that appear in school textbooks. It's an unfortunate editorial tendency that undermines a deeper understanding of the document and the natural law theory that is so fundamental to American constitutionalism.

Another important principle, the rule of law, is manifest in the directive that laws be passed only for the "good of the colony" and that all agree to submit to the law. There is no distinction made in the Compact between rich and poor, occupation, social status, or even religion. The Compact is binding on them all and they promise (to each other and God) to obey the law. Indeed, the very act of writing down the agreement and signing it invokes images of the Magna Carta, with the intent to create an agreement that enforces important political principles and provides the basis of equality under law.

In sum, the Mayflower Compact is the first time in North America that important political principles are codified in a written document for the purposes of governing a free people. The importance of the Mayflower Compact in our constitutional history is often overshadowed by later, more epic events such as the English Civil Wars, the Glorious Revolution, or the American War for Independence. The intellectual influences of the Old World, such as Locke and Montesquieu and Blackstone, are also credited with great influence on the American constitutional tradition. However, all of these influences—both historical and philosophical— postdate the Mayflower Compact.

All this is to say that the Mayflower Compact is a uniquely American creation. This short document birthed a distinctly *American* form of constitutionalism in the New World that predates the major historical and intellectual influences regularly credited for shaping our Constitution. It is not, however, the only instance of an emerging and uniquely American form of constitutionalism. If we think of the Mayflower Compact as the seed of American constitutionalism in the New World, the numerous colonial covenants, compacts, and charters that follow are its flowers.

Covenants, Compacts, and Charters

The constitutional principles of popular sovereignty, natural law, majority rule, and the rule of law found in the Mayflower Compact are evident in other documents used throughout the early American colonies. **Early**

colonial documents usually take one of three traditional forms—covenant, compact, or charter—and provide the fundamental elements for an emerging and uniquely American constitutionalism. These different forms of political documents existed simultaneously throughout the North American colonies, but many of the earliest colonial documents follow the "covenant" form exemplified by the Mayflower Compact. These covenant-style documents focus on the "ends" of political society rather than the "means," and invoke God as the basis of political authority.

A good example of a covenant-style document is found in the Dedham Covenant of 1636. Drafted by settlers in the tiny village in Massachusetts that bears the same name, it starts with a religious invocation similar to the Mayflower Compact. All the subscribers pledge to obey the covenant with "fear and reverence for our Almighty God." The covenant then establishes a commitment to resolve conflicts within the community by the passage of "orders and constitutions" for the common good. Each of the 125 signers pledged to "subscribe hereunto his name, thereby obliging both himself and his successors after him forever…." They don't yet have a government, but they are forming a society with the pledge to create a government in due order.

Another example of a covenant-style document was produced by the colonists of Pocasset, Rhode Island, who drafted a formal document to establish their town (1638) by declaring that they "solemnly in the presence of Jehovah incorporate ourselves in a Body Politic." The intent was to create a binding political order based on a covenantal oath among the signers with God as a party to the oath. There are numerous other examples of these early covenant-style documents in early America.

The idea of people coming together to form a political society—based on the consent of the people, for the good of the people, and in accordance with some higher law—was an idea that permeated the North American colonies, particularly in New England, in the early 1600s. The settlers of that region brought with them a religious tradition of using covenants as the basis for forming churches. An example from the Charlestown-Boston Church (1630) provides a good example of a typical *church* covenant. It reads: "In the Name of our Lord Jesus Christ ... We whose names are hereunder written, being by His most wise, and good Providence brought together unto this part of America ... desirous to unite ourselves into one Congregation, or Church...."

It was a small step for these New Englanders to utilize the same tradition and language used to form churches to form political societies instead. Often the two were so intertwined it was hard to tell where religious and political society differed. In essence, the New England colonists were saying, "we came here as a religious people to set up a Church, now we need to set up a government." They didn't always know what that government would look like, but they would pledge themselves to the enterprise with a religious fervor and devotion that gave great weight to the covenant.

The covenants of early New England quickly evolved to what historians and political scientists refer to as political compacts. While much of the language in these documents is the same as that found in covenants, there are two important distinctions. The first distinction is that references to God, which are central to political covenants, largely disappear and are replaced by an emphasis on "the people" as the binding force behind the political compact. The second distinction is that "the people" codify or write down their fundamental values so as to institutionalize a sense of their identity, often in the form of rights, liberties, and community standards. In essence, if "the people" are the source of authority, then compacts lay out the parameters for what it means to be "of the people."

A good example of a political compact is found in a colony established, ironically, by a very religious people. The people of Rhode Island believed that invoking the Lord's name in the formation of a political agreement was blasphemous. Like a covenant, the signers of the Providence Agreement of 1637 (which effectively established Rhode Island) promise to subject themselves to "all such orders and agreements as shall be made for the public good ... by the major consent of the present inhabitants...." Unlike a covenant, however, this document finds its authority in "We whose names are here under [signed]"—in the name of the people—rather than invoking God as the binding authority of the agreement.

With an increased emphasis on popular sovereignty, political compacts also reflect a more developed sense of community. These documents often provide various regulations and ordinances that reflect the common values of "the people" from whom political authority flows. The Massachusetts Body of Liberties (1641), for example, includes many laws and ordinances that seem foreign to us but were important to the larger Massachusetts Bay community—corporal punishment for blasphemy, regulations regarding the use of farm animals, and treatment of servants, to list a few. Some of the provisions, however, seem surprisingly modern for the 17th century, such as conscientious objector status for military ventures, child protective services, welfare programs for the poor, and prohibition of domestic abuse. And some of the provisions are strikingly familiar—right to a speedy trial, no self-incrimination, right to legal counsel, and right to jury trial—reflecting the influence of English common law on the early American colonies.

The concentration of both the covenant and compact traditions in New England may help explain why that geographic region was so central to the American Revolutionary movement. Having lived essentially under "home-rule" since the early 17th century, New Englanders were not easily persuaded to give up their liberty, which for them was a product of two powerful forces—natural law and popular sovereignty—as reflected in both the covenant and compact traditions. Colonies in the South often held to the established Church of England or ventured to the New World with Royal Charters carried from the Mother Country. As a result, the motivations and allegiances were quite different. This is not to say that the North and South would not eventually converge in the Revolutionary cause, only that they operated on different assumptions and timelines.

The third form of early political documents—political charters—are quite different from covenants and compacts. Their authority stems from the grantor (traditionally the king)—placing obligations on those who receive the charter (an individual or company). As a result, charters read like legal contracts, with one party agreeing to provide some service or product to the other party. They are less philosophical and more legalistic—often establishing geographic boundaries for the respective colony, naming colonial leaders outright, and perhaps setting expectations for colonial success. They place a heavy emphasis on the "means" of government—political institutions and procedures—because the "ends" are explicit in the document and the purpose of the charter. That is, those receiving the charter know exactly what is expected of them, with the charter clarifying how it is to be achieved.

One of the earliest colonial charters is the 1606 charter for the Virginia Company that produced the Jamestown colony. It lays out the mission of the colony—primarily the "propagating of Christian religion to such people, as yet live in darkness" and to "to dig, mine, and search for all manner of mines of gold, silver, and copper" with the return of a specified portion to the Mother Country. The specific boundaries of the colonial grant are provided in miles and longitude and latitude. The charter establishes a colonial council in Virginia and a corresponding council in London, each with thirteen seats. Some individuals with authority are listed by name.

In some ways, the emphasis on institutions and procedures in colonial charters is more familiar to modern Americans than the abstract and philosophical nature of covenants and compacts. The New York charter of 1683, for example, states that "The Supreme Legislative Authority under his Majesty and Royall Highnesses James Duke of York Albany &c Lord proprietor of the said province shall forever be and reside in a Governor, Council, and the people met in General Assembly." After establishing these basic institutions of government, the charter further details the processes and procedures of government. The 1701 Charter of Delaware similarly creates "an Assembly yearly chosen by the freemen thereof.... Which Assembly shall have power to choose a speaker and other officers and shall be judges of the qualifications and elections of their own members, sit upon their own adjournments, appoint committees, prepare bills in order to pass into laws...."

In short, colonial charters provide the institutional and procedural aspects of government that are missing in covenants and compacts. They read more like our own Constitution with its emphasis on the basic structure and operation of government. In fact, the colonial charters of Rhode Island (1663) and Connecticut (1662) actually served as de facto constitutions for years after the colonies had declared their independence from England. Connecticut operated under its charter until 1818 and Rhode Island under its charter until 1842. So while charters may not offer the theological or philosophical depth of their covenant or compact counterparts, they are apparently very practical.

These three traditions in American colonial history—covenants, compacts, and charters—existed and evolved simultaneously during the almost 200 years leading up to the Constitutional Convention of 1787. In many cases, the political documents governing the colonies were a combination of two or more of these different forms, combining elements from the covenants, compacts, and charter formats. For example, the Fundamental Orders of Connecticut (1639) is an amalgam of two different styles. It begins with a covenant that "there should be an orderly and descent Government established according to God, to order and dispose of the affairs of the people…." The remainder of the document is devoted to political institutions and processes like a charter. The Pilgrim Code of Law (1636) blends all three of these forms together in one document. It starts off like a charter, with detailed explanation for various political institutions, but also has elements of a covenant (it directly references the famous Mayflower Compact of 1620) and a compact (claiming sovereignty of the people as the basis of political legitimacy).

The evolution and combination of these early colonial styles into a single document resulted in a completely new political creation— what we now think of as a "written constitution." These "constitutions" contain all three of the original colonial styles in a single document— an invocation of a higher power (covenant), the creation of a people (compact), and the formation of political institutions and procedures (charter). In fact, since the Pilgrim Code of Law and Fundamental Orders of Connecticut are the earliest amalgamation of these different styles, they are asserted by scholars to be prime candidates for the first "written constitutions" in the New World.

Impact on Our Constitution

The U.S. Constitution is a product of the American colonial experience and reflects all three of the colonial formats—covenant, compact, and charter. The compact element is the easiest to identify and probably the most recited part of the Constitution. It is reflected in the celebrated preamble with the words "We the People…." In the tradition of colonial compacts, our Constitution opens with the explicit statement that popular sovereignty is the foundation for the government it establishes. President Lincoln later summarized our emphasis on popular sovereignty by describing our government as "of the people, by the people, and for the people." The addition of our Bill of Rights (the first 10 Amendments) codifies our political values, including things like religious freedom, the right to bear arms, and the rule of law. It reflects our commitment to liberty and limited government.

The bulk of the Constitution establishes political processes and procedures, reflective of early American colonial charters. This is what most people think of when they think of the Constitution. The three primary branches of government are laid out in Articles I through III, Article IV deals with the states, while technical aspects of the Constitution are described in the remaining three Articles. Important processes are described throughout, including the election of government positions, the means for producing legislation, and the amendment process. Much of it seems dry and legalistic, but such is the charter tradition with its emphasis on political institutions and process.

The covenant element in the Constitution is found in the preamble with the words "the Blessings of Liberty to ourselves and our Posterity." The preamble suggests that Liberty is a sacred gift—a blessing—bestowed upon mankind not by government but by a higher power. The second part of the phrase indicates that this gift is promised to later generations—"our Posterity"— and it is the purpose of the Constitution to uphold that promise.

Though the language may sound secular, constitutional preambles in America were used to provide both philosophical and theological justification for the subsequent legalistic and institutional parts of the Constitution. American state constitutions, which preceded the U.S. Constitution by a dozen years, are rife with direct references to God in their preambles as the source of liberty and good government. It is reflective of the covenant language found in early colonial political documents. The Founding Fathers in 1787 would have been intimately familiar with this language, as many of them had a hand in writing their home state's constitution during the Revolution. The covenantal implications of "the Blessings of Liberty … to our Posterity" would have not been lost on the Founding generation though it is perhaps better articulated at the state level than in our national Constitution.

In summary, the U.S. Constitution is an amalgam of three written traditions that originated in colonial North America. While the political, theological, and philosophical elements that informed those traditions was brought with the early colonists from the Old World, the development of a *written* tradition that articulated the fundamental principles and processes of government *in a single document* was a wholly American creation. The early American colonists would continue this tradition of writing on paper their political principles and systems of government so that by the time of the American Revolution, a "constitution" was largely understood to mean a single document that included all the elements of a covenant, compact, and charter. When, in May of 1776 the American colonies prepared for the eventuality of independence by issuing a call for all colonies to draft constitutions as they transitioned to statehood, there was a universal understanding as to what that constitution should contain. Where did we get this grand tradition of written constitutionalism that has been the foundation for our government for over two centuries? We got it not from Madison, or Jefferson, or Franklin. Nor from Locke, Montesquieu, or Blackstone. We got it almost 200 years earlier from a frightened but determined people in the hull of a tiny ship called the Mayflower and the brave colonists that followed in their footsteps.

RECOMMENDED READING

Donald S. Lutz, *Colonial Origins of American Constitutionalism*
(Liberty Fund, Inc. 1998)

Donald S. Lutz. *Origins of American Constitutionalism*
(Louisiana State University Press, 1988)

Nathaniel Philbrick, *Mayflower*
(Penguin Books, 2007)

EARLY AMERICAN CONSTITUTIONALISM

By Chris Hammons, PhD

PROFESSOR OF POLITICAL SCIENCE

School children across America are regularly taught three fundamental untruths about the U.S. Constitution. First, they are repeatedly taught that our Constitution is the oldest written constitution in the world. Contrary to popular belief, however, the U.S. Constitution is *not* the oldest written constitution in the world. That distinction goes to the Massachusetts state constitution written primarily by John Adams in 1780, several years before the U.S. Constitution was ratified. The Adams Constitution is still used by the people of Massachusetts today. Hence, the U.S. Constitution is the world's oldest written *national* constitution, but it is not the oldest written constitution still in use.

The second falsehood students are taught is that constitutionalism—particularly the tradition of a written constitution—is a product of the Constitutional Convention of 1787. This is not true either. By the eve of the American Revolution, all Thirteen Colonies possessed written constitutions as they transitioned to statehood. This was more than a decade before the U.S. Constitution was drafted. The idea of a written constitution was so familiar to the Revolutionary generation that in May of 1776, the Continental Congress called on the colonial legislatures to draft constitutions in preparation for independence from England. When independence was declared two months later, the former colonies adopted their newly drafted constitutions (in some cases they merely tweaked their old charters to serve such a purpose) and became independent states.

The third tale regularly taught to school children is that the U.S. Constitution created our national government, with the implication that we had no national government prior to 1787. To the contrary, the Constitution that we cherish so greatly today is actually our second national constitution. Our first national constitution—the Articles of Confederation—had some real weaknesses but clearly qualifies as a written constitution. Furthermore, we shouldn't dismiss the utility of this first constitution given the fact that the fledgling American nation won its independence under the Articles. In fact, much of the debate over ratification of our current Constitution centered on whether or not we should just keep the Articles of Confederation, amend it, or replace it entirely with a new document.

In short, the use of written constitutions as we think of them today began well *before* the Constitutional Convention of 1787. We learned in the last chapter that American constitutionalism—particularly reliance on a single written document—was the result of a slow amalgamation of colonial traditions. Contrary to the notion that written constitutionalism was invented in Philadelphia in 1787, the practice of writing down fundamental political principles and processes already existed in the colonies for over 150 years. By the time of American independence, written constitutions were in use at both the state and national level and predate the U.S. Constitution by over a decade. In this chapter, we'll take a look at these early state constitutions and the Articles of Confederation to see how they influenced the Constitution we now live under.

Early State Constitutions

The idea of using a written constitution as the basis for good government was not created in Philadelphia during the summer of 1787. To the contrary, the American states already had a long tradition of using written constitutions. These constitutions, as we call them today, developed over many decades as colonies used and adapted their covenants, compacts, and charters to suit a variety of political needs and pressures. By 1776 and American independence, most all states had adopted some amalgamation of the three traditional forms discussed in the last chapter to produce a document that we would now recognize as a written constitution. These documents typically included some statement of political philosophy, a list of political rights, and a framework of government that established institutions and processes. In short, all the elements of a covenant, compact, and charter were present. These same elements are still evident in our state and national constitutions today.

While the philosophical component of the U.S. Constitution is very brief—confined almost exclusively to the famous preamble—early state constitutional preambles often contain lengthy philosophical justifications for revolution and reflections on republican government. These preambles often read like Lockean philosophy or our Declaration of Independence (many scholars argue that the Declaration is actually the philosophical preamble to our Constitution). The lengthier preambles found in early state constitutions reflect the desire to justify rebellious behavior or revolution during the fight for independence. They also reflect the colonial covenant/compact tradition of creating a people as a prior step to establishing a political system and government. In either case, state constitutions from the 18th century have a philosophical orientation to them that results in some interesting and often beautiful political prose.

For example, the opening line of the 1776 Constitution of Georgia reads like a summary of the Declaration of Independence and John Locke's political theory:

> Whereas the conduct of the legislature of Great Britain for many years past has been so oppressive on the people of America that of late years they have plainly declared and asserted a right to raise taxes upon the people of America, and to make laws to bind them in all cases whatsoever, without their consent; which conduct, being repugnant to the common rights of mankind, hath obliged the Americans, as freemen, to oppose such oppressive measures, and to assert the rights and privileges they are entitled to by the laws of nature and reason....

Similar language is found in the New Jersey state constitution (1776) that claims Britain is "depriving us of our natural and constitutional rights" and is "destroying the lives and properties of the colonists in many places with fire and sword...." The state Constitution of Pennsylvania (1776) makes a direct reference in its preamble to the Declaration of Independence, noting that it is setting up a free government because British rule is bent on "reducing them to a total and abject submission to the despotic domination of the British parliament, with many other acts of tyranny, (more fully set forth in the declaration of Congress)." The New York Constitution of 1777 actually reprints much of the Declaration in its preamble. The South Carolina Constitution of 1776 is particularly long and fiery, declaring that the British have "killed many of the colonists; burned several towns, and threatened to burn the rest, and daily endeavor by a conduct which has sullied the British arms, and would disgrace even savage nations...." Even Vermont, which established itself as an independent territory in 1777, got in on the act by declaring that the King of England no longer holds authority over his former domain.

One interesting note about state constitutional preambles that distinguishes them from their national counterpart is that they frequently invoke God, reflecting the covenant tradition of earlier colonial documents. The references to God usually take one of several forms—the Almighty, the Supreme Being, the Supreme Ruler, Divine Providence, or simply God. In most cases these preambles invoke God as the source of good government, appeal to God for help with good governance, or give thanks to God for the blessings of good government. The aforementioned Vermont Constitution of 1777, for example, gives thanks to the "Great Governor of the Universe" for the blessings of democratic government, noting that He alone "knows to what degree of earthly happiness mankind may attain by perfecting the arts of government." Such references are also apparent in later state constitutions, perhaps most poetically in the South Carolina Constitution of 1868, which professes its gratitude to the "Great Legislator of the Universe."

While it is tempting to say that such references merely reflect the literary style of an earlier and more religious American people, the pattern is not restricted to state constitutions used during the 18th or 19th centuries. Of the 50 constitutions currently in use by the American states today, an astounding 90 percent mention God in their preamble. For example, God is mentioned prominently in the preamble to the current Wyoming Constitution, which gives thanks to "Almighty God for our civil, political, and religious liberties...." The current Constitution of Wisconsin is "grateful to Almighty God for freedom...." Washington state's constitution gives thanks to the "Supreme Ruler of the Universe for our liberties...." While establishing their constitution, the people of Texas do so "humbly invoking the blessings of Almighty God...." Utah is "grateful to Almighty God for life and liberty...." New York professes thanks to "Almighty God for our freedom...." Even California operates under a state constitution that invokes God. In total, 45 of 50 current state constitutions mention God in the preamble.

The fact that such a high percentage of previous and current state constitutions explicitly invoke God in their preambles highlights the influence of the covenant tradition discussed in the previous chapter. Invocations of God for the blessings of liberty, order, and government is part of a long constitutional tradition in the United States that dates back to the earliest colonial covenants like the Mayflower Compact. The practice also highlights more clearly the significant influence of our Judeo-Christian heritage on American constitutionalism.

Another unique feature of state constitutions is that while they each possess a listing of rights similar to the Bill of Rights attached to the U.S. Constitution, state Bills of Rights are typically found at the *beginning* of the Constitution rather than appended to the end. The placement makes sense as early American states, having justified Revolution and explained the purpose of government in their constitutional preambles, enumerated rights and liberties to be protected by the governments subsequently established. The practice continues in contemporary state constitutions.

In the current Texas Constitution, for example, Article I lays out the rights of the people, while Article II discusses the powers of the government, and Articles III through V establish the political institutions of government. A similar pattern is found in the current Constitutions of New York, California, Florida, and most other state constitutions as well. The placement of the people's rights *prior* to establishment of institutions and procedures of government highlights the importance of liberty and limited government in American constitutionalism. Political institutions and procedures are meant to protect our rights; rights that exist prior to government and not as a result of it. Hence the placement of the Bills of

Rights at the beginning of state constitutions emphasizes the importance of the people's liberty over the power and processes of government.

Religious liberty amendments in state Bills of Rights provide an interesting contrast to that found in our national Constitution. While the national Constitution uses agnostic language in the Bill of Rights and implies no government endorsement of religion, most state constitutions take a markedly different approach regarding religious liberty. Many state constitutions openly use the word "God" or make direct reference to the "Almighty" in their religious liberty clauses. For example, the New Hampshire Constitution states, "Every individual has a natural and unalienable right to worship God according to the dictates of his own conscience, and reason; and no subject shall be hurt, molested, or restrained, in his peers on, liberty, or estate, for worshipping God in the manner and season most agreeable to the dictates of his own conscience...." The Virginia Constitution reads:

> that religion or the duty which we owe to our Creator, and the manner of discharging it, can be directed only by reason and conviction, not by force or violence; and, therefore, all men are equally entitled to the free exercise of religion, according to the dictates of conscience; and that it is the mutual duty of all to practice Christian forbearance, love, and charity towards each other.

The Nebraska Constitution similarly reads, "All persons have a natural and indefensible right to worship Almighty God according to the dictates of their own consciences." The Oregon Constitution declares, "All men shall be secure in their Natural right, to worship Almighty God according to the dictates of their own conscience." All of the above provisions are still in effect today.

The religious liberty language of state Bills of Rights again highlights the covenant tradition in early American state constitutions, especially when contrasted with the wording of the celebrated First Amendment to the U.S. Constitution. It is interesting to think how different the legal debate over religious freedom in the United States would be if the First Amendment to the U.S. Constitution stated, "Congress shall make no law respecting an establishment of religion, or prohibiting the free worship of Almighty God." The specific reference to God in the provision would prevent an agnostic or atheistic interpretation as often accompanies First Amendment legal cases today.

The early American states also borrowed heavily from each other in terms of constitutional design beyond their preambles and Bills of Rights. In some cases, states copied large sections from the constitutional framework of neighboring states. The result is that the first American state constitutions tend to look very similar to one another, as if a template for American constitutionalism had emerged. They typically share a tendency to be brief, focus on political institutions and processes rather than policy, and exhibit a preference for legislative supremacy. Reflecting the Revolution's emphasis on republicanism, the early state constitutions often gave strong powers to the legislative branch in support of the idea that power should reside with the people and their representatives. These early legislatures are overwhelmingly bicameral (having two chambers), though a select few states (most notably Pennsylvania) adopted a single chamber legislature in the name of democratic equality.

The tendency towards bicameralism is the subject of some debate, but most scholars contend that it reflects the British legal heritage of early America (House of Lords and House of Commons) and the existing practice in colonial charters of relying on some sort of locally elected representatives as well as a governor's council of wealthier citizens. Though technically part of the executive branch, the governor's council had influence over the legislative process, most commonly in the form of some sort of veto power. The use of two chambers to represent the "common people" and the "aristocracy" evolved out of the different constituencies these groups represented, often with the request coming from each group to meet independently to discuss relevant business free from the influence of the other group. As colonies grew in size the simple act of having all these representatives assemble in one room often necessitated breaking them into two separate chambers simply to facilitate meeting. To this end, the adoption of two chambers in early state constitutions seemed a natural extension of long-standing colonial practice.

Another commonality among early state constitutions is that executive power was usually very weak. There was a long suspicion of executive power that stemmed from the colonial experience, so much so that when colonists complained about "the government" they frequently meant the royal governor. In an effort to curb the abuse of executive power that many states had experienced during colonial rule, the executive position was made subordinate to the legislature both in terms of constitutional placement (usually placed in the article after the legislature) and in terms of power and influence.

For example, the executive branch in early state constitutions was often chosen on an annual basis by the legislature. Reflecting the Revolution's emphasis on republicanism, the objective of annual elections in these early state constitutions was to keep the governor beholden to the people through their elected representatives. Executive appointments would have to be approved by the legislature, reducing the governor's ability to control the executive branch. Courts were moved from under the authority of the executive to the oversight of the legislature, and often appointed by the legislature, to keep the courts isolated from executive influence and dependent on the people. As a result, the executive in these early state constitutions was frequently little more than a mere deputy of the legislative branch.

The judiciary often fared no better. Early state judiciaries were typically very weak institutions, again reflecting a belief that political power best resided with "the people" rather than government officials. State judiciaries were often appointed by the state legislatures on an annual basis, effectively making them subordinate to the people's representatives. In several states judges could be removed by the legislature as well. There was no concept of judicial independence, judicial enforcement of the Constitution, nor the idea that judges could use their own interpretation of the state constitution to invalidate the actions of other branches of government. Only three states provided anything similar to our modern notion of judicial review, but the opinion of the court was either advisory and not binding (as in Massachusetts and New Hampshire) or could be overridden by a two-thirds vote of the legislature (New York).

In short, judicial power in early state constitutions was seen neither as a separate or independent branch of government. The judiciary of early state constitutions functioned as a power subordinate to the legislative and executive. In the case of New Jersey, for instance, the governor and his legislative council actually acted as the state's court of final appeals— effectively making the "supreme court" of New Jersey a branch controlled by the executive and legislature.

The period from 1776 to 1787, then, was a period of constitutional experimentation as states tried their best to establish functional state governments. Some states merely operated under revised colonial charters (Rhode Island and Connecticut). Other states (Georgia, South Carolina, and Vermont) would write and ratify a series of constitutions during the last quarter of the 18th century. No one knew exactly what a constitution should look like or contain, so to some extent they were making it up as they went and borrowing heavily from one another. As a result, debates over the proper form and function of written constitutions were rampant during this period, showing up in thousands of pamphlets, essays, and debates.

By the time of the Constitutional Convention in Philadelphia, more than a decade of experience with state constitutionalism provided a foundation for discussing the strengths and weaknesses of different constitutional designs. There was a general consensus that the first attempts at constitution making among the independent American states was a mixed success. Benjamin Rush, the respected physician from Philadelphia, noted at the convention that the early state constitutions reflected the "principles of liberty" quite well but "were ignorant of the forms and combinations of power in republics." In other words, state constitutions could use some improvement. James Madison echoed these sentiments when he wrote in *Federalist #47* that the state constitutions "carry strong marks of haste" and even stronger marks of "inexperience." In other words, Madison too thought improvements were possible.

It was not for nothing. The decade that the American states spent under their own constitutions provided the men who attended the Philadelphia convention with a wealth of information and practical experience in constitutionalism. Rather than a novel creation, the institutions and processes in the U.S. Constitution reflect the Founder's adoptions and adaptations from their existing state constitutions—constitutions they knew quite well. It's as if the Founders were picking from a portfolio of state constitutions the items they most liked most while discarding those things that didn't seem to work so well.

For instance, by the time of the 1787 Constitutional Convention in Philadelphia, bicameralism was largely a decided matter. Just a few days into the convention, Edmund Randolph of Virginia proposed a form of government known as the "Randolph" or the "Virginia" plan. It provided for a national legislature consisting of two branches. Charles Pinckney of South Carolina similarly introduced resolutions for a legislature consisting of two houses, to be known as the "House of Delegates" and the "Senate." With practically no debate on the matter, every state with the exception of Pennsylvania voted in favor of bicameralism. Pennsylvania preferred a unicameral legislature ... just like the one back home.

There was a strong consensus among the convention that executive power at the state level was too weak. The national Constitution would improve on this by adopting a more powerful and independent executive. The Founders debated having the president chosen by Congress, similar to how governors were chosen at the state level. The concern was that the executive would become a mere subordinate of the legislature, as often happened to state governors. Hamilton explains in *Federalist #68* the unique Electoral College mechanism of the presidency by contending that the president might "otherwise be tempted to sacrifice his duty to his complaisance for those whose favor was necessary to the duration of his official consequence." In other words, a president selected by Congress would be beholden to Congress for his job. He would effectively be a subordinate, just like many state governors in relation to their state legislature.

The Founders also decided to avoid the executive council style of government found in many state constitutions. Hamilton argued that executive power is best held by a single person, and the notion of an executive council was ineffective because it diffused authority, led to confusion, and impaired accountability. "I rarely met with an intelligent man from any of the States, who did not admit, as the result of experience," Hamilton writes in *Federalist #70*, that a single executive "was one of the best of the distinguishing features of our constitution." Hence, the Founders learned from their experience under state constitutions and created a more robust chief executive with powers and authority independent of the legislature.

Experience with state constitutions also guided the formation of an independent judiciary at the national level. Whereas many state courts in early American constitutions were subordinate to the legislative branch, the Constitutional Convention proposed an independent judiciary. In *Federalist #78*, Hamilton paraphrases Montesquieu, contending that "liberty can have nothing to fear from the judiciary alone, but would have everything to fear from its union with either of the other departments." James Madison makes a similar argument in *Federalist #51*, noting that "Were the executive magistrate, or the judges, not independent of the legislature in this particular, their independence in every other would be merely nominal." In essence, they would be subordinate to the legislature.

The influence of these early state constitutions on the American Founders cannot be understated. Rather than inventing constitutionalism from scratch, the men in Philadelphia brought with them preconceptions about what the new national Constitution should look like. The broad general structure of the national government reflects what was already in practice in most states. The changes made, such as a more vigorous executive and an independent judiciary, similarly reflects the experiences of living under those constitutions. In addition, there are countless smaller decisions that were made that were also informed by state constitutions. Procedural elements such as staggered terms for the Senate, the legislative process, impeachment, and much of the verbiage related to these and other procedural elements is taken verbatim from state constitutions. **Rather than inventing our Constitution from scratch, the Founders had 13 state constitutions to draw from, and they made good use of them when designing our national Constitution.**

After all the work that went into designing our national Constitution in 1787 and the effort to ratify it (it was ratified in 1789), many states went back and actually revised their existing state constitutions to look more like the new national Constitution—removing the lengthy preambles, reigning in the legislature, bolstering the executive branch, and creating independent judiciaries. In short, the Founders took what they learned at the Constitutional Convention back to their home states to improve their state constitutions. We Americans, it seems, are always looking to improve our constitutions.

The Articles of Confederation

The constitutions that influenced our Founding Fathers weren't limited to just those produced by the newly independent states. By the time of the Constitutional Convention of 1787 the United States had been operating under our first national constitution, the Articles of Confederation, for several years. The Articles of Confederation were drafted during a time of crisis—the American Revolution—in an attempt to create a functional national government where one didn't exist. In fact, the idea of a functional national government was included in the same resolution by Richard Henry Lee on June 7, 1776, that also proposed independence from England.

The Articles of Confederation were set up to create "cooperation and coordination" among the states. The challenge was that the 13 independent states thought of themselves as exactly that—*independent states*—rather than a unified nation. It was a difficult task, philosophically and pragmatically, to unite them all. Indeed, the Articles never really refer to the new United States as a nation, but rather as a collection of states united. You can really see this if you look at Articles II and III.

> ARTICLE II—Each state retains its sovereignty, freedom, and independence, and every power, jurisdiction, and right, which is not by this Confederation expressly delegated to the United States, in Congress assembled.

This article makes it clear that power will remain with the states. That's what they mean by "sovereignty." When the states declare that sovereignty remains with them they are in essence saying they don't answer to the national government. The only powers the national government will have are those that are delegated, or given, by the states.

The idea that the states would retain their sovereignty and delegate power to the national government was a function of two things. First, people tended to view the states as the focus of political power in those days. Travel was basically limited to the speed of a horse on land, so most people didn't go far. A day's journey might be 10 miles. For most of their lives, people stayed within a short distance of where they were born. To this end, people tended to think of themselves as citizens of states rather than citizens of a larger American nation. It was common for people to refer to themselves first as a "Virginian" or a "New Yorker" rather than an "American." They would often refer to their home states as "my country."

> ARTICLE III—The said States hereby severally enter into a firm
> league of friendship with each other, for their common defense,
> the security of their liberties, and their mutual and general welfare,
> binding themselves to assist each other, against all force offered to,
> or attacks made upon them, or any of them, on account of religion,
> sovereignty, trade, or any other pretense whatever.

This third article really gets to the heart of the Articles of Confederation. It creates a "firm league of friendship" among the states for their common defense and mutual welfare. It's a little like the Three Musketeers—all for one and one for all!

While it was better than nothing, and was a genuine attempt to provide some coordinated effort during the war, the Articles were rife with problems. First, the new national government lacked the ability to mobilize an army. The states were supposed to supply the men, but that didn't always work very well. One of the problems was that these men were very loyal to their home states. And while Georgians were willing to fight and die for Georgia, they weren't willing to fight and die for Massachusetts, or even South Carolina. So it was very difficult during the war to count on the army because the status and dependability of the soldiers was always in flux. Men would fight to the finish in their home states but then desert the army when it moved into another state. The army was unreliable and constantly changing in size and strength. It drove George Washington crazy.

Second, there was no real power to raise and collect taxes. States were supposed to contribute money to the national government for the war effort, but you can imagine how well that worked. States could send in all, some, or none of the money that Congress requested. As a consequence, Congress was always broke. George Washington would write Congress asking for munitions, food, uniforms and shoes for his men only to be told that no money was available to purchase such items. Many states would openly refuse to send in the "requisition" money to the Confederation Congress, and there was little the Congress could do about it.

The third weakness of the Articles of Confederation was that there was no power to regulate commerce. Trade regulations were basically just left to the individual states, which regularly passed policies to their own advantage at the expense of other states. For instance, North Carolina might pass a tariff on goods coming through the state to help raise revenue. This not only made goods more expensive but encouraged other states to pass tariffs of their own, resulting in debilitating trade wars. To make the problem worse, as the price of goods increased, the states would often print more currency. An increased money supply devalues the currency so that it takes more of it to purchase things. Terrible inflation combined with trade wars between the states made people wonder if the fledgling American nation would die an economic death even if it won the war!

It became quite apparent that with the lack of finances, inability to field a proper army, and little power to regulate commerce, the United States was off to a bad start. A convention was called for the purposes of discussing the economic problems of the United States. Delegates from all of the Thirteen Colonies were invited to meet in Annapolis, Maryland, to discuss how these problems might be addressed in the Articles of Confederation. Not many people showed up. Some of the states were fearful that tinkering with the Articles might result in a stronger, more powerful central government, which might threaten the autonomy of the states. The idea of a stronger national government was a hard sell after the Revolution.

Even though the Annapolis convention was a bust, a few men who did show up (primarily Alexander Hamilton and James Madison) agreed that the real challenge for the new nation was more than just economic—that the Articles of Confederation were in need of serious revision. In addition, events in Massachusetts known as Shay's Rebellion (where farmers and some veterans of the Revolutionary War commenced an armed rebellion against state economic policies) led many New Englanders to conclude that something had to be done sooner rather than later. The delegates to the failed Annapolis convention of 1786 suggested a second convention for the following year, this time in Philadelphia.

The city of Philadelphia is synonymous with the Constitution. It was chosen as the site of this second convention because it was one of the largest cities in the United States at the time. It was also centrally located on the Eastern Seaboard and accessible by land and water, making it an easy place for delegates to reach. All 13 states were invited to attend, and all except tiny Rhode Island did so. Rhode Island felt that the existing government under the Articles of Confederation was fine just the way it was and boy-cotted the convention.

In the end, 55 men from 12 states showed up in Philadelphia to partici-pate in the convention. George Washington was there. He served as the president of the convention. He was the most famous man in America and his presence lent credibility to the convention. Benjamin Franklin was also there. And if George Washington was the most famous man in America, Dr. Franklin was the most famous American in the world. He didn't con-tribute much to the design of the Constitution, but his presence added a certain gravitas to the proceedings as well. He also lived in Philadelphia, so it would have been a little rude not to invite him.

No man contributed more to the convention than James Madison. Madison, from Virginia, is often called the "Father of the Constitution." Madison spent weeks in preparation for the convention by studying ancient Greek and Roman history, with a particular emphasis on their political sys-tems. He wanted to know everything he could about making constitutions. When the convention finally got underway, Madison came ready with a whole list of ideas and would be instrumental in the convention over the next several weeks. Always the student of history, Madison took a chair at the front of the convention room, facing the other delegates, so he could hear and record for posterity the debate over the creation of our own Constitution. Madison's "Notes on Debates in the Federal Convention" read like a script of the Constitutional Convention of 1787 and provide an invaluable historical record.

It's important to note two famous Founders who were not at the conven-tion. Missing was Thomas Jefferson, who was serving as our ambassador to France during this period. To this end, anytime you hear anybody say, "Thomas Jefferson wrote in the Constitution...." you can stop them right there because he wasn't even in the country. Also missing was John

Adams. Adams, who was instrumental in the Independence movement, was serving as ambassador to Great Britain and did not attend the convention either. The absence of these two men, Jefferson and Adams, meant that two of America's great thinkers and leaders of the Revolution had no input into the design of the U.S. Constitution, though both were instrumental in drafting their state constitutions. It's interesting to speculate how different the final draft of the U.S. Constitution might have been, and what impact that might have had on American history and by extension world history, had these two men been present.

When the convention finally got underway at the end of May in 1787, the 55 delegates gathered in the same room where the Declaration of Independence was drafted a decade earlier—a room not much larger than the average college classroom. **Contrary to the myth that delegates assembled in Philadelphia during the summer of 1787 to invent constitutionalism, the delegates at the convention brought with them a strong understanding of the concept informed through their own experiences.** They had lived under a uniquely American constitutional tradition that had existed since the early 17th century—steeped in history, philosophy, law, and experience. The celebrated summer in Philadelphia was not a struggle to conceive of something new, but rather to sift through a myriad of existing ideas and opinions in an effort to construct some sort of constitutional system that was agreeable to everyone. It was a big task. While most of the men in Philadelphia agreed that the Articles of Confederation was broken, they disagreed strongly on the solution.

The delegates' experience under state constitutions and the Articles of Confederation gave them an excellent source of starting material. Because we're often taught in school that the Articles of Confederation was a terrible failure, its influence on our Founding Fathers and our current Constitution is dismissed too quickly. Not everything in the Articles was useless or discarded. Textbooks sometimes give the impression that the Constitutional Convention of 1787 resulted in a complete replacement of the Articles. To the contrary, a good many of the provisions in the Articles of Confederation were adopted wholesale and carried forward into our current Constitution.

For example, provisions found in our current Constitution like the Full Faith and Credit Clause (Article IV, Section 1), Extradition Clause (Article IV, Section 2), and Protected Speech Clause (Article I, Section 6), are lifted almost verbatim from the Articles. Many of the powers denied to the states in the Articles of Confederation are denied again in Article I, Section 9 of the Constitution. Many of the powers that are provided to the Confederation Congress also find themselves carried over to Article I, Section 8 of the U.S. Constitution. In sum, the ability to borrow provisions on which there was some consensus from the previously approved Articles of Confederation saved the Founding Fathers time and effort that might otherwise have been spent crafting these provisions from scratch.

And yet while the Articles expedited the creation of the Constitution in some ways, in others it slowed the process tremendously. The Articles of Confederation's emphasis on state sovereignty became a huge source of debate for many delegates at the convention. The emphasis on state sovereignty manifested itself in many ways in the Articles but most conspicuously in the equal vote that each state shared in the legislature (each state got one vote), an extremely weak national government, and the general understanding that the nation was comprised of 13 unique states rather than defined by a singular American identity. To this end, while it was relatively easy to take non-controversial operating procedures from the Articles and incorporate them into the Constitution, it was much more difficult for delegates to agree on the underlying principles for a replacement constitution.

The debates over the proposed Constitution of 1787, both at the convention and in the state ratification debates that followed, were largely over the extent to which the Articles of Confederation's emphasis on state sovereignty was or wasn't the right approach to American governance. There were many at the convention and in the states who argued that the new nation was a compact of states. As such, power should remain at the state level, each state should have equal weight in the national government, and the national government should be one of extremely limited powers. Basically they were defending the Articles of Confederation. Men like Patrick Henry of Virginia and Robert Yates of New York argued that the whole purpose of the American Revolution was to throw off centralized power in order to liberate the states, and the establishment of a centralized national government like that proposed by the convention of 1787 was contrary to that end.

When Edmund Randolph of Virginia (with an assist from James Madison) proposed the adoption of a constitution that would provide representation in Congress based on *population,* many delegates felt like this was exactly the type of assault on the Articles of Confederation and the principles of the Revolution that they feared. A government based on population—"the people" rather than the states—threatened to overturn the entire foundation on which the Articles of Confederation was built in exchange for a more nationalistic government that viewed the states as subordinate. In other words, it created an American *nation* rather than a confederation of states.

The debate really came down to whether or not the Articles of Confederation could be salvaged with some amending, or whether it should be scrapped for an entirely new system of government. In response to Randolph's "Virginia Plan," William Patterson of New Jersey tried his hand at introducing what was effectively a spruced-up version of the Articles of Confederation. It called for giving more power to the government (to resolve the tax and commerce issues), but retained the equal vote per state format of the Articles of Confederation. In this manner, the states would still retain control of the political system. This tension between a state-based government and a centralized national government was so intense that it dominated the Constitutional Convention.

The solution to this fundamental tension at the Constitutional Convention came from Roger Sherman of Connecticut and is referred to as the Great or Connecticut Compromise. Historically, however, it's not as innovative as it is often portrayed in textbooks and classroom lectures. Sherman had actually proposed such a system during debates over the Articles of Confederation, when a similar controversy over representation presented itself. Sherman had then suggested a system that based representation on both population and the states. The idea didn't gain any traction during debates over the Articles of Confederation, but when the issue resurfaced at the Constitutional Convention, Sherman was able to revisit the old idea and this time with more success. In short, the structure of our legislative branch in Article I of the Constitution has its origins in the original debates over the Articles of Confederation.

The preamble to our current Constitution also reflects the influence of the Articles of Confederation. The famous opening lines that school children across America have been required to recite for generations are less an abstract philosophical statement but rather a practical bridge between one constitution and the next. The opening line, "We the People of the United States of America …" was originally penned as, "We the people of the States of …" and then went on to list all the states of the Confederation starting with New Hampshire in the North and ending geographically in the South with Georgia. The revised version deletes the listed states and focuses on a singular nation, indicating a conscience decision to transition from a system based exclusively on state sovereignty to one with a stronger national identity. Patrick Henry was apparently furious with the editorial change in the preamble and demanded to know by what right "the people" had been substituted for the "states" in the proposed preamble.

The remainder of the preamble continues to demonstrate the influence of the Articles of Confederation. The phrase "in order to form a more perfect union" is not an abstraction, but a practical statement that the Framers wanted a constitution better than the one that existed under the Articles. The phrase "insure domestic Tranquility" is a promise to avoid the sort of popular uprisings that occurred in Shay's Rebellion and other demonstrations under the Articles. "Provide for the common defence" is a pledge to support a functional and sufficient military, something that had plagued the revolutionary effort under the Articles. The power to tax and regulate commerce would be the first powers granted to Congress under the new Constitution, in an effort to "promote the general Welfare" as stated in the Preamble. Only the phrases "establish justice" and "secure the Blessings of Liberty to ourselves and our Posterity" provide any abstract, philosophical elements, though a case could be made that these elements were lacking under the Articles as well.

The Articles of Confederation served the nation well, at least well enough to help win the war against the British Empire and see the birth of an independent American nation. Its weaknesses and failures are largely a product of the novel attempt to create a written constitution for a continental nation, something that had never been done before. Its emphasis on state sovereignty reflected the passions and fears of a people trying to throw off centralized government. By the Philadelphia convention of 1787, the desire to try something new pushed the delegates to design a Constitution that addressed the weaknesses of the Articles. The proposed Constitution was not without controversy and its passage was strongly contested. In fact, in many states it was barely ratified.

The success of our current Constitution overshadows the important influence of its predecessors. **The constitutions of the early American states and the Articles of Confederation provided the Founders with practical, real-world experience in constitutionalism that informed the theoretical conceptions they gleaned from books and pamphlets. Our existing Constitution is a product of earlier American constitutions.** To paraphrase John Dickinson, a delegate from Pennsylvania, experience rather than abstract reason was the greatest influence on the Constitution.

★ ★

RECOMMENDED READING

George E. Connor and Christopher W. Hammons,
Constitutionalism of the American States
(University of Missouri Press, 2008)

Merril Jensen, *The Articles of Confederation*
(University of Wisconsin Press, 1940)

Donald S. Lutz, *The Origins of American Constitutionalism*
(Louisiana State University Press, 1988)

G. Alan Tarr, *Understanding State Constitutions.*
(Princeton University Press, 1998)

Gordon S. Wood, *Creation of the American Republic*
(University of North Carolina Press, 1998)

CONCLUSION

The Constitutional Convention of 1787 produced one of the most remarkable documents in the annals of history. The very premise of a written constitution, where government is limited by a mere piece of paper, sounds almost absurd. If men are fallen and corrupt, as many of our Founding Fathers believed, then how would words on parchment provide any sort of barrier to tyranny and abuse of power? It seems improbable. And yet while not perfect, our Constitution remains a testament to the idea of self-government and perhaps the embodiment of the ideal itself. It has become the archetype for written constitutions across the globe.

Since 1787 when the U.S. Constitution was written, almost every nation on the planet has adopted some form of constitution embodied in a single written document. There are exceptions—like England, New Zealand, Israel, and Canada—that piece together various historical documents that collectively form the basis of their constitutional traditions, but most nations rely on a singular document that they can point to and refer to as *their* Constitution. Even countries notorious for abusing political power have adopted written constitutions to provide the façade of democratic government. The success of American constitutionalism is highlighted by the failures of so many other nations who merely use written constitutions as window dressing.

Our dedication to our Constitution—the actual written document—is a central feature of American exceptionalism. We really are unlike any other country on the planet due to our serious commitment to this remarkable document. Other nations have strong constitutional traditions—like England—but the American emphasis on a singular document is really unique. Though we often disagree on what each word in the Constitution means, we Americans hold the parchment upon which the words "we the people" are written as a sacred artifact of the American ideal. So much so that each night, this old faded document is sealed up in an impregnable case, lowered by a conveyor system deep into the earth, through atomic-proof blast doors, where it is guarded by armed soldiers—as if the document itself rather than the institutions and process it establishes is the heart of American constitutionalism.

By now you have learned that the Constitution was not the product of a singular event in American history. The Founding Fathers didn't create our constitutional government from scratch. That's the myth that sometimes gets perpetuated from an over simplistic storyline taught to youngsters. From the preceding chapters you've learned that our Constitution is an amalgamation of ideas and institutions informed by history, philosophy, law, religion, and the experiences of colonists and early Americans. When our Founders convened in Philadelphia during that hot summer of 1787, they spent almost 100 days declaiming the strengths and weakness of different constitutional designs, political principles, and institutional arrangements. The time they spent exploring and debating these different ideas wasn't because they knew too little and were trying to come up with this stuff from scratch. To the contrary, the reason they spent so much time in Philadelphia was because they knew too much and were trying to parse it out, make sense of it all, and come to some agreement on the best way to proceed.

The success of the American Constitution was not guaranteed. There were serious misgivings about whether using a written constitution to govern a country the size of the United States (even with only 13 states) would work. Opponents of the Constitution feared it wouldn't sufficiently protect the liberties they had just secured from English tyranny. Through their study of the humanities—history, philosophy, government, law, literature, and theology—the Founders knew that the greatest threat to liberty wasn't the risk of invasions from outside, but the propensity of abuse and oppression from a nation's own government.

Our Founders sought to create a government with enough energy to sustain order but with limited powers so that it would not infringe on the liberty of the people. Rather than hoping for "enlightened statesmen" (they knew from history that such leaders were rare), they designed a government based on their understanding of human nature. They didn't dream of changing human nature or creating utopia. Our Founders saw human beings for what they are—fallen creatures with the potential to do both good and evil, but easily tempted by power and wealth.

All of the mechanisms you are familiar with since you took your first social studies class were incorporated into the Constitution as a means of limiting the abuse of power. These include things like frequent elections, checks and balances, separation of powers, and federalism. The goal was to design institutions that would work with human nature rather than against it. Madison wrote that if men were angels, no government would be necessary. But since we are not angels, the goal of the Constitution must be to allow men to govern men while minimizing the potential for abuse.

What makes our Constitution work, however, is more than just political institutions and processes. While these aspects of constitutional design are indeed worthy of respect, **the success of our Constitution is largely a product of a uniquely American constitutional culture.** This culture developed from the unique combination of English common law, the early colonial experience, the Protestant religion of the settlers, the lessons of history and philosophy, and early state constitutionalism. As a result, our constitutional culture emphasizes natural law, popular sovereignty, liberty, limited government, the rule of law, and equality. It is because these six foundational principles are so ingrained in the American mind that we place such great emphasis on that old piece of paper that serves as our Constitution. In short, our belief in *constitutionalism* precedes our belief in the Constitution. If we didn't hold these fundamental principles as sacred—if we didn't have a strong constitutional culture—the document that governs our nation would literally be just a parchment barrier to tyranny.

Like language, religious traditions, or grandma's recipes, **our constitutional culture must be passed down from generation to generation or else it will be forgotten.** We already witness an alarming number of our young people and fellow citizens who fail to understand or appreciate our nation's history and founding principles. A recent study found that more than a third of Americans cannot name any of the rights guaranteed under the First Amendment, and only a quarter of Americans can name all three branches of government.[1] In addition, many college students graduate without having ever had a course in basic American history or having read the Constitution.

It gets worse. The failure to teach civics in some institutes of higher education has given way to outright resistance. At some colleges and universities across the nation, the very mention of "Founding Fathers" provokes hostility and charges ranging from bigotry to misogyny. The notion of American exceptionalism is seen as nationalistic or predicated on the concept of unmerited "privilege." The Constitution is dismissed as an antiquated

---

1 Americans Are Poorly Informed About Basic Constitutional Provisions, Annenberg Public Policy Center. September 2017.

barrier to social justice, though it is unclear what that means or why social justice can't be obtained under the Constitution. Some schools even offer whole degree programs in "social transformation" but fail to require a single course on the Constitution. In short, widespread understanding and appreciation for the ideas and institutions that safeguard the liberty of the American people is eroding. Some would claim it's intentional. Others would argue it's simply due to neglect. It doesn't really matter. **Something has to be done to preserve for future generations the principles on which our nation was based.**

Our mission at the Morris Family Center for Law & Liberty is to preserve and promote our nation's constitutional culture. We want to make sure that Americans understand that the concepts of liberty, limited government, natural law, equality, rule of law, and popular sovereignty are the basis for a system of government that serves as a beacon of hope for people here and across the globe. In our own city of Houston, people arrive from all over the world—making Houston one of the most diverse cities in America—with hopes of achieving a better life for them and their families. We want our fellow Texans to understand that the principles on which our nation is based provide the best means of achieving that goal. That's why we are so passionate about these principles; we want people to have a chance at a better life.

Our efforts start in our classrooms here on the campus of Houston Baptist University. Students who start at HBU take a class in Greek and Roman history to learn the fundamental stories and lessons that influenced our Founding Fathers. We also require our students to take a basic American Government course that focuses on the Constitution and our nation's Founding Principles. Students who major in Government and Law are required to take advanced courses that focus on our nation's founding documents, a jurisprudence rooted in our Founders' intentions, and the principles of free enterprise. Our students read classic texts that shaped our Founding Fathers' views on history, human nature, and government. In short, we want our students to understand and appreciate our nation's history and founding principles.

Our efforts don't stop in the classroom. The Morris Family Center for Law & Liberty also offers many extracurricular activities on campus throughout the academic year. Each semester we provide a book group moderated by two professors and invite 10 to 12 students to join them in exploring books related to the theme of law or liberty. We've focused on capitalism, socialism, elections, justice, and democracy using both classic and contemporary texts. These book groups provide a great way to introduce students to these concepts (we often invite students from disciplines like nursing, education, or science who don't get as much exposure to these ideas) and engage them in dynamic conversations without the pressure of homework or grades. Some of our best conversations happen in these small group settings.

We also offer to the entire University community, including off-campus guests, a series of faculty lectures each year. The lectures are meant to get our students and fellow citizens thinking about our nation's history while also inspiring them to pursue further study. Our faculty have lectured on the influence that the Greeks and Romans (such as Demosthenes and Cicero) had on the Founding Fathers, on literature (such as Milton and Shakespeare) that influenced the Founding generation, and on women (such as Abigail Adams and Mercy Otis Warren) who made significant contributions to the American Founding. We also host special guest speakers such as public officials, noted authors, public intellectuals, and historical reenactors to engage our students. One of our favorites is a Thomas Jefferson interpreter who encourages our students to remember the important bond we share as Americans, even during tough political seasons. So if you are a student looking for a college and want to engage in serious conversations about the future of our nation, you have a place here at HBU no matter what your major may be.

Through the Center we offer workshops for school teachers. The workshops cover a variety of topics from broad themes such as our nation's founding documents, the American Revolution, and colonial America to more focused topics such as John Locke, executive power, and religious freedom. The workshops allow our expert faculty to present material to high school teachers who cover this material in their own classes. The goal is to provide the content, context, and importance of the material in a way that is informative and useful to the teachers in their own classes while at the same time always emphasizing the importance of our nation's founding principles. We've offered these workshops in Houston, Dallas, and San Antonio with great success and requests for repeated workshops.

To make sure our students understand the sacrifices of the generations that came before us, our American History Travel Program takes HBU students to famous American cities like Boston, Philadelphia, Colonial Williamsburg, and Jamestown. These "study America" tours involve a week of classroom sessions studying the history and significance of the site to be visited followed by a weeklong trip to the actual city. HBU professors serve as guides and are sometimes supplemented by knowledgeable local guides as well. Nothing makes history come alive more than being in the actual spot where famous speeches, important events, or critical battles occurred. Our goal is to instill in our students a lifelong passion for our nation's history while helping them understand the sacrifices of those who gave so much to help build our nation.

We believe so much in the importance of our mission that we are constructing on the HBU campus a classroom building modeled after Independence Hall in Philadelphia. Students will take classes in a replica of the space in which the Declaration of Independence and Constitution were drafted!

Can you imagine the impact on a young person to be seated in the very room where Thomas Jefferson, John Adams, or James Madison sat? What better place to teach students about our nation's founding principles than in the very room where they were forged! This iconic building will also serve the greater Houston area, becoming a field trip destination for area schools, a meeting place for civics groups and the business community, and a place for us to host educational events. What a great opportunity for us to tell the story of America while imparting the wisdom of our Founding Fathers!

Our mission is a labor of love and something we feel very passionately about. In order for us to successfully fulfill our mission, your support is greatly needed and appreciated. You can learn more about the Morris Family Center for Law & Liberty at our website or by contacting us directly. If you have a passion for our nation's history and founding principles, we'd like to partner with you to make sure we can educate as many students and teachers as possible. Passing on our constitutional culture is a big task, but an important one. Together we can ensure that future generations understand that our liberties are a blessing from God, that freedom isn't free, and that while the United States isn't a perfect nation, we must unceasingly aspire to fulfill the promise of our founding principles for all Americans.

WWW.HBULAW.ORG

CONTRIBUTORS

Dr. David J. Davis is an Associate Professor of History at Houston Baptist University. He earned a PhD in History at the University of Exeter (UK) and was recently named a Fellow of the Royal Historical Society. At HBU, he teaches medieval and early modern history courses, with specialized courses on religious history and the history of science. He has published two books on early modern English history, along with numerous academic articles and popular essays in *The Wall Street Journal, The New Criterion, Books & Culture,* and *The American Conservative.* His teaching and research interests focus on the intersection of politics, culture, and religion, and in his current book project (*The Culture of Revelation in England, 1400–1700* [forthcoming from Oxford University Press]) he is examining the role of divine revelation in the writings of figures like John Locke and Isaac Newton. *ddavis@hbu.edu*

Dr. Collin Garbarino is an Associate Professor of History at Houston Baptist University where he teaches courses on ancient Greek and Roman history. He also serves as the Director of Graduate Programs in the School of Humanities, and he received HBU's Opal Goolsby teaching award in 2015. Dr. Garbarino received his undergraduate degree in history from Louisiana Tech University. After spending two years overseas, he enrolled in the Southern Baptist Theological Seminary from which he graduated with a Master of Divinity in 2005. In 2010 he finished his PhD in history at Louisiana State University. Dr. Garbarino's interests involve the intersection of religion, culture, and politics. He has written both scholarly and popular essays for numerous publications including *First Things*, *Touchstone*, *The Federalist*, and *World* magazine. He also writes movie reviews and has appeared on radio and national television to discuss religion in popular films. *cgarbarino@hbu.edu*

Dr. Christopher Hammons is the Director of the Morris Family Center for Law & Liberty and Professor of Political Science at HBU. He teaches courses in constitutional history, political thought, and electoral politics. Dr. Hammons received a BA in Government and History at the University of Texas at Austin in 1991 and an MA and PhD in Political Science at the University of Houston in 1997. He has published articles in the *American Political Science Review*, the *Albany Law Review*, *The Journal of Law & Public Policy*, *Education Next*, the *Houston Business Journal*, *The Federalist* website, and the *Houston Chronicle*. He is currently writing a book entitled *America's Constitutional Culture*. His previous book, *Constitutionalism of the American States*, was nominated by the American Political Science Association for best book in history and politics. Dr. Hammons is the recipient of several teaching awards and is a sought-after speaker on the American founding. *chammons@hbu.edu*

Dr. Steven L. Jones is an Associate Professor of Classics at HBU and holds a PhD in Classics from the University of Texas; an MA in Greek, Latin, and Classical Studies from Bryn Mawr College; and a BA in Greek and Latin from Baylor University. He teaches courses on Roman History, Culture, and Language. He is passionate about helping people realize the modern relevance of studying Ancient Rome. In addition to his expertise in how the Founding Fathers were impacted by the Romans, he also has specializations in Ancient Rome and Early Christianity, as well as in the Greek and Latin Roots of Medical Language, a subject on which he has written two books: *Acquiring Medical Language* and *Medical Language Accelerated*. *sljones@hbu.edu*

Dr. Anthony M. Joseph is a Professor of History at Houston Baptist University. He teaches courses in colonial and revolutionary America, the Civil War, American legal history, and the history of the unborn child. Dr. Joseph received a BA in Plan II Honors (History Concentration) from the University of Texas at Austin and a PhD in History from Princeton University. He is the author of the book *From Liberty To Liberality: The Transformation of the Pennsylvania Legislature, 1776–1820*, and served as an associate editor for the *Documentary History of the Supreme Court of the United States, 1789–1800*. Dr. Joseph has also published articles and reviews in early American legal and political history. He is currently editing the legal papers of James Iredell, one of the first justices of the Supreme Court. *ajoseph@hbu.edu*

Dr. Scott Robinson is an Assistant Professor of political science and the assistant director of the Morris Family Center for Law & Liberty at Houston Baptist University. He received his BA and MA from Louisiana State University, and a PhD in political science from the University of Houston. Dr. Robinson is an award-winning professor whose primary teaching interests are political philosophy and American government, though he enjoys teaching across the spectrum of political science, including international relations and comparative politics. His primary research interest pertains to the influence of political philosophy on culture and civic virtue. He is lead editor of and author of several chapters in *Eric*

Voegelin Today: Voegelin's Political Thought in the 21ˢᵗ Century (Lexington Books, 2019), has published numerous articles about the philosophical influences on American political culture, and is currently working on a book about John Locke's influence on American political culture. He has given many presentations at academic conferences including the American Political Science Association and the Association for Political Theory. Dr. Robinson also serves as associate editor of the internet journal *Voegelin View*.   *mrobinson@hbu.edu*

Dr. John O. Tyler is an Associate Professor of Law & Jurisprudence at Houston Baptist University. He teaches courses in law, jurisprudence, and government. Dr. Tyler received a BA in Philosophy *summa cum laude* from Texas A&M in 1975, a JD from SMU Law School in 1978, and a PhD in Philosophy from Texas A&M in 2012. Dr. Tyler has published leading articles in the *Houston Law Review*, the *Baylor Law Review*, and the *Journal of Air Law and Commerce*. The Texas Bar Foundation and the *Houston Law Review* selected two of these as articles of the year, and Dr. Tyler is a recipient of Texas A&M University's highest teaching award. He has practiced civil litigation since 1978 and is board certified in Civil Trial Law and Personal Injury Trial Law. He has handled cases on three continents. Representative clients include every major oil and chemical company in the world, many of the large financial institutions and school districts in Texas, Texas A&M, the Houston Sports Association (Astros), and Lloyd's of London. His recovery for a group of 12 children with birth defects set a national record and led to the establishment of the Texas Birth Defect Registry.   *jtyler@hbu.edu*

Made in the USA
Columbia, SC
11 December 2021